Better Homes and Gardens®

STEP · BY · STEP
LANDSCAPING
PLANNING · PLANTING · BUILDING

BETTER HOMES AND GARDENS® BOOKS
Editor: Gerald M. Knox
Art Director: Ernest Shelton
Managing Editor: David A. Kirchner
Project Editors: James D. Blume, Marsha Jahns
Project Managers: Liz Anderson, Jennifer Speer Ramundt,
　Angela K. Renkoski

Associate Art Directors: Neoma Thomas, Linda Ford Vermie,
　Randall Yontz
Assistant Art Directors: Lynda Haupert, Harijs Priekulis,
　Tom Wegner
Graphic Designers: Mary Schlueter Bendgen, Michael Burns,
　Mick Schnepf
Art Production: Director, John Berg; Associate, Joe Heuer;
　Office Manager, Michaela Lester

President, Book Group: Jeramy Landauer
Vice President, Retail Marketing: Jamie L. Martin
Vice President, Administrative Services: Rick Rundall

BETTER HOMES AND GARDENS® MAGAZINE
President, Magazine Group: James A. Autry
Editorial Director: Doris Eby
Garden and Outdoor Living Editor: Douglas A. Jimerson

MEREDITH CORPORATION OFFICERS
Chairman of the Executive Committee: E. T. Meredith III
Chairman of the Board: Robert A. Burnett
President and Chief Executive Officer: Jack D. Rehm

STEP-BY-STEP LANDSCAPING
Project Editor: James D. Blume
Graphic Designer: Mary Schlueter Bendgen
Contributing Editor: Stephen Mead/Stephen Mead Associates
Contributing Writers: Monica Brandies, James A. Hufnagel
Contributing Text Editor: David A. Walsh
Principal Contributing Photographers: Jim Kascoutas,
　Perry Struse
Contributing Photographers: Ernest Braun,
　Crandall & Crandall, Stephen Cridland, Jay Graham,
　Peter Krumhardt, Barbara Martin
Contributing Illustrators: Mike Henry, Carson Ode,
　Tom Wegner
Regional Editors: Helen Heitkamp, Cathy Howard,
　Mary Anne Thomson
Contributing Indexer: Hazel Blumberg-McKee
Consultants: Jim Harrold, Jane Austin McKeon
Electronic Text Processor: Kathy Benz

Special thanks to the following landscape architects and
　designers: Phil Chek, Michael Glassman, Ted Lare,
　Matt Moynihan, Gary Orr, Josephine Zeitlin

Special thanks to the following manufacturers and suppliers:
　Black & Decker U.S. Power Tools Group; Echo, Inc.;
　The Toro Co.; True Temper Hardware Division,
　Emhart Consumer Group; Vintage Wood Works;
　Willow Creek Lawn and Garden Center

Special thanks to Ron Hawbaker, Eve Mahr,
　Jill Abeloe Mead, Paul D. Rohrig, Jim Sievers,
　Karen Sievers, Kathy Stevens

On the cover: A brick terrace—surrounded by a low stone wall and connected to the rest of the yard by brick paths—stands on ground formerly occupied by an asphalt driveway. To tie the new brick surface to the landscape, the homeowners planted azalea, rhododendron, and juniper near the wall; forsythia and crab apple behind the terrace; and geranium, impatiens, and begonia throughout. (See also page 169.)

INTRODUCTION

Do-it-yourself landscaping is not only possible, but also pleasurable, when you use *Step-by-Step Landscaping* as your guide. To make the book easy to use, we've focused each chapter on a common landscaping problem or area of the yard. Once you've determined your yard's need—which isn't hard, if you're the typical homeowner—simply look up the chapter that addresses that need. There you'll find text, illustrations, and photographs that compare and contrast various solutions, then show you in detail how to accomplish them.
This handy organization, along with the book's 500 gorgeous and informative photographs, makes *Step-by-Step Landscaping* essential for every homeowner who wants to create a more beautiful and livable yard.

CONTENTS

CHAPTER ONE

CREATING AN ENVIRONMENT

Careful landscaping lets you plan and plant a private world. In that private world, *you* decree where the sun shines and shadows fall and breezes blow. Your world can have the openness of a park, the seclusion of a woodland, or the flavor of a foreign land. As shown here, let the front yard set the mood, offering passersby an inviting glimpse of the world beyond. For help, see Chapter 6, "Front Yards," pages 114–135.

Spreading branches of mature trees provide dappled shade and a frame for the house, adding to its beauty. Beneath the limbs, symmetry and broad, bold lines reinforce the pervading feeling of casual elegance.

The brick walk in herringbone pattern shows fine traditional craftsmanship. The wide, bright beds of orange impatiens pick up sunshine and intensify the colors of the walk and house.

Identical shrubs on both sides of the walk amplify the aura of formality. The planters on the doorstep also enrich the setting and warmly greet both family and guests.

Impatiens thrive in the dancing shadows and bloom continually the entire growing season. Even their seedpods are tidy, which helps keep the surroundings neat.

BACKYARDS

Front yards are formal and public. Backyards are more personal and private. The idea of the backyard as a place to play and to discover ever-changing wonders and terrific new hiding places does not have to pass with childhood. Instead, the enchantment of the backyard should intensify with time.

■ It's *your* backyard

Each family's life-style, needs, and preferences will influence how a backyard is used. One family may want formal beds of show-quality roses; another, abundant fruits and vegetables. Some families design for a woodland or desert or Oriental atmosphere, for the easiest possible maintenance, or for constant experimenting and puttering. Others need sandboxes and room for riding toys, or want pools or hammocks.

Even the smallest backyard can become an additional and special outdoor living room during the warm days, and a contenting place to view year-round. Add a birdbath and feeding area, and it can serve as a focal point while attracting the garden's best helpers.

■ Plan first

However you will use your backyard, start with a plan. For every backyard need or problem, several landscaping possibilities exist to increase beauty, use, and enjoyment, plus add to property value. By making a list of what you want in your backyard, you start with objectives that will help you achieve your goal with a minimum of time, expense, and work. Without such guidelines, you can work forever and are likely to make more mistakes than improvements.

Keep in mind, though, that a backyard is for living, and your needs—and plans—will change as years go by. Sandboxes can give way to basketball courts as children grow. And gardens can revert to lawn or to trees with mulch beneath as time, growth, and interests change.

■ Allow access

No matter what evolutionary stage your plan is in, allow for easy access between its separate outdoor living areas. You won't use spots that are hard to get to. Include paths to assist the walking and enhance the mystery of each area.

▶ *This island of green is an outdoor sitting room with perimeters defined by towering drifts of blue delphiniums and canterbury-bells, white foxgloves, bright poppies, lupines, and coreopsis.*

◀*A well-planned deck, stairs, and landing changed this narrow, sloping backyard from difficult to delightful. The latticework fence permits privacy without closing in the yard.*

PATIOS

Patios—in the form of courtyards—go back to the gardens of ancient Egypt. When lawn mowers came along, yards went largely to grass. But patios, roofed or not, provide a cleaner, drier, and lower-maintenance area for sitting and walking. Patios also make better use of space and resources than do unbroken lawns.

In the front yard, a patio can be an extension of the driveway or the open area around the entrance. It can help direct traffic from the sidewalk to the door without muddying any feet, or it can serve as a spot for sitting.

A patio can turn wasted space along the side of a house into additional outdoor living space, or it can designate an area of the backyard for outdoor cooking, eating, sunning, reading, playing, or resting.

In all areas of the yard, patios make fine focal points and keep garden areas condensed and unified. In a large yard, lawn usually lies beyond. But in a small yard, a patio and its surrounding plantings can eliminate the need for a mower altogether.

■ **Location influences**
Privacy, protection from the sun and wind, and access to the kitchen and family room are all important influences when deciding the location of your patio. You may want more than one patio for a choice of settings: shady or sun warmed, secluded or convenient, small for intimacy or large for entertaining.

Because a patio is a permanent home improvement, check local building codes and zoning ordinances first. Then plan the location and design on paper before beginning construction.

Shape, size, and material should complement the house and the garden style. Work around existing trees and beneath their limbs for immediate shade. Select surrounding plantings to provide interest in every season—color, fragrance, form, and texture—while adding shade and seclusion. Choose plants that will stay in proportion without constant pruning.

For help in selecting patio surfaces and plantings, and for detailed building instructions, see Chapter 8, "Patios and Decks," pages 148–189.

▼*A triangular patio— surrounded by fence and tall evergreens for privacy—turns a narrow backyard into a showplace. Beyond the arches, which bestow a Victorian air, benches offer secluded seating.*

◄*This patio combines with a narrow porch for both protected and open outdoor living. The bright containers and brick pattern emit a colonial charm. Even the garden walk adds to the yesteryear feeling.*

DECKS

The porches and verandas of our past have given way to the wooden deck. As links between the home and the garden, decks combine the comfort and low maintenance of the indoors with the openness of nature more subtly and completely than ever before possible. Often decks continue the level of indoor rooms, permitting easier access to the outside than patios do, an especially important point to the very young or old, or those carrying food and drinks.

Wooden decks shed rain better than patios, and they lend a whole new point of view to both a yard and its surrounding environment. You can enclose them with tall attachments like screens or trellises, or open them to the scenery beyond with low railings.

Bring them alive, too, with containers of flowers or vegetables. Plants in containers need more frequent watering than those in the ground, but the advantages of having beauty nearby far outweigh any hassles.

Where slopes are a problem, decks can provide jutting midair solutions, making tree-root-damaging grade changes unnecessary. Decks also can meander around existing trees; simply cut holes where the trees poke through. Where shade does not already grow, bring in a large tree if there is ample access for the machinery, or build an overhanging arbor. The costs are about the same for both.

Steps, edges, built-in benches, and wide-sided raised planters can provide seating for a crowd or sit-down gardening.

But decks need not be complex. You can build a deck so simple that it can be dismantled for winter or moved from the sunniest spot for spring and fall to the shady east side of the house for the hot summer.

Since most decks are permanent structures, check building codes first. Also be careful to provide safe railings. (See Chapter 8, "Patios and Decks," pages 148–189.)

▶ *A front yard need not be just for welcoming visitors, as this attractive deck proves. Secluded from the street by plantings and a lattice fence (not shown), the deck has side benches to maximize the play area for the young members of the family.*

▶ *This bilevel deck forms an ideal frame for a hot tub—sometimes a better landscape choice than a pool. Raised beds and big tubs of annuals allow nonstoop gardening, plus add interest to the surroundings.*

ENTERTAINING

In a novel or the movies, pulses quicken the moment the gentleman says, "Let's go out for a breath of air." After all, even the largest and most elegant house is but a prelude to the setting of the simplest garden by moonlight.

As such, keep in mind your entertaining needs—whether that means fancy parties or family cookouts—when planning your landscape. Don't plant trees or flowers where children will want to play or people might gather for volleyball.

Making outdoor rooms such as patios or decks too large is a common mistake. They need to be small enough for ease of maintenance and a feeling of intimacy. People can crowd together or spread out on benches or cushions.

Privacy for your party and consideration for neighbors are critical, too. Shrubs will not block all noise or light, but will help considerably.

If much of your entertaining is at night, plan your gardens with plenty of white blooms for a shimmering setting. Fragrance intensifies at nightfall, too.

Garden lighting adds both atmosphere and safety. For constant use, consider permanent lights in strategic places or a series of lamps along the footpath. For occasional needs, string lanterns or buy special candles that stick in the ground. (For more details on outdoor lighting, see pages 92–93 and 212–215.)

A fire pit or space heater will warm your garden on cool evenings to stretch both spring and fall sittings. On the hottest days, overhead fans make porches pleasant.

For large gatherings, a well-thought-out garden plan becomes vital. Allow for open places, then strategically place some refreshments there to encourage people to spread out and mingle.

◄ *A multilevel deck—complete with built-in benches, cabinets, table, and gas grill in a counter/buffet—converted this backyard from a weedy slope into an entertainment center.*

► *With a pit that offers all the benefits of a campfire, including extra heat for cool evenings and just enough smoke to chase bugs, this combination patio and raised deck is as suited for cozy stargazing as it is for fast, fun meals.*

15

SWIMMING POOLS

Nothing adds more fun to a yard or is a more dramatic focal point than a swimming pool. On the other hand, nothing is more expensive to install and maintain—and more potentially dangerous. Careful planning here is vital. Begin with the counsel of professionals and a full knowledge of legal regulations.

If you value relaxation and party punch more than exercise, consider a spa or hot tub. They require less space and cost less than swimming pools, and are easier to seclude. Spas usually offer a longer season of use, too.

Whether pool or spa, also consider the surrounding deck—usually of equal area—which should be nonskid, perfectly drained, fenced, and planted for privacy and attractiveness. If your plan calls for a pool in the future, be sure to leave access now for the heavy equipment.

Choose the site, size, and materials for your pool with landscape harmony, sun and wind patterns, access to bathrooms and changing rooms, soil conditions and drainage, and especially privacy in mind. Surrounding plantings should be nondropping and protected from chlorinated water by raised beds.

See Chapter 9, "Beyond the Basics," especially pages 204–211, for further details.

◀ *A steep slope forced the wall on the right to serve as both pool and retaining wall. Interesting angles integrate the spa, patio, and plantings into a geometric wonder.*

▶ *This 10x40-foot lap pool saves space, yet still allows ample room for exercise. The circular spa at the far end creates a variation in an otherwise boxy and boring configuration.*

GARDEN POOLS

Water in the garden creates new dimensions of beauty, tranquillity, and interest—and with fewer maintenance demands than most people imagine.

Your garden pool can be as simple as a half barrel with water lilies or as complex as a formal pool with statuary and fountains. Between is an infinite array of possibilities.

Since water in any form tends to dominate the landscape, forethought and careful choice are the secrets of success. Do you want a pool for viewing, for reflecting surrounding beauty, for attracting birds, for growing water plants, to stock with fish, or a combination of these?

Will a formal or informal pool fit in best with your landscape? Formal pools are marked by geometric shapes and straight lines. These shapes and lines must agree with other landscape elements to make the formal pool an integral part of the whole. Informal pools, on the other hand, are defined by smooth, flowing lines. These lines must remain uncomplicated. The informal pool looks best when it appears as a natural part of the garden, with lots of plants.

Fountains work well in formal pools (as long as you avoid pretentiousness), but not in informal pools; there, try a gentle waterfall.

In either case, your pool should be designed to be attractive year-round. And don't crowd it among other landscape features.

Location is the most important design decision. Ideally, a waterscape should be easily seen from both inside and out. At least four to six hours of sunlight a day are necessary for water plants to thrive. Nearby trees can pose a problem if they shed too many leaves or their leaves are hazardous to fish or plants.

Place your pool where you'll have easy access to a water spigot, drainage, and perhaps electricity (for a pump and lights). A spot that's naturally wet usually isn't the best site for a garden pool because it may be prone to flooding. Avoid windy spots if you plan to have a fountain. Provide a walkway to your pool for curious visitors.

Despite their shallowness, garden pools can present a hazard to small children. Be sure to check all codes when designing your pool.

■ Pool ecology

The water in a garden pool will not be as clear as that in a swimming pool. A slightly green cast is natural and indicates a balance of life.

Plants will use carbon dioxide and give off oxygen; fish do just the opposite. Snails, clams, and tadpoles will help greatly to keep the water free of decaying matter. Fish, birds, and other insects will eat almost all of the mosquito and other harmful larvae.

Water plants include those that you plant in submerged tubs of soil (such as water lily), floating plants (such as water hyacinth), oxygenating plants that live completely underwater, and marginal plants like iris and reeds that grow beside the pool. For more details, see Chapter 9, "Beyond the Basics," pages 198–203.

▲ *Water lilies enliven this pond, and azaleas, vinca, and blue juniper border it. The irregularly shaped pool is tucked into the corner of a front-yard garden.*

▶ *A black mortar surface and blue stone coping bestow a reflective countenance on this pool. Its quiet demeanor and straight lines add to the formality of the setting.*

CHAPTER TWO

PLANNING AND PREPARING

Turning your yard into your own personal environment means dipping into the broad palette of landscaping possibilities. In this chapter, you'll find an overview of those possibilities, plus a guide to the steps for creating an overall plan. The secret to ultimate success is to first work back and forth from mind to paper; with both, ideas can flow while expenses stay on hold. Once done, your plan becomes the blueprint for the best possible outdoor world for you and your family.

Once a weedy slope, this part of the yard assumed added importance when the owners made the adjoining room their business office. New landscaping tames the slope, enchants clients, and provides added fun for the family.

Bilevel deck and steps provide easy access for business traffic from the street or for sunbathers from the spa. Using the same material for the tub and surrounding planters ties the scene together in pleasant harmony.

The fence couples with a boulder retaining wall to frame the scene with a variety of textures. Trees and shrubs give privacy and absorb noise and lights from the street for a feeling of seclusion from the world outside.

Light fixtures add to the attraction of the scene by day and to the enjoyment of the gardens after dark. When evening relaxation time comes, the lights accent the colors, textures, and patterns of the landscape, creating a sense of mystery.

ASSESSING YOUR LANDSCAPING NEEDS

▲ *Good use of existing trees provides excellent framing and background for this traditional home on a typical lot. Small accent trees, a stone retaining wall, and low, neat shrubs give the setting a simple, well-planned appearance.*

Some landscaping ideas are born full-grown. New homeowners have been known to put in a pool before they unpack their boxes.

But most plans take longer to gain shape. And so they should, because the process of assessing your family's and your yard's needs—and figuring out the best solutions to those needs—is essential to creating an effective landscape.

■ The present
Begin by looking critically at what you've got. As you live in your house through the next cycle of seasons, compile a list of little and large blessings already in place: the shade, bloom, or fruit of a special tree, or the view at sunset or when the winter trees are bare. At the end of 12 months you may be pleasantly surprised at just how long your list is.

A year of surmising your situation may seem excessively long, but taking your time has a built-in advantage: If you move too fast, you could destroy one of your yard's present pluses before you are even aware of it.

During the year also compile a list of dislikes about your setting: lack of privacy or outdoor living space, for instance, or too much wind or too little light. Good landscaping can solve most, if not all, of your yard's shortcomings.

■ Purpose
Next, weigh your family's needs. All landscape improvements—from the planting of a single shrub to the building of a deck and patio system—should add to the ease, comfort, and delight of your everyday living. And this can be true for all members of the family, from indoor grandparents, who appreciate easy entrances and grand views of the grandkids, to children, who play in every inch of yard from the sandbox to the treetops.

Add nothing to your landscape without having a specific purpose in mind—whether that be to solve one of your yard's problems or to accent one of its best features.

We'd like to offer ready-made, detailed plans to solve each reader's landscaping needs. But the combination of site, climate, and family desires makes each yard one of a kind. And even the best-planned yard will change slightly from season to season and year to year as family wants and hobbies change.

No one knows as well as you what your family might require or enjoy. And you will know that much more clearly and completely after some exciting and interesting consideration of the many possibilities.

■ Ideas
To get started gathering ideas, observe the good and bad points of other yards. Drive slowly and carefully; or better yet, ride a bike or walk. You soon will notice details: colors and textures of flowers and foliage, moods of promise and mystery evoked by a winding path or a charming gate, or the way an entrance planting distinguishes a house from all the other similar houses around it.

(continued on page 24)

SOLVING THE TYPICAL LOT

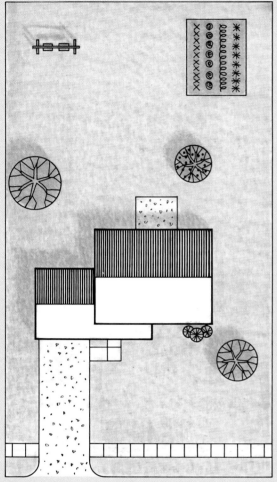

BEFORE

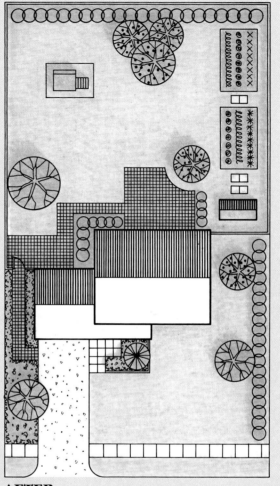

AFTER

A tall fence around the backyard transforms public space to private grounds. The play area is in full view from the house for supervision, but far enough away to give parents peace and children freedom.

With the garage a good hike away, a small shed near the gardens saves steps while offering super storage for tools. Shrubs screen it from the patio. The backyard now offers two service areas (the second one is near the paved side yard), an outdoor living area, an outdoor playroom, and gardens, all neatly divided into zones.

The front yard extends a warm greeting, and a side walkway makes the transition from front to back a pleasant journey.

Many homes sit on a rectangular lot with drive and entrance in front and a larger area in back, like the one above. Landscaping problems for these typical lots include lack of privacy from the sides and rear, narrow side yards where space is difficult to use, and lack of access from front yard to backyard. Also, such lots often offer only a small, open area for outdoor living. Plantings generally include a few foundation shrubs and one or two trees in the front as streetscape. (Lucky is the homeowner who has older trees.) Many times, these homes look unflatteringly similar to one another.

To create an inviting individuality out of such a home, add plantings to one or both sides of the drive, along a portion of the property line, and around the front door. Construct a distinctive entryway. Use structures or plants to subtly divide the backyard into activity zones. Finally, to make sure the yard doesn't end up with a split personality, join the front to the back with a side walkway or other connecting feature.

ASSESSING YOUR LANDSCAPING NEEDS *(continued)*

▶ *A side-entry main door packs the most interest, privacy, and space into this small, narrow lot. Carefully combined details include the raised beds, brick and concrete patterns, and small shrubs. Color accents are provided by the containers, beds, and flowering tree.*

Move your search for landscaping ideas indoors by browsing through this book. Regard pages 30–37 as your landscaping palette and select the colors with which you want to paint your private world. Check out later chapters for specific advice on each of the options.

From magazines and other books, gather photographs, plans, and anything else that might prove useful.

Skim over the pictures and plans the way a clever clothes maker looks at a pattern book, ruling out the completed look of many outfits as unfit, but choosing a collar here, a sleeve there.

Similarly, you can combine a front entry from one plan with a back patio from another; add a certain curve or zigzag border or walk from still another; and choose a grouping of trees for spring bloom, fall fruit, or a woodland feeling from yet another.

You will do much of your initial landscape planning in your head. But to put all that power to work most efficiently, write down your observations, ideas, and expectations as they come to you. This can be done in any form and is mostly for your own use, so don't let formality stop the flow of ideas.

■ Dare to dream
Check building codes, deed restrictions, and setback and easement regulations early in your planning so you can keep them in mind.

Otherwise, don't worry if your landscaping ideas seem muddled at first. The details will come out clear in time. Don't let expense and labor stifle your dreams, either. Planning often makes the impossible possible.

Perhaps you won't wind up with a forest, but you can have a corner where a path and some trees, shrubs, ground covers, and wildflowers make you feel as if you do. And though you can't stretch a small lot into a wide plain, a section of fence along the rim of a slope can visually extend your backyard.

■ The whole site
As the details develop, think of your yard as a whole. Everything should go together with harmony. You don't have to be an artist or know much about the aesthetic principles of line, scale, texture, and balance. These elements of good design are largely common sense. An inner eye will tell you if they are present or not.

Visualize the changes you plan as they will look immediately, in five years, in 20 years. Remember that plans are flat on paper but three-dimensional in reality. Trees and shrubs grow up as well as out. Look up and be sure no electric or phone wires already are in the space where you are thinking of oak branches.

(continued on page 26)

SOLVING THE NARROW LOT

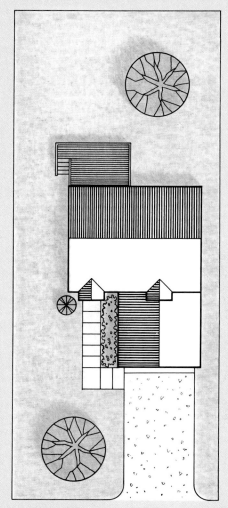

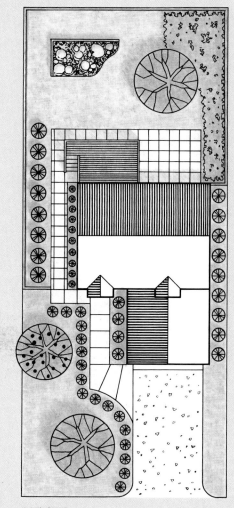

The smaller the space, the more important it is to define zones within the site. Here a street-scaping zone and an outdoor living zone are developed with a concern for detail that brings as much beauty and usefulness as many large yards offer.

The rock garden, with a low fence in front, is a fine focal point and makes the small space seem larger. A taller fence behind it screens an area where equipment can be stored.

Along the property lines, easy-care plants that will not grow out of bounds solve the problem of mowing in narrow places, plus add to a sense of seclusion.

BEFORE

AFTER

Rising land costs make narrow lots the norm in many locations these days. Unfortunately, landscaping problems tend to increase in intensity with such closeness. One wall of the house may rest nearly on the lot line, leaving a narrow, hard-to-plant space on the opposite side. Privacy, though harder to achieve, is more essential than ever. Access and traffic flow within the yard are concerns, too. Every inch of yard on the narrow lot must be used wisely.

To create the illusion of more space, try some visual trickery. Expand the entry as it adjoins the drive to make the space feel larger. Set low-level plantings along the drive and walk to lead the eye to the front door and soften the harshness of one house on top of another.

For outdoor living, build a patio or deck, or a combination. You'll gain a needed sanctuary while retaining an open feel. To provide privacy in the backyard and help absorb neighbors' noise, plant trees and shrubs and build a fence.

ASSESSING YOUR LANDSCAPING NEEDS *(continued)*

▲ *Flower borders make this largely exposed corner yard a showplace, turning a potential problem into an advantage. Front shrubbery and trees on the other side help frame the house and tie it to the site.*

One of the most common landscaping mistakes is planting too close or using plants that will outgrow their allotted space. If you want to avoid the empty look for the present, fill in with temporary plantings—flowers, quick-growing trees or shrubs, vegetables—that you can remove as the choice trees and shrubs grow. Keep scale in mind at all times.

Also keep the same theme throughout the entire yard, whether that be natural, formal, English cottage, Japanese, modern, or any other desired look.

Record the heights, colors, and times of bloom or color interest of all plants, and be sure they complement one another and the structures. If your house is white or gray, you can plant any good combination. But if it is orange or red, you will need to pay careful heed to enhancing and not fighting the existing colors.

Do the same analysis for all structural materials you consider using in your landscape. Wood, concrete, brick, stone, and natural materials all have characteristics that make them fit better in some situations than in others.

Consider, too, as much as you can, your future landscaping needs. You won't be able to do this with crystal-ball clarity, but having the forethought to leave your options open can reap rewards later on. Installation of a swimming pool years later, for example, will be easier if you don't plant any large trees or shrubs now that will block the access of machinery.

Don't worry if you're having trouble visualizing your entire yard. When you put your plans down on paper, as mentioned below and described on pages 38–51, you'll be better able to see and rearrange the parts for the most convenient and beautiful whole.

■ Drawing a plan

Because some decisions will firm up more quickly than others, the sooner you move from your lists and dreams to the actual planning, the better. The day you buy the house, you can begin planting flowers, cover crops, vegetables, small shrubs, and trees that you could remove or move if necessary. These activities, in fact, will help you form and appreciate your plans. But you cannot afford to do anything expensive or permanent until you have an overall plan.

So while all of the ideas are settling, get busy and measure and sketch your yard as directed on pages 38–39. Then draw a map to scale on graph paper as shown on pages 40–41. Over this, lay tracing paper and sketch various arrangements. Try options on the tracing paper just as you would try on clothes, to see what is right for you.

If putting an idea on paper shows that it won't work, the process may bring to mind another idea that will. Then select the ideas that will best fit your plan and your family's way of life.

The pages that follow walk you through this process until, by page 51, you have your own custom-made landscape plan.

(continued on page 28)

SOLVING THE CORNER LOT

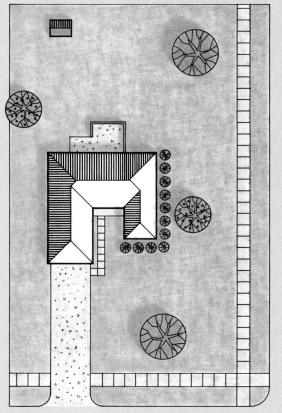

BEFORE

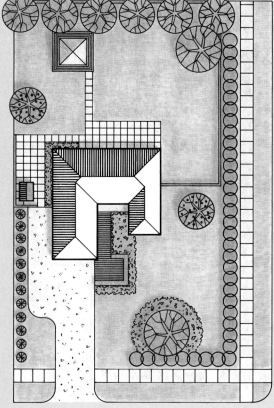

AFTER

A hedge along one side yard and part of the front now shields the homeowners from public display. Trees across the back and a fence along a portion of the hedge bring added privacy.

The planting circling the tree near the corner gives a focal point for the front yard. A wide front-entry walk helps tie the house to the site.

Off-street parking for an extra car uses otherwise wasted side-yard space. The back section on that side has become a service area.

A pavilion and a larger patio yield better outdoor living facilities.

The corner house, bordered on two sides by car and pedestrian traffic, needs careful landscaping to keep it from looking like an island in a sea of lawn. Privacy is a major concern, too, with the exposure in all directions making usable outdoor living space hard to define.

If left open, the lawn on a corner lot all too often becomes a shortcut from one sidewalk to the other. Such lawns may pose great dangers, too: Balls and children are much more apt to run into the street.

To solve many of the problems associated with a corner lot, plant a hedge along the entire side street and the largest part of the front yard. Such a hedge screens the house from the view of passing traffic. It also absorbs noise, blocks headlights at night, and provides a barrier for children playing in the yard or passing by it. Planting the hedge near the sidewalk instead of against the house helps break up the expanse of lawn.

To further absorb noise and visually separate the house from the street—plus stop shortcutters—establish a front-yard focal point in the corner where the two streets intersect. An ornamental tree surrounded by shrubs and flowers often works well. To help expand the house into the site, widen the front-entry walk.

ASSESSING YOUR LANDSCAPING NEEDS *(continued)*

At some point, of course, you'll have to start worrying about what your various landscaping ideas might cost you (see page 50 for more about costs). Estimates are easy to obtain, and are vital before your plans become definite.

Because landscaping can be expensive, it's often done in stages (see pages 50–51). A driveway and a few trees probably will be needed right away. But you can just as well work on and pay for the entryway one year, the back patio or deck the next, the side yard another.

Also as you sift through ideas, you'll want to keep in mind your willingness to work in your yard. Although installation is only done once, maintenance goes on forever.

Few people appreciate that a lawn takes more time, expense, and natural resources (such as water) than any other landscaping option. Cut your lawn down to a workable size with areas of ground covers or mulches around trees and shrubs (see pages 258–261).

Put in a rose garden if you love to work at that, or a vegetable patch or an orchard. But avoid such landscaping features if you just don't have the time.

Patios, decks, walks, and permanent plantings require little work and expense after the initial construction. In return, they give plenty of outdoor living enjoyment for each dollar spent.

■ Professional help
Throughout the process, consider whether you want to consult a landscape professional for help. Such help can come from three types of individuals: landscape architects, landscape designers, and landscape contractors.

The landscape architect is the planning expert and is comparable to a building architect in training and in the time frame when he or she can most help you: while the property is being designed. Although landscape architects do mostly commercial work, many will consult with homeowners on an hourly basis and some will oversee entire residential jobs. Because of their expertise, landscape architects tend to be the most expensive landscaping professionals.

Landscape designers often do much the same work as landscape architects, but they have less training and usually are more plant oriented. The fees of landscape designers employed by nurseries often are absorbed if you buy enough plants from the nurseries.

Landscape contractors do or hire done the actual work. If you work with a landscape contractor, be sure to talk about what materials you must provide and ask for samples of any materials the contractor will supply.

■ Finding good help
Before choosing a landscaping professional, ask the owners of yards you admire for recommendations. Or go to the phone book, call four or five landscapers listed, and ask for addresses that show their work. Then go out for a look. Keep doing this until you've found at least three professionals who do high-quality work, then ask them for bids on your job.

Depending on your own time and expertise, and on your site's complexity, you may not need a professional. But the money spent to consult an expert—especially concerning such problems as difficult grading, sliding hillsides, or high walls or high decks—is often saved many times over in the final satisfying and safe result.

Remember, however, that no professional can know your needs and dreams like you do. That's why good planning becomes even more important when you are putting the results into the hands of a highly paid person.

■ Trees and topsoil
A final note: Be especially careful with existing trees and topsoil when planning and working on your landscape. Both, once lost, take many years to replace.

During construction, protect your trees from machinery, soil compaction, and changes in soil level. Transplant small, choice shrubs and trees that stand in the way.

Before building or making major changes in grade, scrape the topsoil and pile it separately so you can respread it over the finished surface.

SOLVING THE JUNGLE LOOK

In the early stages of planting an empty yard, some homeowners yearn for the look of overgrowth. Others see it too soon in anything but the neatness of near bareness, and do away with possible treasures in their clearing.

Because they grow quickly to maturity, shrubs and vines are the most likely contributors to the jungle look. Beware when planting them. Little potted bushes and seeds of honeysuckle grow so successfully they can take over if placed wrong. When shrubs or vines obscure the best lines of the house or shut out views and light, it is time for rescaling, by either pruning the plants or tearing them out (see page 61).

Trees need thinning less often, but they, too, can become overgrown, particularly in warm and wet climates. Careful pruning for a higher canopy of leaves opens the area beneath the tree to more sunlight and air circulation while preserving the tree's irreplaceable form, silhouette, and shade.

If ripping out plants seems ruthless and extreme, do it in stages. As the advantages of openness appear and you see that new plantings will quickly replace the emptiness, you will gain the needed assurance to press on with the destruction.

Similarly, you don't have to endure walks, drives, or patios that are overgrown, cracked, or outdated, or were out of place to begin with. Yards, like houses, can be remodeled.

BEFORE

◄ *Shrubbery had overgrown the front foundation and overpowered even the porch. The result was a dark, confining, and little-used space.*

An old paved walkway, cracked and irreparable, dominated the front yard and gloomy entry. The deeply shaded lawn was sparse from years of neglect.

Altogether, this house extended an icy greeting to residents and guests.

AFTER

◄ *A glassed-in front porch greatly expands the adjacent indoor family room. Neat, low plantings of holly, azalea, and liriope enhance rather than hide the fine arched windows.*

A low stucco wall and a wrought-iron railing set off a new sunnyside entrance, where a curving brick walk flares into a patio. A high iron gate mimics the curve of the arches.

WEIGHING YOUR LANDSCAPING OPTIONS

STRUCTURES

DECKS
(pages 12–13, 148–189)

Types: Raised, grade-level, multilevel, freestanding, portable; used at entrance, ad-joining house or pool, with a patio, surrounding a spa, as part of play area; usually wooden.

Uses: Decks are an ideal way to gain outdoor living space on level, sloping, or hilly lots. They work best when connected to kitchen, family room, or dining room. They can be built around existing trees without changing the ground level. With various railings and trellises, decks can be made to fit into either natural or formal settings. Avoid creating just a box by rounding or angling at least one corner, by varying the pattern or the levels, and by surrounding with interesting planters or plantings.

PATIOS
(pages 10–11, 148–169)

Types: Brick, tile, flagstone, wood blocks, paver blocks, cobblestones—all usually set in sand; solid concrete or exposed aggregate; pebbles or the like.

Uses: Patios give a solid surface for outdoor living rooms. Connected to kitchen, family room, or dining room, they work well as eating or entertaining areas. They set off the scene around a pool and are great for sunbathing. In front, they serve as a porch or courtyard, and they can reclaim narrow side-yard spaces. Locate them for sun, shade, or wind protection; be sure drainage is good; use plants or railings for privacy, arbors or roofs for shade.

FENCES
(pages 78–95)

Types: Styles and materials vary widely. Can be transparent or semitransparent for ample air circulation, opaque for windbreaks and complete privacy, or a combination.

Uses: Fences frame, accent, and provide background to set off plantings. The many styles, colors, and forms unify the yard and tie various aspects to the house with formal or natural beauty. Fences keep children or pets in, unwanted visitors out. Mix opaque and open styles to cover unsightly views but frame and accent pleasant vistas. Fences can be tall for privacy or short for accent. Cover with vines or espaliers for vertical gardening.

SCREENS
(pages 78–95)

Types: Sections of fence, not necessarily or completely connected. They can be taller and set at different angles.

Uses: Screens provide privacy without the cost and enclosure of a fence. They give focus, emphasis, and vertical interest to the landscape while blocking un-pleasant views or accenting desirable aspects within the yard. By breaking up the open space, they add a feeling of separation to outdoor rooms. They can make a small space seem larger and a large space more intimate. Screens can be made part of patios, deck railings, trel-lises, or storage sheds.

WALKS
(pages 114–135)

Types: Walks can be made of any of the materials used for patios or decks. Loose mulching materials like pine needles, wood chips, and tanbark also work well for walkways.

Uses: Walks lead people around your yard with comfort and safety. In entry and service areas, they should be solid and definite. Farther from the house, they can be more casual. Let them flow with the natural route of traffic, curving by special plantings or leading to hidden nooks. Materials should complement the house and yard. Make walks at least 3 feet wide (wider at curves and ends, if possible). Keep plants or structures beside walks back and low so they don't crowd.

STEPS
(pages 62–77, 114–135)

Types: Made of wood, concrete, or rustic materials like split logs, landscape timbers, or long stones. Ramp steps are a series of single steps alternating with sloping surfaces.

Uses: Steps make a safe and pleasant transition from one grade level to another. Materials should be in harmony with the surrounding area; if chosen well, they can add greatly to the interest. Make steps as broad as the path that leads to them and less steep than interior stairs. For slight grade changes, leave the slope rather than building a single step. Angle treads forward for drainage. A railing on at least one side is recommended (some codes may require it). If the total rise exceeds 6 feet, use landings.

RETAINING WALLS
(pages 62–77)

Types: Can be made of reinforced concrete, timber, or stone laid dry or with masonry. Dry walls are less expensive and can be planted. Mortar makes stronger walls.

Uses: Retaining walls turn difficult slopes into interesting architectural features that also serve to unite the garden with the house. Walls combine well with plants, creating level planting beds above and charming backgrounds below for flowers, foliage, and espaliered trees and shrubs. Retaining walls must be strong enough to hold back the weight of the earth behind them. Be sure to provide for adequate drainage.

ARBORS
(pages 96–113)

Types: Usually wooden; metal available. Sides can be open, latticed, patterned. Arbors can adjoin a house, roof a bench or swing, or form a freestanding accent, gate, or enclosure.

Uses: Arbors provide support for vines or espaliered fruit and increase garden space vertically. They provide shade in much less time and space than trees do and are ideal places to hang plants, lights, or hammocks. Used to roof part of a patio or deck, they give the ideal choice of shady or sunny space. With vined or latticed sides, they increase privacy yet let the air circulate. Sides also can have louvers or panels.

(continued on page 32)

WEIGHING YOUR LANDSCAPING OPTIONS *(continued)*

STRUCTURES *(continued)*

OVERHEAD SUNSHADES
(pages 96–113)

Types: Can be freestanding or attached to the house; usually wood, but can be combined with canvas or other shading materials. Varying styles; can drastically alter a house's looks.

Uses: Overhead sunshades give instant and permanent shade that can greatly improve the comfort and usefulness of both outdoor rooms and adjoining indoor ones, especially where glass doors connect the two. Adding deciduous vines increases the summer shade and still lets plenty of sun warm the house in winter. Like arbors, these can give yards the advantages of some sunny and some shady areas.

SCREENED ROOMS
(pages 220–231)

Types: Parts of porches, patios, or decks connected to the house; freestanding summer houses or gazebos. Screening can combine with almost any style of architecture.

Uses: Screened rooms offer the ultimate in protection from insects. They also provide a measure of privacy and protection from the elements that makes them almost like additional indoor rooms. But they have all the advantages of open air, cool breezes, and nearness to the garden. Combine with gentle vines like Virginia creeper or clematis to give additional shade and summer interest.

GAZEBOS
(pages 192–197)

Types: Usually freestanding and wooden, gazebos can combine with bridges, fences, decks, or other structures. Colors, shapes, railings, floors, and ceilings can be chosen to fit any yard.

Uses: A gazebo is a definite garden accent and focal point, and as such should be in scale and harmony with the rest of the yard. It provides a separate outdoor room ideal for relaxing, entertaining, dining, or quiet seclusion. To avoid having the gazebo look too obviously out of place, tie it to the rest of the yard with architectural touches or walkways. Cloth and even portable gazebos are now available.

SWIMMING POOLS
(pages 16–17, 204–211)

Types: In-ground pools: Gunite, concrete, fiberglass, or vinyl lined; most any size or shape. Aboveground pools: less costly and permanent, fewer shapes, usually smaller and safer.

Uses: Swimming pools offer the ultimate in outdoor recreation, relaxation, and exercise. They usually are the focal point of the yard and often of indoor rooms as well, so surrounding decking and plantings require as much planning, care, and expense as the pool itself. Study soil type and sun and wind patterns, and consult experts as you plan. Screening the area around and above will keep a pool cleaner, especially with trees nearby.

GARDEN POOLS
(pages 18–19, 198–203)

Types: Clear reflecting pools, fishponds, water gardens. Can be made of poured concrete, PVC liner, or preformed fiberglass.

Uses: A pool opens new worlds of fish, foliage, and flowers to the garden; to add the music of trickling water, outfit a pool with any form of fountain or falls. Always delightful and dramatic, garden pools can be used as either accents or focal points. They take less upkeep than most people think, seldom need emptying, and can be heated in the winter. A sunny location is best. Water plants include submersible, surface, and poolside types.

LIGHTING
(pages 92–93, 212–215)

Types: Lights on the regular house system include porch, door, post, and floodlights. Low-voltage floodlights, accent lights, mushroom or well lights, drive or walk lights available.

Uses: The essential lights allow homeowners to come or go at night with sure steps and no fear of intruders. Additional garden lighting can effectively extend outdoor living and enjoyment into the evening hours, and create striking views. Choose the fixture types and positions that best fit your purpose: providing security, lighting recreational space, accenting plantings, or dramatizing architectural features.

STORAGE UNITS
(pages 232–239)

Types: Tool or potting shed separate or adjoining the house; or space in a portion of the garage, under a bench or deck, or in a handy corner.

Uses: Proper and convenient storage can save time and frustration for the gardener; rust and wear on tools; and, by providing a secure place for chemicals, even the life of a child or pet. Ideal storage is about 60 to 100 square feet and includes racks and hanging space, shelves, compartments for soil and compost, a potting bench, and floor space for wheelbarrow and lawn mower. If designed to harmonize with the house and landscape, a shed can be an attractive garden feature.

DRIVES, PARKING AREAS
(pages 232–245)

Types: Concrete, flagstone, tile, brick, asphalt, or aggregates like gravel. Circular is good for large or formal yards. Straight, L, or T shapes can double as play or entry areas.

Uses: Driveways must be clearly visible and easy to turn into and negotiate in any weather. Gentle curves may add visual interest, but also cost and time. Where needed, curves reduce the steepness of a slope and add to the formality of the house. Out-of-the-way parking is a great convenience. A place to turn around so motorists can enter traffic head-on is a good safety plus; it's a necessity in areas of heavy traffic or short visibility. Plantings can screen parking areas from the street.

(continued on page 34)

WEIGHING YOUR LANDSCAPING OPTIONS *(continued)*

PLANTS

SHADE TREES
(pages 98–99, 108–110, 301–306)

Examples: Ash, cork tree, edibles (such as cherry, cherry laurel, crab apple, nuts, persimmon, plum), ginkgo, golden-rain tree, honey locust, magnolia, maple, oak, tulip tree.

Uses: Besides filtering or blocking the summer sun for cooling comfort, shade trees, more than any other option, give needed framing, privacy, and vertical or skyline interest to the landscape. Shade trees tie a house to its site, give a sense of oneness with nature, and provide protection from the elements. Deciduous trees let the winter sun in to brighten and warm the scene. Plant one or two of the largest you can afford. Use quick growers for temporary shade until choicer selections grow enough.

ACCENT TREES
(pages 108–110, 118, 301–306)

Examples: Apple, birch, cherry, cherry laurel, crab apple, dogwood, hawthorn, holly, Japanese maple, magnolia, pear, persimmon, plum, redbud (in photo), serviceberry.

Uses: Accent (also called specimen or ornamental) trees are ideal for perking up a front yard or creating a focal point in a backyard. Place them in center-stage locations for best results. Spring-blooming trees work well where they can be clearly seen from indoors, the street, or the entrance. Keep fruit trees away from the driveway or patio. Accent trees work well against a house, fence, or evergreen background. Keep mature size and scale with your house in mind.

SCREEN SHRUBS
(pages 80–83, 307–313)

Examples: Clipped: barberry, hazelnut, juniper, privet, yew. Unclipped: arborvitae, azalea, blueberry, boxwood (in photo), bush cherry or plum, currant, elderberry, quince, roses.

Uses: Shrubs make fine screens because they quickly grow into place. You can choose them for any height; for open, dense, or thorny growth; or for their flowers, fruit, or foliage color. Some places, like a side window or front door, will gain enough privacy from a single specimen. Other areas will need a group of plants. For maximum effect, make the grouping all the same; for maximum interest, judiciously mix the selections. Choose sizes that will not overgrow their sites.

ACCENT SHRUBS
(pages 82–83, 307–313)

Examples: Clematis, cornus, cotoneaster, fringe tree, holly, honeysuckle, hydrangea (in photo), mahonia, rhododendron, viburnum; all tree-form, weeping, or espaliered shrubs.

Uses: Accent or specimen shrubs are so lovely they often steal the garden show. Use them as focal points in the yard, at the entrance, or at a corner of the house. The shrubs listed at left, and many others, offer something striking for at least two seasons: flowers and fruit, summer or autumn foliage color, general form, and winter twig, bark, or foliage. Make your selections according to when you'll see the shrubs most often. Accent shrubs also can serve as privacy, screening, or foundation plantings.

VINES
(pages 106–111, 166, 314–316)

Examples: Bougainvillea (in photo), clematis, passionflower, and wisteria for flowers; bittersweet, grapes, kiwi for fruits; Boston ivy and Virginia creeper for fall foliage; evergreen ivies.

Uses: Vines are wonderful for giving shade and privacy in a short time and in a narrow space. You can choose vines that have fragrant or outstanding flowers, bountiful fruit, or open or dense growth. You also can choose according to tolerance for dry or wet conditions. Some are annual, some perennial. Some are soft wooded, some hard. Many grow easily from seeds or cuttings. Choose carefully to minimize pruning and maximize interest in the season you want it most.

GROUND COVERS
(pages 67, 260–261, 317–319)

Examples: Artemisia, barberry, bellflower, bishop's weed, bugleweed (in photo), cotoneaster, herbs, ivies, juniper, lily-of-the-valley, mint, pachysandra, phlox, strawberry, yarrow, yew.

Uses: Grow easy-care ground covers in narrow areas or on steep slopes, where mowing is difficult or dangerous; also grow them under trees where it is too shady for grass. Save mowing time and watering expense—and add interesting textures, colors, and blooms—by using ground covers to reduce the size of a large lawn. You can choose among ground covers a few inches to a few feet tall, annual or perennial, evergreen or deciduous, edible or ornamental, and for shade or sun, wet or dry soil.

LAWN GRASSES
(pages 256–261, 296–297)

Examples: Cool-season grasses include bent grass, bluegrass (in photo), fescue, and ryegrass. Warm-season grasses include bahia, bermuda, centipede, St. Augustine, and zoysia.

Uses: Lawns give a clean, attractive look to the yard, and a living surface that will take more walking and playing traffic than any other plant. Lawn grasses hold the soil and are the most common outdoor carpets. Few yards would be complete without at least some areas of green grass. But grass takes much time, water, and work—more so than other plants—so don't seed or sod more than you want to mow or irrigate.

ORNAMENTAL GRASSES

Examples: Blue fescue, cloud grass, foxtail millet, job's-tears, liriope, mondo, plume or pampas grass, quaking grass, squirreltail grass, tall cordgrass, tasseled fountain grass.

Uses: Low-maintenance ornamental grasses make dramatic edgings or accents. When dried, they work well in winter bouquets. They come in a wide variety of colors, forms, and heights. Know what each will do before you plant because some are extremely hard to remove once established. Use clumps of different types at intervals for balance, blooms, and interesting textures. Pick seed heads to keep under control.

(continued on page 36)

WEIGHING YOUR LANDSCAPING OPTIONS *(continued)*

PLANTS *(continued)*

PERENNIALS
(pages 90, 129, 320–321)

Examples: Aster, bleeding-heart, candytuft, columbine, coralbells, coreopsis, delphinium, iris and poppies (in photo), lily, peony, phlox, Shasta daisy, veronica, viola.

Uses: Perennials make fine focal points when combined with shrubs or ground covers. They form the backbone of most flower borders because they come up every year. After planting, they take minimal care. Some can be divided every few years. Others will stay happy for decades. Some like shade, some like sun, and some thrive in both. For greatest appeal, combine them with height, color, and time of bloom in mind. Many will bloom again if cut back. Use in bouquets.

ANNUALS
(pages 90, 129, 322)

Examples: Alyssum, amaranth, bachelor's-button, calendula, cleome, coleus, cosmos, dahlia, geranium, impatiens, larkspur, marigold, petunia, portulaca, salvia, snapdragon, zinnia.

Uses: No other flowers bloom as abundantly and continually as do annuals, so they are ideal for color accents. Use them in massed plantings, as edges and hedges, for cutting, or in containers. Buy started plants for earliest use. Start seeds indoors or out if you need a large quantity. When choosing types, keep in mind height and color. Mix spike and round flowers for balance and drama. If you remove dead blooms, many plants will flower until frost.

BULBS
(pages 90, 129, 323)

Examples: Caladium, canna, crocus, dahlia, Dutch iris, gladiolus, grape hyacinth, hyacinth, lily, narcissus (in photo), scilla, snowdrop, tuberous begonia, tulip.

Uses: Bulbs, a loose grouping that includes corms and tubers, give generously of their striking, often fragrant, flowers. The early bloomers increase rapidly; daffodils, snowdrops, scillas, and grape hyacinths will spread for carpets of bloom. Bulbs make fine accents in flower or shrub borders. Cut off deadheads; let the foliage die down naturally. Let annuals, grass, or ground covers spread and cover fading leaves. Tender bulbs must be dug up and stored inside over winter.

HERBS
(pages 260–261, 317–319)

Examples: Basil, catnip, chamomile, chives, cress, dill, fennel, garlic, lemon balm, lemon grass, marjoram, mint, nasturtium, oregano, parsley, rosemary, sage, tarragon, thyme.

Uses: Herbs can be used in special gardens, as shown at left, or be planted in containers or among other flowers and shrubs. Keep herbs used for flavoring near the kitchen for easy access. Plant others for their textures, foliage and flower colors, interesting forms, and wonderful fragrance. Put aromatic ones like lemon balm and rosemary where you will brush against them. Use chamomile and mint underfoot, but beware of mint. Plant it where mowing or barriers will control it.

FERNS
(pages 203, 318)

Examples: Asparagus, climbing, common, crested wood, hay-scented, holly, lady, maidenhair, mountain wood, narrow beech, New York, ostrich, resurrection, royal, sensitive, staghorn.

Uses: Ferns grace many garden settings, especially those in the shade, though some will take a little sun as well. Ferns thrive as ground covers and accent plants, in rock gardens and woodland shade, on the banks of streams or the edges of water gardens, or in boggy sites. Many are so easy to grow that they flourish in such unlikely places as beneath decks. They offer a variety of textures and colors, as well as fine foliage for indoor arrangements.

HOSTAS
(pages 203, 321)

Examples: Narrow plaintain lily, Siebold plaintain lily, royal standard; many hybrids and cultivars with such names as 'Blue Skies,' 'Daybreak,' 'Lemon Lime,' 'Shade Master.'

Uses: Hostas lend a sense of serenity to a summer setting that few other plants can match. Most require some shade. Excellent for whole gardens or as accents, as ground covers in shady areas, or as plantings at woodland edges. Many sizes, colors, and textures are available. Some also have showy or fragrant spikes of white or lavender bloom. Easy to grow.

CONTAINER PLANTS
(pages 166, 186)

Examples: Annuals such as begonia, geranium, petunia, verbena, vinca; bulbs; herbs; roses; vegetables; dwarf and tender trees; strawberries; fruits; and houseplants.

Uses: Containers are perhaps the best way to add color to patios, decks, poolsides, and entryways. Annuals give the most and longest-blooming flowers, but ferns, fruits, herbs, and vegetables work well, too. Move containers (put castors on large ones and light soil or soilless mixtures in all) from sun to shade and vice versa to put color where you want it and to transfer plants past their prime to places they prefer. Move tender plants indoors for the winter. Check moisture needs daily.

FRUITS
(pages 110, 301–310, 314–316)

Examples: Apple, apricot, blueberry, cherry, citrus, fig, gooseberry, grape, kiwi, mulberry, nectarine, peach, pear, persimmon, plum, quince, and strawberry.

Uses: Fruits—whether in tree, shrub, vine, or ground cover form—can be used with or instead of ornamental plants for an edible landscape that has all the color, bloom, interest, texture, fragrance, and beauty any plan needs. They take no more space than similar nonfruiting plants and comparable feeding and watering in most climates. Plan for the most produce over the longest times to balance fresh eating with winter-preservation needs.

MEASURING YOUR EXISTING SITE

Transforming a bare or bedraggled yard into a private paradise is more than a willy-nilly procedure. It's a step-by-step operation that involves measuring and drawing a map of your site, sketching the new landscape possibilities, choosing a final plan, and, lastly, staging the work according to personal priorities, logical work order, and budget.

■ Taking measurements

A map of your lot may already exist. Check with the builder or architect, with the local FHA, VA, or mortgage office, or with your deed. Your town or county building department may have a property survey on file, too. Check any plan for accuracy, especially if it is old. If you find plans, ask also for any topographical data that may show grade changes and drainage.

If no plans exist, don't worry. Just follow the directions below, and in less than an hour you can do the measuring. Or hire a surveyor (especially if property lines are in question). Most people, however, can do their yards themselves.

Take a notebook, the largest measuring tape you have, and a pen or pencil, and head for the outdoors. Someone to hold your tape and double-check your measurements will help immensely, but you can do it alone. Just use an ice pick, a skewer, or a large rock to hold your tape.

If your yard is large, pace off the measurements. To be most accurate, measure a strip 50 or 100 feet long. Walk this and count your steps. Then convert paces into feet (for example, 50 feet at 20 steps equals 2½ feet per step).

First, make a rough sketch of your house and property. Next, accurately measure property lines, then locate the house by measuring from each corner perpendicular to the two nearest property lines. Finally, measure and mark all other structures and all trees and plantings you plan to keep. Put the figures on your rough sketch as you go.

Now or later you will want to mark the eaves, first-floor doors and windows, downspouts, meter locations, relevant utility and water lines, and anything else that may affect your plans.

◄ *To pinpoint a tree, measure a right triangle, beginning at the corner of a nearby structure and positioning the tree at the apex. To make sure the angle is square, use a carpenter's square and heavy string.*

▼ *Record the distances from one structure to another. Sight from post to corners of both structures to make sure you're standing square.*

◄Record your measurements as you go. Accuracy counts for more than neatness at this point. Be sure to locate all structures, trees, walks, drive, overhead and underground utilities, and any other relevant information.

◄To measure the grade of a slope, mark a board in feet, then butt it against a stake at the top of the slope. Level, then measure from board bottom to ground. This grade is about 2:5, 2 feet vertical drop to 5 feet of horizontal distance.

DRAWING A MAP OF YOUR EXISTING SITE

With the rough sketch of your property drawn and accurate figures gathered (see pages 38–39), you are well on the way to redesigning your yard's landscape. Now, go back inside and turn the rough sketch of your yard into a detailed, drawn-to-scale map. The sooner you do this, the fewer trips you'll have to make back out to recheck any measurements.

This base plan will give you a good picture of your yard as a whole.

A drawing board and T square will make the job easier, but they aren't essential. All you really need are any flat surface (a breadboard or large piece of cardboard makes a fine portable one) and a piece of paper large enough to draw your yard on. Most yards up to a half acre can be drawn on graph paper 18 to 24 inches square or vellum 17 to 22 inches square.

Use a scale of 1:4 (1 inch equals 4 feet or ¼ inch equals 1 foot) for a small yard down to 1:20 (1 inch equals 20 feet) for a half-acre lot. The larger the second number of the scale, the smaller everything will appear on paper.

Graph paper and vellum come with 4, 8, or 10 light grids per inch. These will not reproduce on a blueprint but will be helpful prior to that stage.

If your yard is very large, you may want to make one map of the whole yard at a small scale

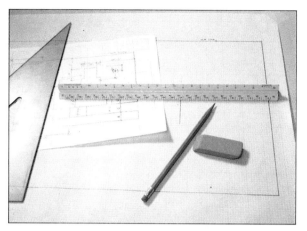

◄ *To make your base map, you must have a large piece of paper, pencils, an eraser, and a ruler. If you like, visit an art or drafting store to get large sheets of graph paper or vellum, an architect's or engineer's scale like the one shown, a compass, and a triangle or two.*

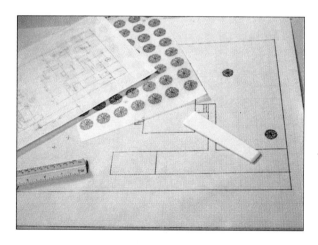

◄ *Draw the property lines first, structures next, then existing walks, drives, trees, shrubs, and plantings. Use the symbols shown below or buy press-on stickers, which you apply with a burnishing tool (both shown at left).*

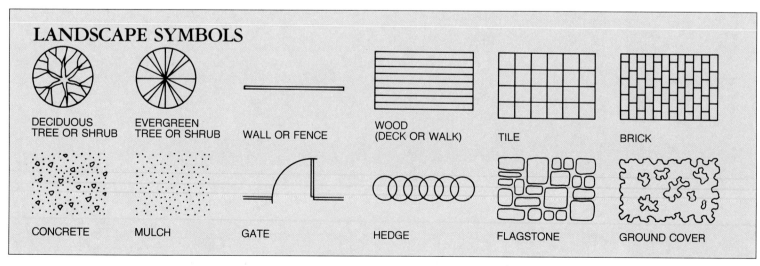

LANDSCAPE SYMBOLS

DECIDUOUS TREE OR SHRUB

EVERGREEN TREE OR SHRUB

WALL OR FENCE

WOOD (DECK OR WALK)

TILE

BRICK

CONCRETE

MULCH

GATE

HEDGE

FLAGSTONE

GROUND COVER

first, then later make separate plans of individual areas at a larger scale.

As an aid, you can use a professional scale (see photo, opposite, top). An architect's scale is calibrated in eighths of an inch, an engineer's in tenths. You can buy one scale that combines both. Or you can just use a ruler.

Tape your paper to your surface with a sturdy but removable tape such as masking tape.

Draw an arrow pointing north. You can, of course, fill this in later, but it is best to have the north point at the top or side of your paper for quick reference. It will tell you much about the sun patterns and govern many plant and placing decisions (see pages 96–113).

Then, using pencil, draw your map, starting with the property lines. Fill in the lines of the house and other structures. Measure with scale, compass, or ruler and make dots on the plan.

Join them for lines. Mark the trunk positions of the trees and shrubs you plan to keep. You also may want to sketch in the present branch lines with thin but solid lines and keep the possible future spread lines in mind.

(continued on page 42)

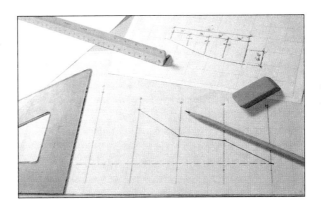

◄*A scale or ruler and triangle allow you to transfer any slope measurements to a formal drawing like this for help in deciding about grades. You can use the same methods to make elevation sketches (see page 45).*

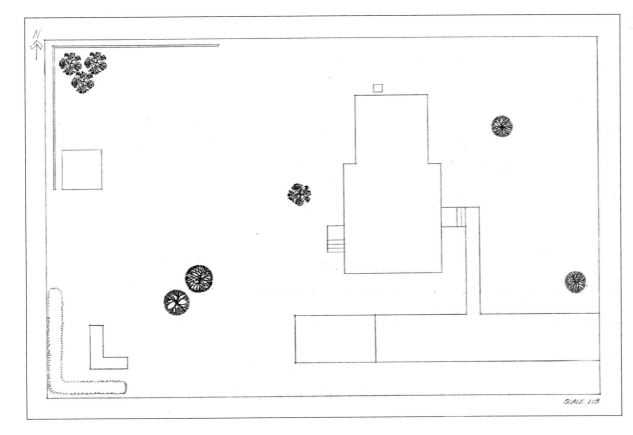

◄*Here is the formal base map drawn from the measurements recorded on pages 38–39. Once you complete your plan, make several photo- or blueprint copies for you and any contractors to work with. Put the original in a safe place.*

DRAWING A MAP OF YOUR EXISTING SITE *(continued)*

Having drawn your base map, you now have done more professional landscaping than most people ever accomplish. The next step is to tape a piece of tracing paper over your base plan and go outside again.

This time, on the tracing paper, make notes about your yard, similar to those shown below. Indicate any feature that may affect your landscape decisions: sun, wind, good and bad views, privacy needs, soil, topography, and any other problems or special features your yard presents. Put in arrows to indicate directions or intensity.

Also include here any notes about the adjoining properties that may be relevant to your plan: nearby trees, for example, or noise, erosion, or drainage problems.

Next, to make sure you fully analyze your lot, go back indoors. Check the views from the windows in the rooms where you spend the most time, and from your entryways, noting all the pluses and minuses of each view.

Get out any lists of likes and dislikes you've noted about your yard over the years (see page 22). Write everything of importance on the piece of tracing paper.

If you are doing this plan after studying your yard for a full cycle of seasons, you are ready to proceed. If not, the plan will help you notice more keenly how such features as sun, shadows, wind, and views change with the time of day and time of year. Put your plan in a handy spot so you can add to it as needed.

Only after doing such a plan can you put the information in the rest of this book into the climate and context of your yard. Combine the possibilities with your own realities, and you will make decisions that will enhance the best and change the worst landscaping features.

► *This tracing page puts our original base plan into the context of the lot's unique climate and surroundings. Pin your own "problem plan" up on a wall or some other place where you can refer to it easily.*

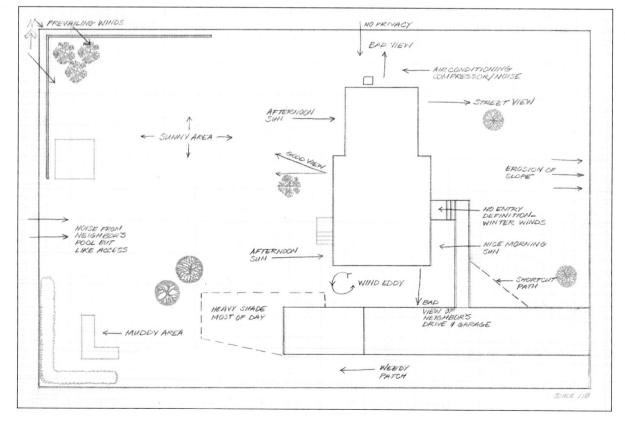

DESIGNING YOUR NEW LANDSCAPE

The initial design stage is the most important, creative, exciting, and forgiving of all the landscaping steps. Let it be the most fun as well.

The process is a simple one: Lay tracing paper over your base plan, sketch all sorts of ideas, then select or change ideas based on how they fit together and how they solve the problems or accent the features you highlighted on your problem plan (see opposite).

■ Ideas

Be sure to give your plan time to evolve. You'll find that ideas may seem limited at first, but that they multiply as you play with them and they interact with each other. (See pages 22 and 24 for hints on generating ideas.)

You'll want to decide early on if there's a single landscape style—formal, natural, English cottage, etc.—you'd like to adopt. To help you with this decision, check to see whether your ideas seem to be tending in one direction. Once you've selected a style, you can more readily choose and reject ideas. This saves you time and helps you develop a more unified design.

■ Bubble tracings

At the start, instead of sketching specific ideas on the tracing paper, draw bubbles representing the possible general use areas you see for the yard: entry, outdoor living, service, etc. (see illustration, below). Most of the front and perhaps some of the side, for example, could be entry area. Most of the back and perhaps part of a side yard could be reserved for outdoor living and entertaining. Drawing such bubbles keeps you from thinking in too many specifics too early on in the process.

(continued on page 44)

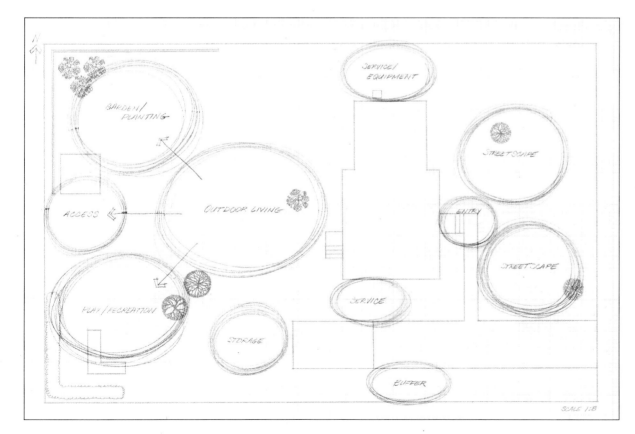

◄ *Still looking at your yard as a whole, begin to consider the separate uses you'd like your landscape to serve. Draw bubbles representing general use areas—and erase and redraw them—until you find the locations that work best for function and looks.*

43

DESIGNING YOUR NEW LANDSCAPE *(continued)*

◄*Continue to trace over the base map, trying new options and erasing or tossing rejected solutions until you come up with several feasible combinations.*

▼*A handy way to check how your plans will actually look: Lay tracing paper over an enlarged photo of your house or other yard site and draw sketches of proposed additions.*

As you do your bubble tracings of general use areas, you may also want to cut out some smaller bubbles—from any kind of slightly thicker paper—to represent areas that will have a specific use, say a patio, deck, or pool. You can move these patterns around easily, trying different arrangements within the broader space you've allotted to that general use.

Be sure when you're considering the general uses for your yard that you set aside space for a service area or two (see pages 232–251). These are the areas in your landscape that will accommodate everything from trash cans, boats, and drying clothes, to pets and fireplace wood. Try to put these service areas in the least conspicuous but most convenient spots possible.

As you sketch the bubbles and as you begin to draw more specific ideas on your tracing paper, don't forget to refer to your problem plan (see page 42). Double-check all dimensions to be sure the pieces you're considering still fit in the whole. Refer, too, to any lists you made of your family's outdoor needs. Ask often what the rest of the family thinks about the plan. Considering everyone's ideas and desires will help in assessing and implementing the plan, and in the ultimate success of the landscape.

Concentrate on problems and solutions at this stage, not fine detail. Think of the plants as architectural forms: background or specimen trees, high or low screens. Save the decisions about varieties for later.

■ Three-dimensional thinking

Remember that your scale plan is accurate, but flat. Expand on it by walking around the yard and pacing off proposed changes, and by sitting on the step and visualizing the finished scene.

Use some props, too. Lay out hoses to indicate the edges of patios. Put up sheets to mark the height of fences. Go out after dark and shine a flashlight to give the effect of night lighting.

Draw some simple elevation sketches. They don't have to be as accurate as those shown below, though you can use the same tools and methods you used for your base plan to make your elevation sketches just as detailed; and the greater the detail, the easier it will be for you to picture the results.

Or, for a quick elevation view, blow up a photo of your house, lay tracing paper over it, then sketch in possible changes (see bottom photo, opposite).

This may be a good time to make separate, large-scale plans of various sections of the yard.

At some point, you also may want to draw up specific plans indicating lighting, drainage, or other special construction needs. These detailed plans will greatly help those doing the work.

■ **Long-term thinking**
When testing the pros and cons of all ideas, think of how things will look not just at the time the work is completed, but also in five years, in 10 years, in 25 years. Consider, too, how your landscaping needs may change over time. After all, landscaping is an evolutionary art form that's never really finished.

▼ *Simple elevation drawings like these can help you make decisions and better visualize the results of the plans. Note how the height and spread of planting materials relate to the size of the house.*

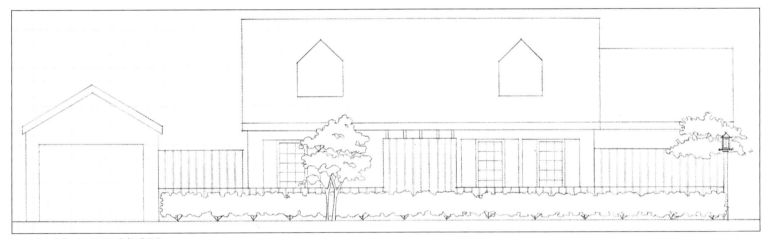

FRONT ELEVATION

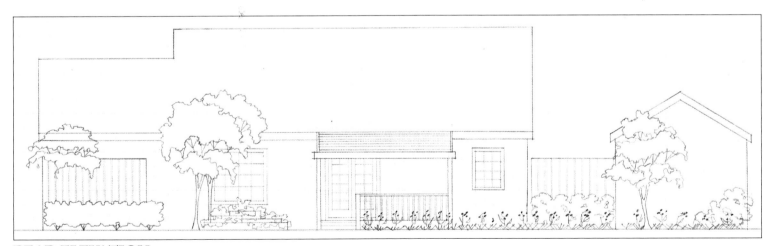

REAR ELEVATION

CHOOSING YOUR FINAL PLAN

If you diligently dream up different solutions to your site problems and different ways to achieve the functions that your family wants to enjoy, you're bound to come up with several possible landscape plans.

Your alternative plans probably won't be as definitely drawn as those shown opposite and on the two pages following, since you will have been automatically condensing and eliminating as you went along. We formally drew our plan options so that you could see three approaches to the same problem plan (see page 42).

You may say, "If it were my house, I'd definitely choose Plan B." Or you may as definitely eliminate that as "Nice, but not for us," and prefer the first or the third or a combination.

The main point is that each of these plans accommodates all the notes presented on the problem plan. Be sure that the options you finally choose do the same for your problem plan.

■ Further study
While you are moving from concept to final plan, you will want to carefully read the relevant parts of the rest of this book.

Interesting homes and yards that you quickly drove by before will demand more detailed study now. You'll find yourself driving past certain places so slowly and so often that someone may get suspicious. Do it anyway.

In fact, feel free to park and make a sketch of concepts you like. Or get out and ask the homeowners about their yards. Most people will be flattered and more than willing to expand on how and why they did what they did.

Go to the library and check books and plans again. Check prices at home-supply stores and in catalogs. Get estimates from contractors as you approach the final decisions.

■ Keep drawing
By drawing through your ideas, you will keep the concept developing toward its final stage. No one can say for sure when you reach that point. When you think you're getting close, ask yourself these questions:

■ Does the plan meet all building codes, or deed, setback, or easement restrictions?
■ Have I solved all of the problems presented on my problem plan?
■ Are my choices realistic in view of the cost, work, and time involved to implement them?
■ Will the yard I've planned provide for all of the functions my family wants, or at least the most necessary ones?
■ Is the plan in keeping with our life-style? Does it fit my family? Will my family fit it?
■ Can we safely move cars (or trucks and other needed equipment) onto and off the property and park them where needed?
■ Is there a usable and pleasing sequence: easy access from car to kitchen or front door, from indoor rooms to outdoor living areas, from garden to shed?
■ Will the yard be pleasant to the eye, ear, nose, sole, and soul in every season? From indoors looking out? From the street looking in? From the outdoors looking around?

No plan is perfect. It doesn't have to be. It only has to be the best one that you can come up with at the moment for your site, your climate, and your family.

Nor is any plan ever completely finished. As you, your family, and your trees grow and mature, you will no doubt have to make some minor changes. Maybe you'll even decide to make major changes. That's OK, too. This is paper, not stone; a guide, not a law.

■ The final plan
When you're ready, place a new piece of tracing paper directly over the base plan and draw your final plan. Try to make your plan neat and concise now. Make sketches and notations bold enough to read easily.

You can still indicate plants by general type. Remain vague about structure design and materials, too, if you like. Workers at your local nursery and building-supply center can help you make decisions about specific plants and structural details after looking at your final plan.

In this logical and problem-solving scheme, the backyard includes well-defined play/storage and lawn/visual zones. In front, the inviting streetscape gives the house distinction.

This clump of trees adds interest to the new deck, making it more usable and enjoyable. Walkways and surrounding plantings tie the deck to the site. The walks provide access to the yard.

The deck itself is on the same level as important rooms inside. The vined arbor shades the deck, softens the summer shadows indoors, and lets in full sun in the winter, when it's needed.

This short bit of fence gives privacy from the house next door. Trees soften it and buffer noise from neighbors. Shrubs around the air conditioner soften sound and improve the sight.

A new concrete retaining wall solves erosion worries, eliminates the need to mow the slope, and adds visually to the streetscape. Topped with a low hedge, it turns at the drive.

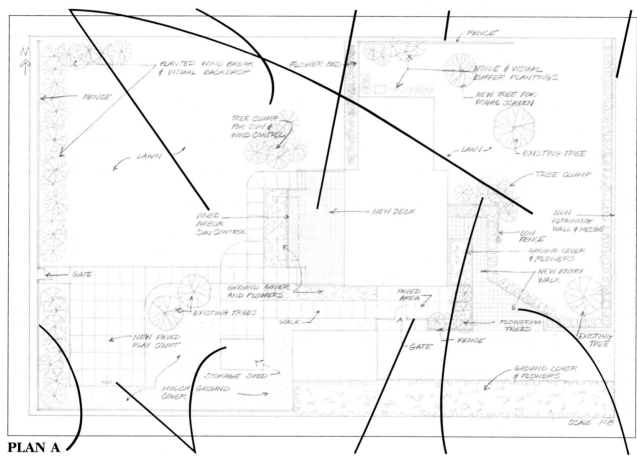

PLAN A

The fence across the back and around to the garage provides the utmost in privacy for the backyard. The gate saves good neighbor relations. Trees buffer noise and stop prevailing winds.

Shady and muddy areas where few plants would grow are ideal for a storage shed and play court. The existing trees make the walkway system seem natural and keep the court from looking so bare.

This high fence screens the view of the neighbors' drive and blocks the wind eddy where groceries are unloaded. The gate adds interest and access. Flowering trees create a pleasant view for those inside the house.

This clump of trees gives scale, beauty, and distinction to the front of the house. It keeps the winter wind from whipping the front storm door out of the hand on blustery days.

A wider entry takes in the shortcut path. Low flowers and ground cover and a low fence separate the yard from the entry without blocking the morning sun. They also add color and elegance.

CHOOSING YOUR FINAL PLAN *(continued)*

This plan uses many of the same elements as Plan A (page 47), but is more formal. Here, the outdoor living, service, and streetscape zones are defined more clearly. The play area is out of sight.

A gazebo provides a focal point and also serves as a windbreak. A pool and rock garden separate main deck and gazebo for two outdoor rooms, yet provide visual and audio interest for both.

This angular deck and walkway also are more formal and elaborate. Notice the symmetry and balance. As on Plan A, the deck adjoins and is on the same level as the important rooms indoors.

Fence and clumps of trees give privacy and quiet to the bedroom end of the house, create a pleasant view from inside, separate front yard and back, and make the house seem longer.

A retaining wall again solves the erosion and mowing problems on the slope. Of brick instead of concrete, it blends with the tone and style of this plan. Turf replaces the shrubbery of Plan A.

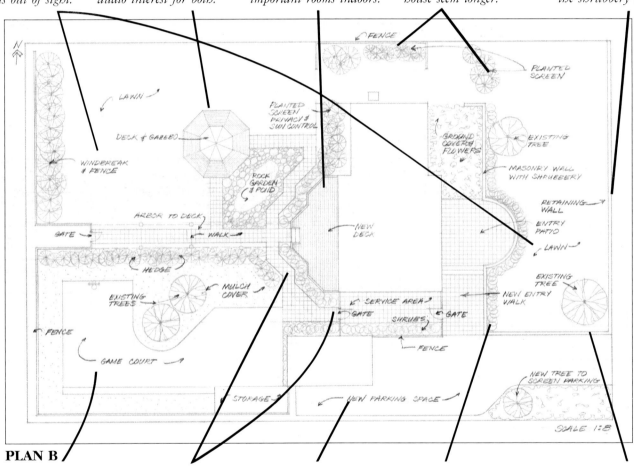

PLAN B

The game court is more elaborate and is separated from the passive lawn area with a hedge and arbor. Existing trees are used and protected. The plan still resolves mud and shade problems.

A patterned and formal walkway system of brick unites the entire yard. From the deck to the back gate, it is covered by an arbor that gives visual interest, shade, and separation.

Additional parking space covers the weedy patch. The tree at its approach helps to screen, soften, and shade the greater expanse of paving. The tree is back from street so as not to block an exiting motorist's view of traffic.

Hedge at retaining wall in Plan A is at entry patio wall here to give a look and feel of substance. Flowers and ground cover at the far end eliminate mowing and look lovely from bedroom windows.

The wall continues along driveway and entry for continuity of the streetscape and to block the shortcut. This and the simplicity of the front lawn help bring the house visually closer to the street.

One way to assess subsurface drainage is to test your soil's porosity. To do this, dig a hole about 2 feet deep and fill it with water. After the water drains out, fill the hole again. If all the water disappears within 24 hours, the soil is too porous. If water remains after 48 hours, the soil is too dense. If the water level gradually rises, the water table is too high.

Some subsurface drainage problems can be cured by improving surface drainage—directing runoff to parched areas, for example, or away from low spots. Other subsurface problems call for below-the-surface solutions, such as correcting soil that drains too poorly or too quickly, or installing underground drain lines, as shown at lower right and discussed in more detail on page 54.

■ Wet basement

If the floor or walls of your basement are chronically wet, improving surface or subsurface drainage, or a combination of the two, could dry them out. The box at right shows the steps to take. But first, here's how to evaluate which steps are appropriate for your situation.

■ *Seepage* oozing through a basement wall at or near grade level is probably the result of a grade or downspout problem, both easily corrected, as shown at right.

■ *Leaks* farther down the wall or at floor level usually indicate that subsurface water is building up around the foundation and forcing its way in through cracks. Dig down to the level of the leaks—to the footings for floor-level leaks—and install perforated drain lines to carry the excess water away.

■ *Subterranean water* starts out as a thin, barely visible film of moisture on the basement floor. A spring or high water table is forcing water up from below under high pressure, turning your basement into a well. Drain lines around the footings may help reduce subterranean water, but you also may need to install a sump pump.

(continued on page 54)

IMPROVING FOUNDATION DRAINAGE

Use fill to create a gentle slope away from foundation walls. The grade should fall a minimum of ¼ inch per foot for a distance of at least 4 feet from the wall. Use topsoil if you intend to plant here. For more about correcting a grade, see pages 56–57.

If splash blocks aren't keeping rainwater away from the foundation, dig a trench, layer it with gravel, then run flexible drainpipe to a remote location. A special adapter connects the pipe to the downspout outlet. Cover the pipe with more gravel, then fill the trench with earth and cover with sod.

Intercept subsurface water flowing toward a foundation wall with a drainage trench alongside the wall. Dig to the depth of any leaks. Lay a bed of gravel, install perforated drainpipe, then top with more gravel, earth, and sod. The drainpipe should slope at least ⅛ inch per foot toward its outlet.

SOLVING DRAINAGE PROBLEMS *(continued)*

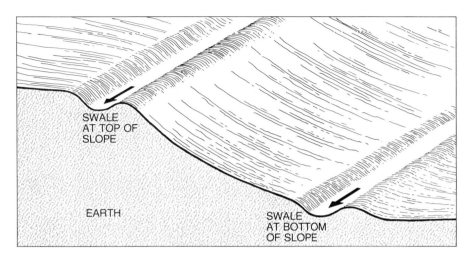

SWALE
AT TOP OF
SLOPE

EARTH

SWALE
AT BOTTOM
OF SLOPE

▲ *Swales divert water coursing down a hillside. Dig shallow trenches pitched in the direction you want water to go. Mound and compact earth on the downhill side of each trench, then lay sod or plant with ground cover.*

▼*Baffles slow runoff. Dig zigzag trenches across the hillside. Make the trenches slightly shallower than the thickness of landscape timbers. Set the timbers so their tops tilt back into the slope.*

Pages 52–53 help identify areas where good landscaping could improve surface or sub-surface drainage. Here, let's look at specific ways you can recontour the terrain or siphon off underground water.

■ Reshaping slopes
Plan carefully before you cut into a slope. Aim to either slow runoff or redirect it; attempting to dam up water only causes flooding. If you're redirecting runoff, make sure you don't discharge it onto a neighbor's property, which may be a code violation and could cause ill feelings. Most codes permit dumping rainwater into a storm sewer, but not a sanitary sewer.

Locate swales at the top and bottom of a slope, as shown at upper left. Make trenches about as wide as a spade, using the earth you excavate to create berms along the swales' lower edges. If swales will cause a mowing problem, plant them with a hardy ground cover.

Baffles impede water's descent, giving it more time to soak into the slope. Install them as shown at lower left. Baffles also can control erosion, as can bevels and contours (for more information, see pages 66–69).

■ Installing drain lines
Flexible plastic drainpipe (see page 53) offers one good material for underground drain lines. Clay tiles are another. For either, dig a trench about 4 inches wider than the pipe's diameter and at least a foot deep. Slope the trench ⅛ inch or more per foot of horizontal run.

Lay 2 inches of gravel in the trench, then install the pipe. If it's perforated, lay pipe with the holes down to keep soil from clogging the line. Set clay tiles end to end and cover tops of the joints with roofing paper to keep out soil.

After installing drain lines, cover them with several more inches of gravel, then replace soil and sod. As an alternative, you can dispense with the soil and sod and fill the trench to the brim with gravel.

DEALING WITH SPECIAL DRAINAGE PROBLEMS

Contouring and installing underground drain lines remedy most drainage problems, but some situations require more extensive measures.

What do you do, for example, about a low spot where water chronically collects? What if your yard has compacted, poorly draining soil, or a discharge from drain lines that can't reach a disposal area? Is your soil too dry to support plants?

Each of these situations calls for one of the special approaches listed below.

■ Catch basins

Drain a swampy low spot with a catch basin like the one illustrated at right. Water falls through a grate at ground level and collects until a sloping (⅛ inch per foot of run) drainpipe can carry it off to a proper discharge area. A sediment trap snags leaves and other debris that also wash through the grate.

You can buy a ready-made catch basin or you can form and pour your own. Choose its location and the location of the drainpipe carefully, as well as the discharge point.

Because sediment piles up in catch basins, they need periodic cleaning.

■ Drainage chimneys

Improve the absorbency of dense, slow-draining soil with drainage chimneys. Dig 8- to 12-inch-diameter holes, spaced 2 to 4 feet apart. Make each hole deep enough to penetrate the hard soil up top, but don't go down to the water table. Fill the holes with gravel or crushed rock. To hide the chimneys from view and give your yard a finished look, top off the holes with sod or other plants.

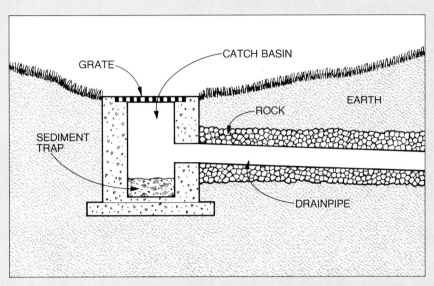

■ Dry wells

What can you do with drain lines—from downspouts, for instance, or along a foundation—that can't be emptied into a storm sewer or natural drainage area? Answer: Connect them to a dry well, which is simply a large hole filled with rock and covered with a concrete slab or other impervious material.

Local codes, pegged to regional rainfall data, dictate the size of dry wells, but 2 to 4 feet wide by 3 feet deep is typical.

■ Irrigation

Contouring and underground drain lines can bring water to dry areas of your lot, but if there's simply not enough rainfall to keep your lawn and gardens green, you'll need to irrigate them. One good way to do this is with an underground sprinkler system that automatically supplies moisture at optimum times of day. To learn about installing an underground sprinkler system, see pages 262–265.

▲ *In a low spot prone to heavy flooding, install a catch basin. Cover it with a grate, or fill the basin with crushed rock. Extensive low-lying areas may need several catch basins for good results.*

CORRECTING THE GRADE

Improving surface-water drainage, adding contours to a flat site, and digging for a new walk or patio all require some remodeling of your lot's topography. Making changes in grade is the necessary—and sometimes arduous—first step in a wide variety of landscaping projects.

Work out a complete grading plan, from lot line to lot line, before you begin excavating. This way you can conserve soil and effort by moving earth from high spots to low ones. A comprehensive grading plan also can save money if you must order additional soil or have excess hauled away; many suppliers and truckers add a surcharge for quantities of less than 5 cubic yards (for more about purchasing soil, see the opposite page).

For safety's sake, mark the locations of all underground telephone, gas, sewer, water, and other utility lines before digging. Many utility companies will come out and mark their lines for you, usually at no charge. Also, file with your building department for any permits you might need.

■ Moving earth
All but very major regrading can be accomplished with a pick, shovel, rake, wheelbarrow, and other simple hand tools. To make the job easier, consider renting equipment such as a power tiller to break up the soil or a front-end-loading garden tractor to push it around.

If you decide to do the job the old-fashioned way (and give your body a modern-day workout), plan short sessions of digging and hauling. Spread them out over several weekends, if need be. Dig when soil is slightly moist, neither heavily laden with water nor caked and unyielding. To conserve strength, don't overload the shovel or wheelbarrow, and lay a path of planks from excavation to fill sites.

Professional excavators can move a surprising amount of earth in a few days. Be warned, however, that heavy machinery can do lots of damage to landscaping around the area to be

1 Lay out the slope with string, as explained opposite. Here, we are correcting a slope adjacent to a foundation, so we also snapped a chalk line at the new grade level. Measure to determine how much fill you will need.

2 On our site we were able to shift soil from a spot higher than the final grade to build up lower areas, a process known as cutting and filling. If you can't cut and fill, you'll have to haul soil from another area in your yard that needs lowering or buy it.

3 After you've moved soil and compacted it, rake to shape the final grade. We filled to slightly below the chalk line because we plan to add a layer of crushed rock on top. If you plan to lay sod, allow for its thickness as well.

excavated—not a problem for jobs with easy street access, such as a driveway, but you probably wouldn't want a heavy tractor crunching across an established lawn or garden.

■ Laying out a slope
To drain properly, any grading you do must slope away from the house or other structure at a rate of no less than ¼ inch per foot. With rough recontouring projects, you can visually estimate the fall, making sure that it doesn't drain toward areas where water would puddle.

For greater precision, use stakes, string, and a level, as shown opposite and on pages 74–75. Drive stakes at the top and bottom of the new slope, stretch string between the stakes, and level it. Measure the string's length. Finally, slide the string down the lower stake at least ¼ inch for every foot of length. Bear in mind that even a nearly level project, such as a patio, must have some pitch to it.

■ Making the grade
After you've determined the slope, grading proceeds in three phases. First you strip away the sod, if any, shovel up topsoil, and set the two aside for reuse. Next, you establish the rough grade by removing or adding subsoil. Finally, you replace the topsoil, smooth it, then lay sod or plant.

Skim sod by slicing into it with a pointed spade held almost parallel to the ground. Separate sod from the soil underneath with short, jabbing strokes, rolling it up as you go. If you have lots of sod to deal with, rent a power-driven sod cutter. As you remove topsoil under the sod, chop it up to destroy any grass roots.

Attack subsoil next, driving the spade into the earth at about a 45-degree angle. Push the handle downward, then lift and pitch soil into a wheelbarrow or low spot. After moving the subsoil, break it up into chunks measuring an inch or less. If you encounter rocks, split them with a

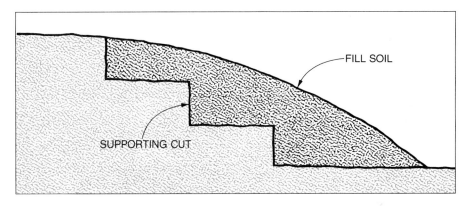

sledge or use them as fill. Mound the fill slightly, then compact it until it's even with surrounding undisturbed soil.

After you're satisfied with the rough grade, spread out the topsoil you've saved and smooth it with a steel rake.

■ Purchasing soil
If your grading project will require extensive filling, you may need to buy additional earth. First, determine how many cubic yards to order; 1 cubic yard will cover 300 square feet to a depth of 1 inch.

Look for soil that approximates the texture of the existing soil. Differing textures can cause drainage problems because water does not move easily from one soil texture to another. Soil quality and prices vary widely, so check with several suppliers, and be sure to take a look at the merchandise.

Test soil by crumbling it in your hand. Soil that breaks down easily into uniform particles works best. Avoid compacted, sandy, or poor-quality earth, which could be contaminated by weed seeds and other soil problems.

Before the soil is delivered, plan a route for the truck so you can get the load as near as possible to the work site. If a truck can back into the site, the driver can spread out the earth, saving you lots of work.

▲ *To make a steep slope more gradual, dig a series of stair-stepped supporting cuts first, then add fill. The supporting cuts help hold the fill, protecting against erosion until grass or ground cover establishes itself. For more information about controlling erosion, see pages 62–77.*

LAYING OUT PROJECT SITES

Now—after you've assessed your landscaping needs, developed a plan, and solved any drainage problems your lot might have—comes the moment when you begin to get your ideas off the ground. The chapters that follow proceed step-by-step through dozens of landscaping projects—everything from rustic paths to raised decks. But all start in the same way: You mark the site, then square and stake corners. Let's take a look at how to lay the groundwork for a successful project.

■ Siting basics
To lay out the site for a landscaping project, arm yourself with two 50-foot tape measures, chalk line, a line level, mason's level, plumb bob, carpenter's square, sledge, and stakes made by cutting points on the ends of 1x3s. You'll also need a helper and chalk, lime, or sand. The job doesn't take long, but don't rush: A measurement that's off by just an inch at the outset can compound itself into feet down the line.

Begin by marking an approximate outline of the project's boundaries with stakes and string. Use rope or garden hose to mark curves. This outline gives you your first full-scale look at

how a new fence, patio, or other improvement will affect its surroundings. If you don't like what you see, making changes at this point is as easy as pulling up stakes and erasing a line on your landscape plan.

Once you're ready to formally measure and mark the layout, consider using batter boards to locate any corners, as shown opposite, bottom right. Batter boards make special sense for decks, fences, and other projects where height or slope is a factor. Batter boards also come in handy for in-ground projects like patios if you prefer to remove the strings for digging, then put them up again to see if edges have strayed.

Just run string from batter board to batter board, and—if you're building an attached structure—from batter boards to the house.

If your terrain is level and so is your project, you can dispense with batter boards and lay out the project with strings and stakes. In fact, if your design has a curve or two, this is just about the only way to go. For straight edges, simply stretch strings from stakes at each end. For curves, stake garden hose in position. For precisely radiused curves, use a stake and string as a compass. Locate the stake equidistant from the beginning and end of the curve, then swing the string in an arc, driving stakes at 1-foot intervals.

(Note: When putting up strings for concrete patios and walks and other projects that require forms, be sure to mark a perimeter several inches outside the actual planned slab to allow room for form boards and stakes.)

■ Checking corners
Whether you lay out your project with simple stakes or use batter boards, you'll want to be sure that any corners are exactly square before proceeding. Use a simple geometric formula.

As you probably recall learning in school, the square of the hypotenuse in a right triangle equals the sum of the squares of the two shorter sides. This means that if one leg of a triangle measures 3 feet (3 squared = 9) and the other 4 feet (4 squared = 16), the diagonal hypotenuse must be exactly 5 feet (square root of 9 + 16).

▼To mark the perimeter of a project, stretch string between stakes a few inches above ground level, square any corners, then pour powdered chalk, white sand, or lime along the line. This tactic works best on level land; to deal with a slope, see pages 74–75.

▼One way to position posts on a slope: Mark 1-foot intervals on a 2x4. Butt this against the starting stake at the slope top. Level the board, drop a plumb bob, then drive a stake at that point. (See also pages 74–75.)

► Use the principle of the 3-4-5 triangle to assure that a corner is square. First, mark a spot 3 feet over from the corner. Extend a tape measure 4 feet along the string line. The diagonal between these points must be 5 feet.

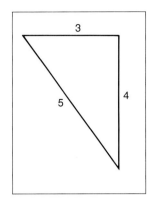

▲ The sides of a triangle with a square corner always relate to each other the same way. You also can use multiples of 3-4-5 (6-8-10, 9-12-15).

◄ Make batter boards by nailing crosspieces to stakes. You'll need two assemblies for each corner, situated a foot or so beyond the corner. Stretch strings, square them, and drop a plumb bob to position each corner stake.

Using the principle of the 3-4-5 triangle, you can check a corner for square as shown at upper right. If necessary, adjust strings and remeasure.

After you turn a second corner and plot locations for a third run of posts, as you would with a square or rectangular structure such as a deck, measure diagonally from both sets of opposite corners; these measurements must be equal.

■ **Marking for digging**

For patios and other projects requiring excavation, once you know the corners are at right angles, sprinkle powdered chalk, lime, or sand along the strings, as shown opposite. These marks will guide you as you dig. Also adjust the string to the proper grade so you can use it as a reference when determining how deep to dig.

For projects that require posts, measure along the strings, drop a plumb bob, and drive stakes.

ERECTING POSTS

After the site is laid out, the next step in the construction of many landscaping projects is the erection of posts.

Posts for a deck, fence, or other structure must be absolutely plumb and firmly rooted in the earth or bolted to a concrete footing. To ward off rot, posts should be of heartwood or pressure-treated lumber, and steps should be taken to assure that water drains away from the posts. To prevent the posts from heaving, post-holes must extend below the local frost line.

■ Step-by-step

Begin by digging holes at the points you've staked (see pages 58–59). Choose your digging equipment based partly on how hard or rocky your soil is, and partly on how deep you must go to reach your area's frost line. For shallow holes in soft earth, use a clamshell digger like the one in the photo at upper right; for hard soil or holes deeper than about 30 inches, you'll need a hand- or motor-powered auger. Most rental outlets offer all three of these tools.

Next, you'll need to determine whether you want to set the posts in the ground, as shown here, or on top of separate footings. Separate footings require more concrete because you must completely fill the postholes. You'll also need to insert anchors into the tops of the wet footings (see pages 100 and 159). Local codes may dictate one method or the other.

To set posts in the ground, first soak the holes, then drop in 2 to 3 inches of gravel. Put tubular forms in the holes, if you like, so you can extend the concrete above ground, which helps keep surface water away from the posts.

After you set each post in place, adjust until it is plumb in two directions, then secure the post with two diagonal braces nailed to the post. If necessary, use string tied to end posts to check the alignment of intermediate posts.

Recheck that the posts are plumb, then pour concrete into the holes, poking with a rod to remove air pockets. At the top of the hole or form, round off the concrete. Let the concrete cure 24 hours before doing any other work.

◄ To ensure posts are an even height, you can dig holes to a uniform depth or cut posts after concrete cures. To check depths, make a square as at left and stake a level string. Cut square's longer arm to reflect desired depth; shorter one rests on string when you reach that depth. For cutting posts, see pages 74–75.

◄ Once posts are braced in position, backfill around any forms, then pack holes or forms with concrete. After the concrete has set for about 20 minutes, check the posts for plumb again and adjust if necessary. Leave the braces in place until you're sure the posts are fixed.

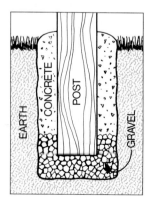

◄ Good drainage begins at the bottom of each posthole you dig. Wet down the hole, then pour in 2 to 3 inches of gravel. This prevents groundwater from collecting at the base of the post.

DEALING WITH EXISTING PLANTS

Most sizable landscaping projects demand that you first tear out a sizable amount of existing landscaping. Aim to reuse what you can—and decide in advance what you're going to do with the debris you don't need. If more than a few cubic yards of branches, bushes, earth, or other materials must go to a landfill, consider renting a refuse container.

Leave big or dangerous jobs, such as major grading and removing big trees, to professionals with the equipment and know-how to handle them. You can also rent a power-driven sod cutter, mulcher, small tractor, or other machinery to make clearing jobs easier.

Spray plant materials with herbicide several weeks before removing them, then water well so chemicals seep into the soil and kill the roots. The best time to remove weeds and many other plants is in early spring, before they go to seed.

Clear ground covers by mowing them flat with a rotary mower or cutting off tops with a sickle, hedge shears, or weed trimmer. Then dig up the roots with a spade or power tiller.

■ Transplanting

Want to relocate choice shrubs and trees? You may need help lifting them out of the ground and setting them in again, but shrubs of medium size and trees no taller than 6 feet, with trunks no larger than 1 inch in diameter, lend themselves to amateur transplanting. And, with professional help, you can safely transplant trees many feet taller.

Spring and fall are the best times to move shrubs and trees, but if you keep the roots moist, you can shift plants in the summer, too.

Use a sharp spade to cut a circle around the roots, then shape them and surrounding soil into a ball by undercutting lower roots. When the ball is free and can be rocked to one side, wrap it in burlap, then fasten with twine.

After you've set the plant in its new home, remove the twine. Fill around the roots and give them a good soaking. In hot weather, mist the plant daily with a hose for the next two weeks; avoid overwatering. Then water weekly.

◄ *To tear out a deep-rooted shrub that's outlived its usefulness, dig around and under the plant, chopping through roots as much as possible. Wrap chain around the roots, hook it to a garden tractor, and pull the shrub free.*

▼ *If a small dug-up shrub can't be transplanted right away, mothball it in a mound of soil and mulch. Be sure to bury all the plant's roots. Build the mound in a well-shaded spot, and keep it moist.*

The flower and shrub garden bursts forth with the color and natural feeling of California native perennials. Potted plants on the deck, stairs, and balconies add accenting color.

CHAPTER·THREE

SLOPE SOLUTIONS

Tilt your world a bit and you get a whole new landscaping perspective, invigorating and challenging. The first rule of designing new surroundings is to study and work with site conditions. If your land includes slopes, your design begins and certainly will end with a more interesting scene. Take full advantage of the sometimes superlative views or the feeling of enclosure. Let initial problems push you to creative solutions.

62

For easy access to the outdoors and a delightful treetop view, a deck opens from the dining area and balconies open off the sleeping floor.

The dry walls of large natural stone hold the soil in place for the plantings. They also add character, economy of space, and a mood of natural permanence.

ASSESSING SLOPE SOLUTIONS

If you have slopes on your property, you know that they can pose landscaping difficulties. But be assured that they also can offer tremendous opportunities.

Properly used, slopes add interest to a landscaping plan. They can screen views, buffer noise, and direct the eye. They can even create illusions: a rail fence along the top of a gentle slope can make the yard within seem to extend to the edge of the world.

A sloping yard also gives you more planting ground in the same lateral space, and slopes sometimes create microclimates—sunny south-facing slopes, shady northward ones—that enable you to grow a wider variety of plants.

Some flat lots, in fact, could use artificially created mounds to generate a little interest.

Slopes, though, can be limiting. For instance, if your site slopes so much that you'd use the word "hillside" to describe it, you'll want to choose a natural, flowing landscape design instead of a symmetrical, formal plan.

And slopes, if left untreated, can create erosion problems, limit outdoor living space, and hinder plant growth.

■ Controlling erosion

All lots must have at least some slope. The land must slope away from your house at least 4 inches every 10 feet to assure that water does not seep into the basement. To learn how to determine slope, see page 39. For solutions to drainage problems, see pages 52–55.

If your concern is slowing water to prevent erosion, rather than diverting water to improve drainage, you'll want to add plantings, baffles, terraces, or retaining walls to your slopes.

Plantings, at least those with root structures that bind banks, usually are the easiest—and least expensive—erosion-control measure to install (see pages 66–67). Ground covers and low-growing shrubs are the best choices.

On slopes where plantings may not stem erosion, consider installing rows of stones called *riprap,* or plastic or wood baffles (see pages 66–67). The baffles or riprap act as small dams, slowing water and encouraging soil to build up.

To check the soil on medium-grade slopes, put in contours or bevels—two types of miniterraces (see pages 68–69).

For sharply sloping land, retaining walls are the best option, despite their expense and engineering demands (see pages 70–73). They take less room than a bank and are easier to maintain. They also yield level space for play or plantings. Keep in mind, though, that retaining walls must be carefully built if they are to withstand the tremendous pressure put on them by the soil they hold back.

Position retaining walls so they disrupt the site as little as possible. Be sure the walls you build are in scale and harmony with your house and the rest of your garden. Brick or stucco walls work well in formal gardens or near houses of the same materials. Rock walls fit into more-natural plans. Wood can blend with either. In general, the simpler its construction, the better a wall looks.

Select materials for strength, too, not just appearance. Wood walls can't be as big as masonry walls because they can't hold back as much dirt. Uncut stones work without mortar or footings unless the wall is taller than a couple of feet. Poured concrete yields the strongest walls.

Because low walls are cheaper to build and their design is less crucial (they retain less dirt), you're better off stepping a series of low walls down a hill than building one high wall.

■ Outdoor living

If slopes limit your outdoor play space, consider decks, paved or unpaved terraces (basically, patios or retaining walls), and steps.

Decks fit best into informal landscaping styles; paved terraces or patios work best in formal landscape designs. (See Chapter 8, "Patios and Decks," pages 148–189. For decks, also see pages 74–75.)

To save on time and money, build decks and patios that fit rather than fight the existing slopes. For decks, if you plan several levels instead of one, you'll use fewer materials; for patios, you'll move less soil.

Steps, besides allowing access to areas above or below, can act as erosion-controlling bevels. Any necessary landings can act as terraces. Make garden steps less steep than indoor stairs and as wide as the walk that leads to them (see pages 117 and 124–125). Again, use material that harmonizes.

If you're building your house new, situate the floor levels of your house to adjoin the flat areas, if possible. Locate your gardens, service areas, and play areas on the flats and use the rising slopes as gentle walls to enclose or the falling slopes as windows to open vistas.

To install a pool, you may have to do some grade changing. Use any soil you dig out to fill necessary grade changes or create interesting new ones.

Plan driveways and walks to make use of level land or gentle slopes. Neither should exceed a 10 percent grade. If you let your driveway wind across the contour of a slope, it will slow water runoff and help hold the hillside. Be sure the drive surface slopes for good drainage to prevent ice formation. Grade to make the approach to the road one with full vision both ways, and make a turnaround, if possible, to avoid backing into traffic (see pages 240–245).

For fencing, choose an open style, such as a split-rail fence, if your slope is steep. For gently rolling terrain, choose a slightly open fence style, such as one using lattice or louvers; avoid a closed style.

To create a secret nook or cranny, put a bench or arbor at the top or bottom of a hill, perhaps out of sight of the house.

■ **Plantings on slopes**
Lawns are fine on slopes, except those too steep for mowing. You can safely mow an incline as long as the ground does not rise more than 1 foot for every 3 feet of horizontal slope.

To establish turf on a hillside, use sod. If you can't afford sod and plan to use seeds, the grass is more likely to become established if you first divert the surface water at the top of the slope by running a turf gutter—a slight ditch with a lip on the downhill side—across the slope. Then, to further slow water runoff, lay a few strips of sod across the slope at intervals of 4 to 6 feet all the way down.

For extensive slopes, consider using a process called *hydroseeding.* Mixes of grass seed or various flowers are combined with fertilizer and a wood fiber to make a spray-on slurry. Transportation departments use this method to plant highway embankments.

If your slope makes mowing dangerous, plant ground covers (see pages 66–67, 260–261, and 317–319 for recommendations). They're easy and inexpensive to start. If your slope is very steep or long, or your soil is heavy clay that could wash down, seek advice from experts.

Here are some other tips for planting slopes:
■ Land too steep for a lawn is great not only for ground covers, but for trees, shrubs, and wildflowers, too. Put bird feeders and a birdbath on the edge nearest the house for the best bird watching.
■ Gentle slopes, particularly those facing a house or patio, look great with crocuses, other bulbs, or wildflowers planted among the grass.
■ If your landscaping plans require you to change grades, build walls or wells around the roots of choice mature trees to avoid damage.
■ For cultivated plants, use beds that follow the contours of the slopes. Or, create terraces.
■ If you have a slope facing south, use it to stretch your growing season. With more sun and natural wind protection, the south-facing slope will warm earlier in the spring, enabling you to grow tender plants, like dogwoods, where they otherwise might not be hardy. Watch out, though, because that same spring sun will lure some early bloomers into premature growth, and a late frost may take a greater toll. Avoid peach, almond, and other early-blooming fruit trees on south-facing slopes. Grow them instead on north-facing slopes, where they will stay safely dormant until spring truly arrives.
■ Because cold air collects in low-lying areas, don't plant frost-sensitive fruit trees there.

CONTROLLING MINOR EROSION

If erosion is a problem on a gentler slope, try one of these four techniques to keep soil from washing away.

Baffles work well on slight to medium slopes and can vary from small pieces of plastic edging to landscape timbers. Partly buried across the hillside, they slow runoff water, giving it more time to soak into the ground. Use a trowel to install small, lightweight baffles by hand as you plant. For large timbers, dig a slight ditch with a spade and put the soil removed on the uphill side. Position the baffle before planting.

Use *retaining cloth* on slopes where the erosion is more severe. It can be any porous material from burlap to the mesh used on steep highway banks. The latter is rather expensive, but topsoil is beyond price. The greenkeeper at a nearby golf course can give you a source. Avoid using plastic on steep slopes because it drastically cuts rainwater penetration into the soil. Planting will be easier if you soak the ground well, remove unwanted growth, and loosen and smooth the soil before laying the cloth.

Mulch, good on flat land, slows runoff on minor slopes. It also keeps down weeds, and, if organic, adds humus. Spread it thick, at least 4 to 5 inches, and renew organic mulch often. On slight slopes, use mulch alone; on steeper slopes, use mulch with baffles.

Stone riprap can be made with handpicked rocks or concrete rubble, and can cover the steepest area of a hillside or the whole expanse. The rocks act as a permanent mulch and slow water runoff. Plant roots will wind through and under the rocks to further hold soil in place.

Remember, when setting out plants on a slope, always leave water-catching lips on the downhill side to conserve precious water.

▼*Minibaffles—here made from pieces of plastic edging cut to lengths of a foot or so—reduce soil erosion. With your trowel, cut into the slope and set the baffles to make a series of small walls and terraces.*

▶ *To use retaining cloth, prepare and water the soil, then lay and stake the cloth in position. Use scissors to cut holes for plants, then plant with a trowel. This can be an awkward chore, but the results are worth the effort.*

For basic information on plants and planting, see pages 292–299.

► *Mulch holds rainfall like a sponge, stopping the runoff that could otherwise carry away your soil. Just pour the mulch out, before or after planting, then smooth it evenly over the surface and up around the plants.*

▼ *Stone riprap works like a small retaining wall. Dig troughs across the slope and place large stones so they are half buried. Scatter smaller stones, if desired. Pack soil and plants tightly into the spaces between the stones.*

EROSION-CONTROL PLANTS

Alpine strawberries *will start from seed sown indoors and give you both flowers and berries the first year. Spreading by crowns instead of runners, they create a colorful, edible carpet.*

Pachysandra *includes alleghany and Japanese spurge, both 8- to 10-inch-tall perennials that thrive in moist soil and like shade. Leaves yellow in full sun. 'Silver-Edge' is less vigorous.*

Rockspray cotoneaster *is less than 2 feet tall, has horizontal branches in a pattern resembling fish bones, and has bright red fruit. This sun lover's small, glossy leaves turn red in fall.*

Vinca minor *or periwinkle has dark, shiny, evergreen leaves and lavender flowers in mid-spring. It grows in sun in zones 4 to 7, in shade in all areas, and in almost any soil.*

Also try shrubs like juniper, leucothoe, cranberry, lingonberry, some jasmines, and rock rose; vines like winter creeper, ivy, honeysuckle, and Virginia creeper; and ground covers like bearberry, Carmel creeper, and lantana. (See pages 307–319 for more details.)

BUILDING CONTOURS AND BEVELS

To check erosion on an intermediate slope, you can ripple it with contours or terrace it with bevels cut into the hillside and fitted with wood planters. Contours intercept the flow of water and direct it elsewhere. The planters serve as miniretaining walls. Both can add design interest to your landscaping plan.

■ Contour basics

Building contours calls for little more skill than expertise with a shovel, rake, and wheelbarrow. Give thought, however, to where water absorbed by the contours will go. Drain lines must slope away from the house, and codes (as well as courtesy) probably prohibit dumping water onto a neighbor's property.

For the drain lines inside our contours, we drilled ½-inch holes in 4-inch-diameter rigid PVC pipe, which can be solvent-welded into runs of any length. You also can buy flexible plastic drainpipe, which shapes easily into bends, but could collapse under heavy pressure.

To assure that the line doesn't clog up with silt, plan a drop of at least ⅛ inch per foot of length. Cover the upper end of the run with screening and leave it accessible so you can flush or use a snake to rout out any debris that might build up inside.

■ Bevel basics

Bevels call for very elementary carpentry skills. You construct a series of bottomless boxes, notch them into the hillside, fill with earth, and plant with flowers or ground cover.

For the boxes, buy only construction-heart redwood, construction-heart cedar, or ground-contact, pressure-treated common lumber; anything else will rot away in just a few years. To retard rust, assemble the boxes with galvanized nails, screws, and corner brackets

Excavate bevels carefully, keeping all cuts straight both horizontally and vertically. Set soil aside and use it to fill the planters after you've set them in place.

CONTOURS

1 Establish a horizontal reference line with stakes and string. To carry away runoff, the contours must cross the slope at a slight angle. Excavate to 4 inches or so and lay a 2-foot-wide bed of crushed rock or coarse gravel. Scoop out a slight depression in the bed of rock and set drilled PVC drainpipe in place.

3 Unroll the sod and tack it with stakes on the uphill ends so that it doesn't slide down the slope. Water again. After several rainfalls, remove the stakes.

2 *Mound soil over the pipe and rock bed to a depth of about 4 inches. Rake the fill to establish a smooth drop down the hillside. Moisten the soil and tamp it well. Tamping greatly lessens the chance that the contour will cave in or lose its shape.*

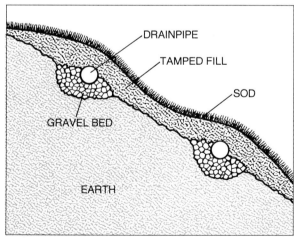

DRAINPIPE

TAMPED FILL

SOD

GRAVEL BED

EARTH

4 *To control erosion, step several contours across a steep slope. Gravel beds and drainage pipe prevent erosion by capturing water and diverting it from its destructive path.*

BEVELS

1 *Lay out bevels with stakes, string, and a tape measure. Use a spade to cut precise notches. These should be as close to 90 degrees and as nearly level as possible.*

2 *Build boxes with rot-resistant lumber and galvanized corner braces. Lay plastic to control weeds, then set the boxes in place. Secure them by driving stakes as shown. Hook the stakes over nails to prevent sideward shifts.*

3 *For drainage, in each box lay about ½ inch of gravel, then fill with soil. Plant with shallow-rooted annuals. Since roots will be above ground level, avoid using perennials; they could suffer winterkill.*

For basic information on working with wood, see pages 276–281.

BUILDING RETAINING WALLS

Check with your community's building department before setting out to build a retaining wall. Many codes require a permit for any structure that holds back what amounts to thousands of pounds of earth, and most limit the height of an amateur-built retaining wall to 3 feet. If your slope needs a higher wall or requires extensive grading, call in a masonry or landscape contractor—or terrace the slope with two or more lower retaining walls.

■ Drainage basics

Water is a retaining wall's worst enemy. Without proper drainage, water soon will buckle any structure you put up. Come winter, alternating freeze-thaw cycles also can wreak havoc on a retaining wall.

Each of the three walls we constructed uses a different drainage system. For the poured concrete version shown at right, we installed perforated PVC drainpipe, illustrated opposite, top right. Loose-masonry retaining walls (page 72) drain naturally through chinks between the stones. Our timber wall (page 73) expels water via weep holes near the base, a solution that works equally well with concrete or mortared masonry walls.

■ Material options

To construct a concrete-block retaining wall, consult your local building code and adapt the steps for pouring a concrete retaining wall, at right. You'll need to pour a footing below the frost line for the block wall and tie the wall's courses together with steel reinforcing rod, known as *rerod*.

We built our loose-masonry wall with ashlar stone; other, less-regular cuts work equally well, though you might want to tip the wall farther back into the slope for stability, and, for looks, fill gaps between stones with plantings.

For our wood retaining wall, we used pressure-treated 8x8 fir timbers. Construction-heart redwood or cedar timbers are other good options, but avoid railroad ties; these are treated with creosote, which is harmful to some plants and makes the ties messy to work with.

CONCRETE RETAINING WALL

1 Dig a trench into the slope to a depth that's just below the frost line for your region (local building authorities can give you that measurement). Make the trench wide enough for the wall you plan to pour; dig enough space, too, for you to work.

4 To strengthen the wall, drive lengths of rerod into the ground every 18 inches. Tie rerods to the spreaders with No. 8 or 9 wire. Tie horizontal rerods to the vertical ones every 18 inches. If you plan to cap the wall with concrete, let the vertical rerods protrude an inch or so above the spreaders' bottom edges.

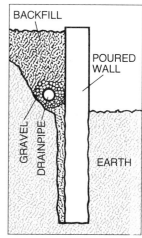

2 Cut ¾-inch plywood into panels 3½ inches taller than the height your wall will extend above the ground (the earth below provides the form for the footing). Coat plywood with motor oil for easier removal. Nail studs of 2x4 lumber to the plywood, spacing them 24 inches apart.

3 Assemble the form with end pieces of plywood and interior spreaders of 2x4 wood. Set the form in place, make sure it's level and plumb, then brace it with outriggers and stakes. Push the form into place with one foot while you drive the stakes.

One way to provide drainage for a retaining wall is to bury perforated drainpipe behind it at ground level. Slope the pipe at least ⅛ inch per foot.

5 Pour the concrete. We built a wheelbarrow ramp to the top of the form. As you pour, have a helper tamp the concrete to squeeze out air bubbles. After the concrete has set slightly, smooth its surface with a float.

6 After the concrete cures, remove the forms, install perforated drainpipe as shown in the illustration at upper right, then backfill. Cap the wall with brick, wood, or precast concrete coping, if desired. Use the terrace created by the wall for gardening or other activities.

For basic information on working with concrete, see pages 282–287.

BUILDING RETAINING WALLS *(continued)*

LOOSE-MASONRY RETAINING WALL

1 Lay out the wall with stakes and string, then dig a shallow trench, cutting its back side at a slight angle to the slope. For drainage, lay about an inch of gravel in the trench. Our wall will turn a corner, but the same techniques apply to straight walls.

2 Lay your longest stones on the bottom; the fewer the joints in the first layer, the less frost will heave it. As you lay stones, level them as best you can by tapping with the handle end of a sledge. (To prevent possible injury, use your legs, not your back, to lift heavy stones.)

For basic information on working with stone, see pages 282–287.

3 Lay succeeding courses so that each stone bridges a joint below. If you must cut a stone, use a sledge and chisel, as explained on page 287. If a stone wobbles, stabilize it by troweling loose soil underneath.

4 Dig a hole into the slope every 4 to 6 feet and lay a long stone crosswise to the wall. Pressure from earth above these stones will tie the wall to the soil behind it. Finish laying the stones, then backfill as necessary.

WOOD RETAINING WALL

1 Cut a beveled trench into the slope, wet the trench, and tamp well. Set the first timber into place and level it. This course will be completely buried in the ground. We planned our wall to turn a corner; the same techniques apply to a straight wall.

2 Set a second timber on top of the first and bore a hole through the two timbers. (Use a heavy-duty drill with an extension bit; small drills burn out on long holes like these.) Drive ¾-inch rerod through the holes and into the ground.

3 Continue to place the timbers, staggering joints from one course to the next. Drill holes and use rerod to pin each timber to the one below on each side of every joint. When needed, cut timbers with a sharp chain saw, wearing goggles to protect your eyes from flying chips.

4 Backfill as necessary. For drainage, drill weep holes every 4 feet along the wall's length. One row of holes about a foot above ground is fine. Instead of drilling holes, you also can provide drainage by leaving 1-inch gaps between ends of timbers.

For basic information on working with wood, see pages 276–281.

BUILDING STRUCTURES OVER SLOPES

Thinking about sinking posts for a fence, deck, gazebo, porch, or other structure? Unless the terrain is absolutely level, you need to locate several points that are, literally, in midair—and sometimes at quite widely varying heights from the ground. How can you determine how high each post should be? And how can you be certain your layout is square?

Actually, neither job is as difficult as you might think. First you establish points where you'll want posts. Then you dig holes and set posts that are taller than they need to be. Finally, you cut off the tops of the posts so all will be at the same level. At corners, some elementary geometry assures that rows of posts will be precisely at right angles to each other.

■ 3-D layout
To plot a structure that will be built on a slope, you need the same tools required for a level-ground layout (see pages 58–59), plus several stakes that are about two feet longer than the elevation at the downhill edge.

Start at the uphill edge. If you're building a deck or other project that will attach to the house, tack strings to its ledger (see page 172). For a gazebo, shed, or other freestanding structure, drive stakes and tie strings to them, as we did at right.

At the downhill edge, maneuver the taller stakes until they are at perfect right angles to the house or—for a freestanding structure—the string that marks the uphill edge. To be sure the corners are square, use the principle of the 3-4-5 triangle, as explained opposite and on page 59.

After you've found all four corners, double-check that they are square by measuring from each corner to the corner opposite it. If the corners are square, these diagonals will be equal in length. If they are not, go back and check each corner with the 3-4-5 triangle principle until you find the one that's out of square, then readjust the layout.

1 Drive a stake at the starting point, tie a chalk line to it, then extend the line downhill. Have a helper hold a carpenter's square to the starting stake to assure that the line meets it at a right angle. Tie the chalk line to a taller stake located several feet beyond the spot where your last post will be. Drive this stake into the ground, then adjust the chalk line until the bubble in a line level is centered.

4 After digging holes for posts and adding gravel, set and plumb the posts using a level and side braces, then pour concrete. For more about this, see page 60.

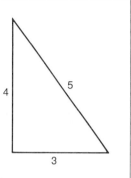

2 Measure from the starting stake to the point where you want the second post, drop a plumb bob from the line at this point, and mark the location with a stake or by spraying an X on the ground with aerosol paint. Locate and mark other post sites in the line the same way.

3 If your project will have posts at corners, use triangulation to square them up. Here, our original line was 12 feet (4x3), so we measured 9 feet (3x3) out from the corner. We then maneuvered the 9-foot tape and another one stretched from the starting stake until the diagonal measured 15 feet (5x3). Their inter-section showed exactly where to drive a stake to stretch a line for the second run of posts.

To square a corner, measure 4 feet (or a multiple of 4) one direction from the corner and 3 feet (or the same multiple of 3) another direction. Adjust the diagonal between the two un-til it measures exact-ly 5 feet (or the same multiple of 5).

5 Level the chalk line at the height you want to cut off the posts, then snap it against each one. Draw a line all the way around each post.

6 Use a chain saw or reciprocating saw to trim posts to the proper height.

For basic information on working with wood, see pages 276–281. For working with concrete, see pages 282–287.

GALLERY OF SLOPE IDEAS

◄ *This modern house sits high on a steep hillside to capture forest views. Outdoor-living areas include balconies and decks. Broad, shallow steps give easy access, and walls check the slope.*

► *To create sizable outdoor-living space on their sloping lot without making their house look like a wooden fortress, these homeowners chose to build a multilevel deck that jogs out and down.*

► *The patio, the broad, simple steps, and the deck below extend well the classical elegance of this house. Lush plantings plus pots and planters of colorful annuals eventually will make the starkness regal.*

◄ This steep, narrow slope becomes a flower festival with candytuft, basket-of-gold alyssum, armeria, heather, thyme, coralbells, moss phlox, crested iris, aubrieta, and violas. The low hedge at the bottom gives a neat outline.

▲ Long platform steps zigzag down this slope for easy, pleasant garden walking. A layer of gravel underneath each level aids drainage. Bricks are set in sand and held in place by 4x4 lumber.

With other houses so close, this 30x40-foot yard would have had a fishbowl rather than a family feeling were it not for deliberate measures to obtain privacy. Vines and fence combine for instant, unobtrusive seclusion.

The wisteria vines rise well above the fence yet fit into a narrow space. Their overhang is airy and open, and they are especially beautiful in late spring when dotted with purple panicles of bloom.

The weathered fence has just the right, quiet touch here. A more ornamental or painted fence would make this yard feel closed in, rather than comfortably enclosed.

Law requires that pools be enclosed so neighboring children cannot wander in and drown. But fences for safety need not be prisonlike. They also can lend beauty, privacy, and other pleasant qualities to a yard.

CHAPTER FOUR

PRIVACY AND SECURITY

The greater your measure of seclusion, the more personal and individual your environment becomes. What walls, roof, and window coverings are to the house, privacy plantings and structures are to the property as a whole. Outdoor living, no matter how innocent, is limited by exposure to the eyes of neighbors. Outside, as well as indoors, we want to be able to see the world, but we don't want the world to see us.

ASSESSING PRIVACY SOLUTIONS

Traditionally, enclosing gardens in America seemed both unfriendly and unpopular. People sat out to be seen and to visit. Yards were substitutes for the European public square.

As modern traffic changed neighborhoods, and life-styles became more individual and intense, yards began to change. Most people now have an overdose of public exposure and need areas for retreat, outdoors as well as in.

Don't be afraid to demand and design for privacy. It starts with planning.

■ A good start

Your first step should be to figure out where you need privacy and what visual intrusions you need to block. Usually, that means the areas of your backyard where you'll relax and entertain. Your property also might dictate the need for blocking views into front or side windows. Or, you may want to separate parts of your garden from one another (do this carefully, especially where space is limited, because too much division can cause confusion and crowding).

Next choose the method. Privacy most often is obtained with plantings, fences, or screens.

And always remember the golden rule. If your plans will affect your neighbors, talk to them early in the planning stage. For instance, where fences are few, people may just need reassurance that your intentions are not unfriendly. The neighbors may be as amenable to the idea as you and even agree to share the cost.

If a tree that will give your patio privacy also will block your uphill neighbor's view, try another solution, such as an overhead arbor.

Before starting to build or plant, it always is best to know exactly where property lines lie. Check laws and regulations, too, concerning the placement and height of fences, walls, and other permanent structures.

■ Methods

Whether you choose fences, screens, or plantings to obtain privacy, you'll more than likely want a plant or structure that's just above eye level or taller. Six feet usually is a good height for a privacy fence. If your concern is privacy only when sitting, say for patio dining, 3- or 4-foot plants or structures will work. Worst is something just below eye level—5 feet or so—because of its distracting height.

Plantings usually are a cheaper way to obtain privacy than fences or screens. Maintenance demands depend on the type of project: a clipped hedge is more work than a weathered fence, but a painted fence is more work than an informal shrub border.

Shrubs and trees, of course, provide a lovely green type of privacy, but fences and screens can do the same if they're climbed by a vine or used as a backdrop for flowers, ground covers, and smaller shrubs (see pages 90–91).

If you must always be assured of complete privacy, plantings alone may not be a good choice because diseases and other problems can create future gaps.

Screens, which can be anything from sections of fence to individually designed panels, are particularly effective when you desire a lighter look than fencing would provide.

■ Plantings

For maximum privacy using plants, you'll usually want to grow a border or hedge of shrubs (see pages 82–83 and 307–313). If your need for privacy extends into the winter, you'll want to choose evergreen, not deciduous, plants.

Shrub borders can be formal and clipped or informal and mixed. The first has the advantage of being narrow, but requires trimming, a time-consuming and often-repeated task. Formal hedges usually offer only a foliage background.

Untrimmed shrub borders, on the other hand, can spread to 8 feet or more. They will need less maintenance at longer intervals and can offer flowers, fruit, and fall color, as well as a variety of forms.

Choose shrubs carefully, paying particular attention to ease of maintenance. Make sure, too, that the mature size of plants won't overpower your house or landscape. Where space is limited—in a side yard, for example—use narrow, columnar-shaped shrubs.

When mixing shrubs in a border, select no more than three compatible species, with at least two or three of each type.

Don't limit yourself to shrubs, though, when seeking privacy. Vines on trellises can yield quick, inexpensive privacy and are especially effective in narrow spaces (see pages 106–111 and 314–316).

Even single trees or shrubs, carefully situated, can solve many privacy problems. Or choose flowers, particularly tall ones or those suited to raised beds. The seasonal privacy they offer may be sufficient for a patio or summer cottage.

■ Fences

Unlike plants, fences give instant privacy, and they can offer great architectural interest. Select from a wide variety of ready-made panels or design your own (see pages 84–85 and 88–89).

When planning a fence, you'll want to keep a number of considerations in mind.

Solid fencing yields the most privacy, but it also cuts off light and breezes. Slightly open fences, such as those with louvers or latticework, can let in the sun and the wind, yet still screen views into a yard. The slight openness also can provide an inviting transition from street to garden.

Some homeowners combine the best of both and erect a fence with a solid bottom and an open top.

To be most neighborly, you'll want to choose a design that looks as good from your neighbors' yards as it does from yours. Keep in mind, too, that if you're enclosing a large area, you might want to incorporate occasional variations in your fence so it doesn't become monotonous. And, to make a large expanse of fence less imprisoning, add plantings.

Be sure your fence style matches your house style: red-brick homes go well with redwood fences; clapboard homes gain with fences of similar boarding. If your fence will run close to or abut your house, consider painting it the same color or a complementary one.

SECURITY SOLUTIONS

Most homeowners know that well-placed lights can deter crime (see pages 92–93). But many don't consider the importance of keeping shrubs and trees well trimmed.

Clip shrubs near windows and doors low to deprive prowlers of cover while trying to enter your home. Locate trees away from the house and remove lower limbs that could serve as a ladder. And avoid screening neighbors' views of your front door and driveway.

Pay attention, too, to the character of your neighborhood. Whether it's rustic or sophisticated may go a long way toward dictating fence style—weathered or painted, open or closed.

■ Gates

When designing your fence, carefully plan the location and style of gates (see page 85).

Points of access, of course—whether from front yard to backyard or from your yard to a neighbor's—will determine location.

The style of gate you choose depends on how much attention you want it to draw. To extend an invitation to passersby, design your gate to contrast with the fencing. Change the spacing or size of the boards, make the gate taller, add color, or cap it with an arch. If privacy is paramount, build a gate that blends with the fencing.

Finally, consider width. Will a riding lawn mower pass through the gate? How about cars?

■ Screens

Screens usually are used within the yard rather than as boundary markers. As with fences, they can block views from outside in or from one section of yard to another. But they take less room, allow more feeling of openness, and restrict air movement less than fences. In design, they can be taller than fences, yet still be lighter in appearance and weight (see pages 86–89).

CHOOSING PLANTS FOR PRIVACY

BORDER, HEDGE, AND SCREEN SHRUBS

ARBORVITAE
Thuja species

Type: Columnar evergreen
Height: 40–60 feet or more
Zones: 3–8
Soil: Prefers rich and moist
Light: Medium shade to full sun

Comments: Slow growing, arborvitae makes a good formal hedge because it bears clipping well. Unclipped, it makes a semiformal hedge, a good screen, or, in clumps, an effective buffer. Use single plants as accents. The foliage is bright to dark green or yellow-green in flat sprays. Except for certain cultivars, the yellow turns unattractive in the winter, so be selective. Arborvitae has few problems, but watch for bagworms. Also, be sure it keeps a central leader; prune competing side branches.

BARBERRY
Berberis species

Type: Evergreen and deciduous
Height: 2–9 feet
Zones: 4–8
Soil: Average
Light: Prefers sun; tolerates light shade

Comments: Barberry species include a large group of dense, spiny shrubs widely used for barrier or hedge plantings. Most have small, bright yellow flowers, either single or in clusters and borne in great profusion. The fruits are small berries—some brilliant red, some purple or black—about ¼ inch long. Many are decorative all winter. Deciduous barberries have deep red fall color.

HONEYSUCKLE
Lonicera species

Type: Deciduous to semi-evergreen
Height: 3–15 feet
Zones: 3–10
Soil: Average to dry
Light: Prefers full sun

Comments: Fast growing and fuss free, honeysuckle has many species and varieties, but only a few are recommended. Tartarian varieties with upright, arching habit and white to pink flowers are considered the best. Many have very fragrant flowers and showy red fruit that attracts birds; most, however, lack autumn color. Use in shrub borders or as single plants. Twining honeysuckle vines are good on arbors. Prune as needed. Some can become rampant in favorable climates.

ROSE
Rosa species

Type: Deciduous
Height: 3–15 feet
Zones: 3–10
Soil: Average to rich, well drained
Light: Sun; late-afternoon shade

Comments: The most-used and -loved garden plant in the world, the rose—available in both shrub and vine forms—is ideal for arbors, archways, and informal hedges. Shrub or species roses are hardier, easier to grow, and have far fewer pest problems than the hybrids. Many have beautiful autumn color as well as exquisite flowers and fragrance. Orange to red fruits—or hips—are edible and easily made into a drink rich in vitamin C. Shown here is belinda, a musk rose that flowers repeatedly.

VIBURNUM
Viburnum species

Type: Mostly deciduous
Height: 5–12 feet, a few taller
Zones: 3–9
Soil: Does best in moist, well drained, slightly acid
Light: Prefers sun

Comments: A handsome shrub that is easy to grow, viburnum is an asset in the mixed border, near the foundation, or as a specimen plant. Its year-round interest extends from flat to snowball-shaped clusters of small flowers in May, to good green summer foliage, scarlet fall color, and bunches of red berries that last into the winter. Viburnums provide food and cover for many birds. Flowers are mostly white or cream; fruits are red, yellow, blue, or black. Some can become small trees.

YEW
Taxus species

Type: Needled evergreen
Height: 3–20 feet
Zones: 2–7
Soil: Average to below average; well drained with no wet feet
Light: Sun or shade

Comments: For a trouble-free evergreen, the yew is hard to beat. Its dense, dark green, 1-inch needles are complemented by red berries (inedible; some thought to be poisonous) in midsummer to fall. Yews can be found in globe, vase, columnar, pyramidal, or ground-hugging shapes. They provide privacy as clipped or informal hedges or screens, or in mixed borders. Yews grow slower than deciduous shrubs. Males produce no berries.

Because the number of shrubs appropriate for borders and screens is almost limitless, you should consider mixing several different types. Try one or two of those listed above and opposite with edibles like cherry, currant, blueberry, or quince. Add a hardy ornamental with interest for all seasons: dogwood, azalea, holly. Plant shrubs in a mixed border farther apart than shrubs in a formal hedge to emphasize the individuality of the plants; let lines meander. *(For more shrub recommendations, see pages 307–313.)*

PLANTING A FORMAL HEDGE

Start your formal hedge right by choosing a spot where the plants will receive good light and air on both sides. Also plan to set plants at least half their mature width from property lines.

Lay a string line as shown. For the cleanest edge, strip the sod. Dig a trench or large holes as deep as the root systems. Prepare the soil well, adding humus generously. Lay plastic to control weeds, cut holes as needed, and insert plants. Set them to the same level as at the nursery. Adjust each plant to keep it vertical and in line. Spacing varies with shrub type.

For basic information on plants and planting, see pages 292–299.

BUILDING FENCES AND GATES

Putting up a fence is a satisfying project that doesn't require any special skills or tools. The hardest part is digging the holes; after that, the structure takes shape quickly. Besides a rented posthole digger, you'll need only a circular saw and ordinary carpentry tools.

Designs vary widely, but just about all fences consist of the same basic elements: A series of *posts* sunk into the ground and connected by *rails* top, bottom, and usually in the middle as well; and *fencing* boards or panels that are nailed to the rails to give the fence its character.

Privacy fences usually require 4x4 posts. Rail and fencing lumber can be almost any size.

Lumberyards sell prefab sections of fence in many styles, but custom design and construction usually yield a better-looking fence. See page 88 for some sample fence styles.

■ Check codes
Before proceeding, check community building and zoning codes. Many specify maximum fence height, distances you can build from property lines and the street, and even the materials you can and can't use.

Once you've chosen a design and established a location, stake out and measure the site. Plot post spacing for the most efficient use of lumber. Six- or 7-foot spans usually work well; never set privacy-fence posts more than 8 feet apart.

If you're building your fence on a slope, plan to step the fence down the hill, setting each section lower than the one preceding it. Only if the slope is slight—and the fence design won't suffer—should you follow the contour.

■ Fence materials
When you order lumber, specify construction-heart redwood or cedar or ground-contact, pressure-treated wood for all posts and bottom rails; upper rails and fencing can be less expensive grades of rot-resistant lumber. To minimize rust, buy hot-dip galvanized nails and fittings.

If you want to paint or stain your fence, apply the finish to posts, rails, and fencing *before* you nail up the fencing. Besides saving time, you'll get better coverage.

For basic information on working with wood, see pages 276–281. For working with concrete, see pages 282–287.

FENCE

1 Lay out the site, dig holes, and set posts, starting with the end posts. (See pages 58–60 and 74–75.) Check each post for plumb by holding a level to two adjacent faces; nail braces to hold posts upright. Check, too, that posts are aligned by tying string from end post to end post.

3 Attach the rails to the posts. We used galvanized rail clips; page 89 shows other joinery techniques. A line level and combination square assure that each rail is level and square with the posts.

2 As you shovel concrete into the holes, have a helper tamp the concrete to remove bubbles. Round off the concrete so water will drain away from the posts. After the concrete cures, cut posts to a uniform height, if necessary (see pages 74–75). Shape tops of posts so they'll shed water.

4 Measure carefully and use a square to mark locations on the rails for each fencing board. Wood scraps squeezed between boards maintain uniform spacing. Have a helper align boards—in this case flush with the bottom—while you nail them to the rails.

GATE

1 Build a frame ½ inch narrower than the gap in the fence. Square the frame, secure corners with angle brackets, and install a brace from the bottom of the hinge side to the top of the latch side.

2 Add finish boards to match the fencing. Measure carefully and install hinges, taking care that they are square with the edge. All but very lightweight gates should have three hinges.

3 Prop the gate into position on blocks. Plumb it and have a helper mark each hinge position. Remove the gate, drill holes, and hang the gate. Finally, install latch hardware.

BUILDING LATTICEWORK SCREENS

Designs for wooden privacy screens can be as varied as those for wooden fences. A screen, after all, is really just a section of fence. But for a particularly striking effect, consider lacy latticework screens, which provide privacy without blocking balmy breezes. Lattice screens also offer sound support for climbing plants, which increases privacy even more.

Lattice is inexpensive and demands no special expertise to build—you can install it with only simple hand tools and an electric drill/driver.

The term *latticework* refers to any decorative pattern made with narrow, thin strips of wood (drawings on page 89 show four typical patterns). Latticework designed to give privacy has 1½-inch openings; with garden-spaced lattice, the openings are 3 inches.

■ Prefab versus homemade

Most lumberyards and home centers sell 4x8-foot prefabricated lattice panels for a cost that often is less than that for the lath alone. These panels are easy to install because the cutting and nailing already has been done.

Inspect prefab latticework carefully before you buy, however. Cheaper varieties often are made with lath much thinner than that sold in individual pieces, and the staples holding cheap lattice together may be thin and dislodge easily.

For the photographs on these pages, we used a prefab panel. To make your own latticework, build a frame like the one shown at top right. Then, if desired, paint or stain the frame and the strips of lath you'll use for the lattice. If you prefer to leave the wood natural, coat it with a wood preservative.

Once the paint is dry, lay the lath against the frame diagonally, placing the strips so each strip touches the next to form a solid screen. Nail every other strip, then remove the pieces not nailed. Repeat this process for the second course of lattice, starting in the opposite corner. For garden-spaced lattice, nail every third strip.

To avoid splitting the extra-thin strips, blunt the tips of nails by pounding on them with a hammer. After nailing all strips to the frame, trim the ends with a crosscut or circular saw.

1 *After you've set the posts (see pages 58–60 and 74–75), measure the distance between them and build a 2x4 frame. Square each corner, using temporary wood braces to hold the corners square. Then nail the frame together at each corner.*

4 *Purchase a prebuilt panel at a home center (or, as discussed at left, make your own lattice; see page 89 for style choices). Prime and paint the latticework with a brush, or immerse it in a large, shallow pan of paint. If your plans call for painting the frame and stops, do them now, too.*

2 *Remove the braces one by one, check each corner again with a square, and secure the joint with a metal strap or angle. Use only galvanized screws and hardware.*

3 *Now attach the first stop to the inner side of the frame. Align it with one edge, predrill holes at foot or so intervals, and drive screws through the 1x1-inch lumber.*

5 *After the paint dries, lay the panel atop the frame's first stop, then install a second stop on top of the panel. If desired, attach the lattice to the first stop with a staple gun before adding the second stop.*

6 *Fasten the frame to the posts with lag screws spaced about a foot apart. Predrill holes and, for a neater appearance, countersink them as well. Fit each lag screw with a washer before driving it. If you painted or stained the frames, touch up around the screws.*

For basic information on working with wood, see pages 276–281. For working with concrete, see pages 282–287.

CHOOSING A FENCE OR SCREEN STYLE

FENCE AND SCREEN STYLES

(Far left) Vertical board fences and screens are popular and easy to construct. Nail all boards to one side, as we did on pages 84–85, or alternate them as shown here.

(Near left) Basket-weave panels come ready-made from home centers and lumberyards. Many also sell vertically grooved posts that the panels fit into.

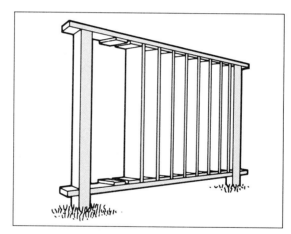

(Far left) Grooved posts also work well with a horizontal board design. As an alternative, you can face-nail boards to the posts and to 2x4 rails top and bottom.

(Near left) Louver-style fences and screens offer beauty and ventilation. The verticals— usually 1x6s or 1x8s—are angled and overlapped slightly. The degree of the angle determines the degree of privacy.

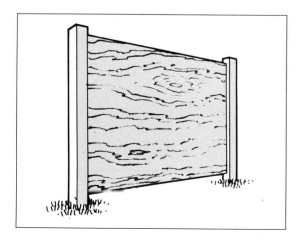

(Far left) Fit plywood panels into grooved posts, or face-nail them to posts and rails. Install the panels vertically or horizontally.

(Near left) For an open-slat design, space 1x3s their own width apart, then secure the boards at the top, bottom, and middle with rails made of bigger-dimension lumber.

LATTICEWORK STYLES

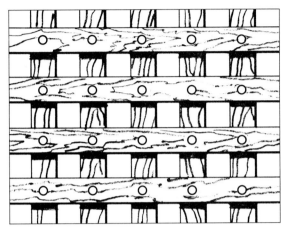

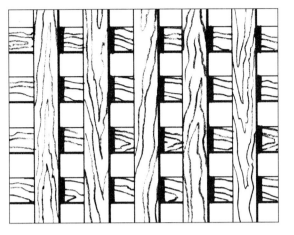

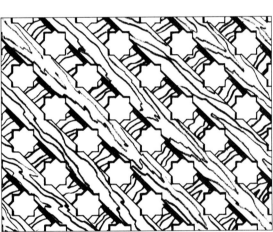

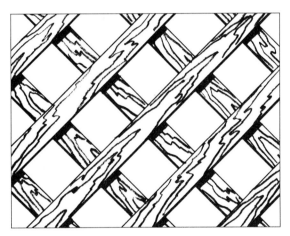

(Far left) Latticework lends itself to a variety of decorative effects. To interplay round and square openings, bore holes at the points where strips intersect.

(Near left) Vertical and horizontal strips make a strong grid pattern. If you don't mind a rough texture and variations in thickness, buy "fall-down" lath, inexpensive wood left over when lumber is milled.

(Far left) Notched lattice strips create an interesting design motif. You can purchase panels made from notched lattice, buy notched strips, or notch the strips yourself.

(Near left) Garden-spaced latticework doesn't provide a lot of privacy until vines begin to flourish. If you choose latticework for a trellis or arbor overhead, construct it with 1x2s, not lath.

JOINERY TECHNIQUES

If you don't like the looks of the metal rail connectors shown on page 84, attach rails to posts with one of the joints shown here. All work equally well. Choose based on your tools and skills. To make a *dado joint,* cut away part of the post so the rail will be flush (or nearly flush) with the post. For a *block joint,* nail a short piece of 2x2 to the post, rest the rail on top of it, and toenail through the block into the post. For a *butt and toenail joint,* drive nails at an angle through the rail into the post.

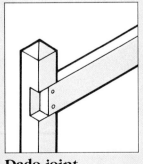

Dado joint

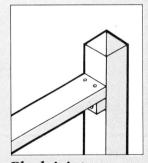

Block joint

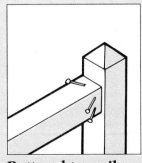

Butt and toenail joint

FENCE AND SCREEN PLANTINGS

Besides providing the perfect backdrop for plants, fences and screens need plantings to soften their angular appearance. Working together, plants, fences, and screens can set the mood for a garden. Roses on a post-and-rail fence sing one song; on a picket fence, a slightly different tune.

■ Plant pointers

Keep the following in mind when deciding how best to use plants near your fence or screen.
■ Your yard will seem larger if you group flowers and shrubs as near to the structure as practical, leaving an open central area. Place the tallest plants in back and graduate down to the shortest in front (see chart at right).
■ Shrubs and trees can overpower a fence. Select open and narrow varieties for minimum pruning, and plant them far enough from a fence for uncramped development.
■ Vines are especially good on fences and screens. They will climb wire or thin trellis unaided. To get some of them to grow up a wood surface, you may need to attach string support.
   Vines can completely cover a chain-link fence, but more-elegant structures look better with vines that accent, not hide, them. Also consider the strength of the fence or screen when selecting vines. (See pages 106–107 and 314–316 for more information on choosing vines.)
■ Colors come alive against a fence or screen. Blue delphiniums, lost without a background, stand out when displayed against white.
■ Fences and screens can create new microclimates, resulting in new growing opportunities. For example, a solid structure protects downwind plants for an area equal to its height. Latticework allows some wind penetration, but protects a larger area. Heat is reflected or stored depending on color and material.

■ Maintenance

Since mowing or hoeing under a fence is difficult, remove all plants and roots before you build. To keep out new roots, bury edging a few inches from the fence. Or place plastic or tar paper covered with gravel under the fence.

RECOMMENDED PLANTS

Plants with spike, simple, or striking blooms benefit most from a vertical background. (See pages 301–323 for more plants.)

4 to 5 feet	1½ to 4 feet	2 inches to 1½ feet
Andromeda	Bachelor's-button	Celosia
Camellia	Blue flax	Daffodil
Cosmos	Cleome	Heather
Delphinium	Columbine	Hosta
Fire thorn	Daphne	Marigold
Hibiscus (mallow)	Dictamnus	Nasturtium
Hinoki cypress	Forsythia, dwarf	Rose, miniature
Hollyhock	Iris	Salvia
Japanese maple	Leucothoe	Sweet william
Liatris	Rose	Tulip
Rose	Snapdragon	

Remember to put the tallest plants nearest the fence, then the midsize varieties, and finally the short plants in front.

◀ *Though vines would work on this fence of lattice and brick, the owners didn't want to hide its good looks. Instead, they used airy perennials like Japanese iris and astilbe to accent the fence without obscuring the design or blocking the airflow.*

▶ *The purple-red, semidouble spring flowers of the rose 'Magnifica' leap into focus against the wood fence. A shrub rose, 'Magnifica' has foliage that forms an attractive backdrop the whole growing season. When choosing rose varieties, keep scale and harmony in mind.*

◀ *A small-leaved ivy is neatly espaliered up the side of this privacy screen. The grape vine that covers the arbor between the hedge and screen is a fuller, but more reserved garden wall. Ferns, annuals, and perennials in front fill the corner with color.*

▼ *Potted petunias fit into openings in this fence, extending a friendly greeting to viewers, no matter which side they're on. The low shrubs and cascading ground covers at the fence's base contribute to the visual treat on the street side, while also helping to absorb auto noise.*

INSTALLING SECURITY LIGHTING

Effective outdoor lighting brings four benefits to a landscaping scheme: 1) It discourages intruders; 2) It prevents accidents; 3) When done creatively, it can enhance your landscaping scheme; and 4) Perhaps best of all, it increases the time you can enjoy your outdoor surroundings. (For more information on lighting for aesthetic reasons, see pages 212–215.)

■ How much?
The illustration at right identifies points on your property that need illumination for security purposes. In general, don't be afraid to install too many lights. Outdoor fixtures are not terribly expensive, especially if you install them yourself. Operating outdoor lights, however, can be costly, so try to provide separate switching, perhaps with a master switch that controls all.

When you shop for outdoor fixtures, you'll find an abundance of choices. *Post lights* illuminate walks and drives. *Step lights* prevent stumbles. *Floodlights* mount on poles, in trees, or high on house sides and back. *In-ground lights,* placed below plants, can erase burglar-hiding shadows.

■ Installation
Check your community's electrical code before ordering materials for a 120-volt project such as the one opposite. Some codes allow the use of UF cable buried in a trench at least 12 inches deep; the cable, however, must be protected by conduit at points where it is out of the ground. Other localities require that all outdoor wiring run through plastic, thin-wall EMT conduit, or heavy-wall rigid conduit; rigid conduit requires a trench only 6 inches deep.

Most codes also require you to protect outdoor lights and receptacles with a *ground fault circuit interrupter* (GFCI), a device that senses any shock hazard and shuts down a circuit. A GFCI in your home's service panel protects all outlets on that circuit. If you decide to tap into an existing outdoor receptacle, a GFCI there will serve the receptacle and all outlets beyond it.

Much simpler to install but less versatile is 12-volt lighting. For more information on this option, see pages 214–215.

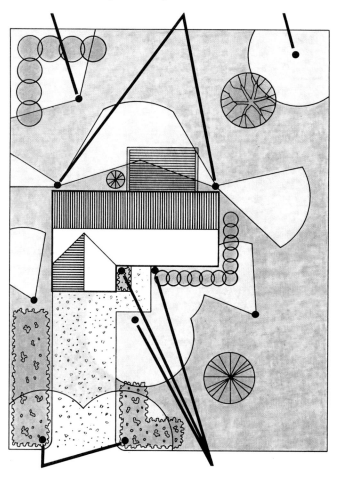

Dark bushes can provide cover for anyone contemplating a raid on your home. In-ground lights here wash away the cloaking shadows, plus play up plantings.

Floodlights at each corner of your home's rear exterior can brighten outdoor living areas and illuminate substantial sections of the remainder of the backyard.

Light far corners of your property with post lights or floods in trees. Aim the lights so they don't shine into neighbors' yards or windows.

Driveway entrance lights provide a cheerful welcome and supplement street lighting. Be sure to shield fixtures here so they won't blind approaching drivers.

Front steps, door lock, and house number should be lighted with fixtures on both sides of the door and at any turning in the approach. The extra door fixture serves as a backup in case a bulb burns out.

1 Draw up a detailed plan of your installation and take it to an electrical supplier for help in getting just the right fittings. The LB and L fittings at left enable you to make 90-degree turns.

2 Dig a trench from the nearest electrical box to the fixture site, then measure the length of conduit you will need. Use a rented auger to dig under sidewalk, if needed. We tapped into an existing exterior box. You might have to bore through the foundation and connect to a box in the basement.

3 Bend conduit with a bending tool wherever necessary. Cut the tubing to length after bending, lay it in place, and use fittings to attach it to the boxes at either end. Push 12-gauge wiring through the conduit in the trench.

4 Shut off current to the circuit and make final connections with wire nuts. We added a GFCI receptacle (see opposite) to our fixture, which required a third wire. A switch controls the light, but not the GFCI. Pour a concrete collar around the fixture post for stability.

For basic information on working with wiring, see pages 288–291.

GALLERY OF PRIVACY IDEAS

◄*Lattice fencing, together with vines and other plantings, makes this spa area an exclusive home resort. The inviting brick-floored outdoor room is tucked into a corner of a pocket-size piece of property.*

▼*An eye-catching gate enhances an otherwise hard-to-landscape portion of a side yard, plus provides privacy and security for the backyard. A camellia at left and azalea on the right soften the structure's lines and color the scene.*

►*A large, pink-flowered rhododendron, a Japanese maple, and a higher-than-usual railing combine to add seclusion and beauty to this front-yard deck.*

◄ *A once painfully plain backyard was excavated for this sunken octagonal center. The vine-covered fence makes it as private as an indoor den. The benches also serve as retaining walls for the gardens beyond.*

◄ *A solid-bottomed, open-topped fence like this one offers privacy in a more-inviting, less-forbidding way than completely solid fences often do. Detail work on the tops of the posts adds the right accent.*

▲ *This private dining nook is better than a booth at the fanciest restaurant. Behind the curved seat is a convenient, cleverly hidden potting and utility area. You can build a retreat like this almost anywhere.*

CHAPTER FIVE

SUN AND SHADE

The pattern of sun and shade on your yard and house is vital to your personal world. It determines not only the placement of every plant and landscape feature, but often, too, your outlook on life. Yet that pattern changes subtly with time of day, season of year, growth of plants, and addition or removal of structures. The ultimate enjoyment of your surroundings depends on using sun and shade well. Too much of either throws your environment—and you—out of harmony.

Structures—including the neighbors'—are big shadow makers on most lots. The closer they are to important yard space, the more they affect landscape plans. Keep in mind that temperatures can vary widely from one side to another.

Overhead sunshades can immediately better the climate of an outdoor living area like this deck. Indoor rooms, especially those with glass doors, become more comfortable, too, with cooler temperatures and dappled light.

Existing trees are a gift to cherish. If their shade is excessive, the least choice and the least well-situated can be moved or removed. Pruning of others for a higher or thinner canopy of foliage can make a big difference to the world beneath.

Vines offer cool shade and lovely foliage in summer. In winter, they disappear, admitting all the sun's warmth. As a bonus, in spring, this wisteria creates a fragrant ceiling of clustered lavender or white flowers.

ASSESSING SUN AND SHADE SOLUTIONS

A yard needs both sun and shade to modify otherwise uncomfortable weather. Sitting in the sun on a crisp autumn afternoon is uplifting and invigorating. But if fated to spend that time in shade, we'd soon retreat indoors for needed warmth. On a hot summer day, though, the exact opposite is true.

How best to plan then for ideal sun and shade? As with most landscaping decisions, take your time and study the given conditions first.

■ A full year

You may get a pretty good idea whether a yard needs more sun or shade the minute the real-estate agent drives you up in front. But do not make expensive, irrevocable decisions until you have studied sun and shade patterns in your yard for a full year.

The homeowner who considers only the uncomfortable heat of the high summer sun may miss an opportunity to take advantage of the low, warmth-giving winter sun. Winter-sun watchers may not give a thought to what their problems will be in summer. Besides, knowing the sun and shade patterns on a yard (from spring to fall, at least) is essential to knowing what plants will grow where.

First, orient yourself to the north point and other compass points of your yard. Then make notes of sunrise and -set and the shadows on different parts of the yard at different times of the day and year.

In the meantime, if you have spots that just must have some shade, plant vines or even some of the tallest annual flowers and vegetables, like sunflower. These plants provide shade within a single summer. Many vines can be trained on makeshift stakes or wires until you're sure about the placement of elaborate trellises and arbors.

Shrubs are almost as fast growing. To avoid constant pruning, select shrubs with the mature height and width you want and set them far enough from walls, walks, patios, and property lines. Most deciduous shrubs will reach mature height within three growing seasons; evergreens take a little longer.

Trees, of course, take much longer. But as a stopgap measure, you can plant fast-growing species like poplar, silver maple, willow, and Chinese elm. Unfortunately, most of these quick-maturing trees are weak wooded, short-lived, and inferior in quality. Plan on planting them among slower-growing trees, then cutting them out as the better trees grow tall. (To prevent clogged pipes, keep willows or poplars away from water pipes or septic fields.)

■ Options

Once armed with the knowledge of year-round sun and shade patterns, you can start considering your options.

If your problem is too much shade, be glad that you can remedy the problem quickly. But do not do it rashly. Call in a tree specialist and discuss which, if any, trees should be removed.

Careful pruning can work wonders. By having lower branches removed from large trees or doing it yourself from smaller ones, you can open new vistas and increase the light and air circulation that reaches your living areas, indoors and out. By raising the canopy of leaves, you preserve the shade you need and the health and shape of the trees.

If your problem is too little shade, consider capturing some with either structures or plants.

For instant and permanent shade, build an overhead sunshade (see pages 100–103), arbor (see pages 104–105), or trellis. Such structures are particularly appropriate if you have just a small area to shield or if you don't plan to stay in your house long enough for a tree to grow. They can be built over patios, decks, paths, or a corner of the garden; they can be attached to your house or freestanding.

A well-designed, well-positioned sun structure screens out the summer sun, yet lets the winter rays stream through. Match the material, size, and shape of any structure to your house, lot, and other landscape features. As with most projects, the simpler the design, the better.

If you build an overhead structure, choose a canopy that fits your sun or shade needs (see page 103). Loosely spaced boards let in more sun; tightly spaced boards do the opposite. Or, for even more sun protection, select a solid material like canvas or fiberglass.

To soften a structure's lines and obtain additional shade, drape it with vines (see pages 106–107). In winter, vines vanish, letting in warmth.

■ Trees

The most graceful and natural way to obtain shade, of course, is with a tree or large shrub.

If you're building a new house on a lot with existing trees, decide which ones are keepers and spare no expense to protect them. Money cannot buy their years of growth.

If you're faced with an empty yard, resist the temptation to plant lots of young trees and shrubs close to walls and each other. Unless you think about the mature sizes of plants, your bare yard can quickly become a jungle.

When choosing shade plants (see pages 108–111 and 301–316), consider how their shape, texture, and color will blend with the rest of the landscape. Make sure their mature sizes will be in scale. Weigh maintenance needs.

Decide whether the plants you're considering provide the type of shade you want: Large-leaf species like maple and sycamore may shade so much that little else will grow near them; fine-leaf trees like honey locust or mountain ash, on the other hand, provide filtered shade. A deciduous tree on a house's south side blocks summer sun, then sheds its leaves and admits winter light. An evergreen shields light year-round.

Give prime consideration, too, to the growing conditions in your area. Seek the advice of local nursery workers and extension-service personnel. Use reliable native trees.

■ Position

When positioning shade trees, keep in mind that they will spread their branches about as wide as their height and send their roots much farther. So, in general, for ideal growth, allow as much as 65 feet between spreading trees, 35 feet between nonspreaders.

A walk in any timber, however, will show you how nature adapts. With careful pruning and control, and planned crowding, you can plant many more trees or smaller trees in a yard. Just plan on cutting some of them out as they grow. (With weeping trees, avoid any thought of crowding lest their special effect be lost.)

Plant shrubs at least 3 to 4 feet from the house, making sure to check the drip line. Within it, you will have to water the plant more often. Right under it, the plant could drown if no gutter catches the runoff from the roof.

■ Care

Your woody plants will grow faster and claim their own space sooner if surrounded by mulch. Cultivated plants are the next-best choice for around the trunk. They will remind you to feed and water the plant, and soften the emptiness of the new landscape at the same time. Lawns or wild plants are the worst early companions. They lead to lawn-mower damage or neglect.

Don't hesitate to have a trained and well-recommended tree expert treat pests, diseases, and wounds. Get a second opinion if an expert suggests removal too quickly. Tree care is more important than most homeowners realize. The loss of a mature tree can devastate the best-planned landscape and take decades to replace.

■ Plants in sun and shade

As your landscape plan develops and the woody plants grow, you will have to adjust your gardening below and around them. Every plant has different sun and shade needs. Some thrive in a wide range of light conditions; others perish in the wrong exposure. Some survive in shade but need sun to bloom and bear fruit.

Take maximum advantage of the conditions at any given time. Put shade-loving plants—like hostas and woodland wildflowers (see page 323)—in the darkest spots. Place adaptable plants—daylilies, for example—in partial-shade areas. Save the bright spots for vegetables and sun-loving flowers. If need be, plant sun lovers in containers and move them around.

BUILDING OVERHEAD SUNSHADES

ATTACHING A SUNSHADE TO A HOUSE

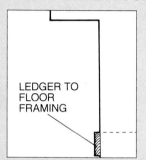
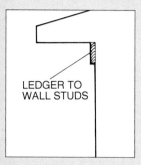
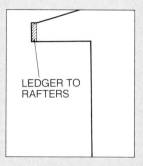

Two-story house:
Lag-screw the ledger to second-floor framing, as you would a deck to the first floor (see pages 176–177). To locate joists, measure up from a window, inside and out. Add the thickness of ceiling materials.

One-story house:
Screw the ledger to wall studs. This will put the sunshade several inches below roof level. If your home has lap siding, remove one course so the ledger will lie flat. In brick or stone, drill with a masonry bit.

One-story house:
Or, remove the fascia board that covers the ends of the rafters, and attach the ledger to them. Protect the ledger from water by covering its top edge with metal flashing tucked up under the roofing.

ATTACHING TO AN EXISTING DECK

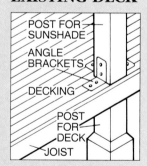

Locate sunshade posts directly above those that support the deck. Secure the new posts with angle brackets or post anchors. Use posts that are several inches longer than the plan calls for, then trim their tops as shown opposite.

ATTACHING TO A NEW PATIO

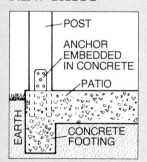

Pour a concrete footing along with the patio and embed a post anchor in it (see page 159). Don't rest posts on a patio that has no footings underneath; the concrete could crack. Let concrete cure a week before erecting posts.

ALONGSIDE AN EXISTING PATIO

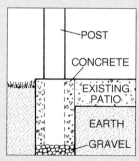

Rather than break into an existing patio to pour footings, position the posts just outside the patio. Dig to below the frost line; put gravel in the holes for drainage. Set the posts in concrete (see page 60).

The best time to think about an overhead sun structure is while planning a new patio or deck. Then you can provide footings for its posts, or simply extend a deck's posts 8 feet or so to carry the load.

If you need to shade an existing patio or deck, check out the drawings at lower left for post basics, then assemble the framing as shown opposite and on pages 102–103.

Because no one will be walking around up there and because canopy materials are relatively lightweight, framing for a sunshade needn't be as strong as the underpinnings for a deck. It must be sturdy enough, though, to withstand strong winds and avert a potentially dangerous collapse, especially in snowy areas.

■ Two ways to go
Like decks, sunshades can be joined to your house with a ledger or be freestanding (see box, opposite). Where you attach the ledger depends, in part, on whether your house is one or two stories high (see illustrations, top left). Our photos depict an attached sunshade going together; for a freestanding version, substitute posts and another beam for the ledger.

■ Shades of difference
Give thought, too, to the sort of canopy material you'd like to top your sunshade with. The box on page 103 discusses five popular alternatives to the 2x2 treatment we used, and there are at least a dozen others—ranging from a simple, eggcrate layout to angled louvers to snow fence.

Aesthetics will play a big role in your choice, of course, but consider several practical matters as well. First, just how much shade do you need? A deck or patio on a treeless southern exposure could require protection all day long; a deck on an east or west side can get by with only partial shade. Assess, too, whether a covering you're thinking about will allow adequate ventilation or darken interior spaces too much.

1 *Determine post placement (see pages 58–59). Erect posts and, if needed, ledger. Pull level line from ledger to posts or post to post. Mark cut lines, allowing for rafter and beam thickness.*

2 *Cut the posts to the proper height. Make two passes with a circular saw. Don't use a chain saw; standing on a ladder, you won't have enough leverage to safely operate it.*

For basic information on working with wood, see pages 276–281. For working with concrete, see pages 282–287.

3 *Nail a metal post cap to the top of each post. You also can bolt beams to the sides of posts, as shown on page 178, or make wooden cradles by nailing 2x4 splints to the sides of the beams and posts.*

(continued on page 102)

ANATOMY OF A SUNSHADE

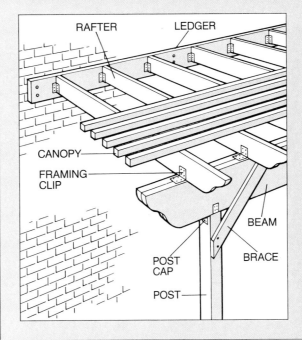

RAFTER LEDGER

CANOPY

FRAMING CLIP

POST CAP

POST

BEAM

BRACE

With an attached sunshade, 2x6 rafters fasten to a 2x8 or 2x10 ledger at one end, and rest atop a beam of doubled 2x12s at the other. Diagonal braces strengthen the post-beam connections. The canopy consists of 2x2s nailed to the rafters. A freestanding sunshade has beams at either end, and no attached ledger.

101

BUILDING OVERHEAD SUNSHADES *(continued)*

4 *Construct beams by sandwiching a strip of ½-inch plywood between two 2x12s. First, nail the plywood to one 2x12, then nail the beam together from both sides. Sandwiching the boards creates a member that's 3½ inches thick, the same dimension as a 4x4 post. For design interest, we scalloped the ends of the beam and rafters with a jigsaw.*

5 *Set the beam into the post caps. Check it with a level and shim if necessary. Check for square, too. Then drive nails through caps into the beam. You also can attach beams as discussed on pages 101 and 178.*

8 *Cut rafters to length and scallop their ends with a jigsaw, if desired. Install the rafters level; or, to slope them away from the house, measure and cut notches at each end of the rafters, as shown above.*

9 *Nail through framing clips into the rafters. Framing clips will be structurally adequate if you'll be using rigid canopy material. If not, brace between rafters with short lengths of 2x6.*

6 *Post caps alone won't handle the stress of post-beam connections. Cut diagonal 1x4 braces and nail them to one or, for stronger support, both sides of the posts and beam. Other techniques for post-beam joinery don't require any bracing.*

7 *Attach saddle clips to the beam and joist hangers to the ledger, if any. For 2x6s, space the clips 16 to 24 inches apart, depending on the weight of canopy materials. Consider not only the weight of the completed canopy, but also the water or snow load it must bear.*

10 *Cut 2x2s to length and nail them to the rafters, using a length of 2x2 as a spacer between slats. For other canopy possibilities, see the box at right.*

CANOPY ALTERNATIVES

Lattice: Crisscrossed slats of lath offer a lacy effect (see pages 86–87 and 89). Paint the strips or use inexpensive grape-stake lattice, which has a rough, furry texture.

Reed or bamboo: These inexpensive materials have a limited life span. Prolong their use by rolling them up and storing them inside during winter.

Shade cloth: Meshed fabric coverings provide filtered shade from sunlight, but let air and moisture through.

Canvas: Heavy cotton duck provides some protection against rain, but must be stretched taut so water won't collect.

Fiberglass: Corrugated plastic panels are easy to cut and nail. Slope the canopy so water will run off.

BUILDING ARBORS

If you're looking for a leafy way to put a special part of your yard in the shade, why not construct an arbor and drape it with a gracious canopy of vining plants?

To give you an idea of the variety of shapes an arbor can take, we built two. Our teahouse version at right goes together like a miniature barn, complete with roof trusses; the much simpler structure shown on the opposite page consists of just two posts topped off with a 2-foot-wide slatted sunshade.

Add a bench or two to the teahouse, and it becomes a mini-gazebo. The simple arbor can frame a special view, serve as an inviting gateway, or provide a verdant boundary for a patio or deck.

■ Arbor basics

Erecting either structure takes only a couple of days, several days apart: one to dig postholes and set the posts, another—after the concrete cures—to cut and assemble the components. We used pressure-treated 4x4s for the posts and, to add to the beauty of the arbors, redwood for the superstructures.

Making the teahouse's trusses isn't as tricky as you might think: You simply miter one end of two rafters, lay them out on a flat surface, then measure and cut the cross brace. For the short, vertical stud, make *two* miter cuts on one end. This creates a point that fits up into the peak, providing rigidity.

Secure the joints with special galvanized-metal truss nailing plates, available at most lumberyards and home centers. Some plates come with separate nails; others have sharp prongs that you pound into the wood.

Space the posts for either of these arbors no more than 6 feet apart. If you want to extend the distance to 8 feet, increase beam sizes from 2x6 to 2x8.

To learn about selecting the right vines for your arbor and training them to grow on it, turn to pages 106–107. (Also see pages 109, 111, 166, and 314–316.)

TEAHOUSE ARBOR

1 Site and erect four posts, as explained on pages 58–60 and 74–75. For beams, we notched a motif at the ends of 2x6s and lag-screwed them to the posts. Check frequently to be sure that everything is plumb, level, and square.

3 Set each truss in place and toenail it to the beams. For appearance' sake, arrange the trusses so the nailing plates holding them together face the arbor's interior.

2 Angle-cut 2x4s and assemble roof trusses with nailing plates as shown. You'll need plates on only one side of each truss. Our design calls for a total of three trusses.

4 Nail 2x2s to the trusses and posts. Use a 2x2 to ensure equal spacing between boards and a short scrap of wood to assure that the ends of the boards extend the same distance beyond the outside trusses.

SIMPLE ARBOR

1 Erect two posts (see pages 58–60 and 74–75). Lag-screw two short lengths of 2x6 to each post. Check to be sure crossbeams are square with the posts before tightening screws.

2 Use a jigsaw or router to shape a decorative motif at the ends of two longer beams. Drive at least two nails through these into the ends of each crossbeam.

3 Cut 2x2s to length and drive one nail through each into each of the longer beams. To minimize measuring, use spacers, as shown in step 4 at left.

For basic information on working with wood, see pages 276–281. For working with concrete, see pages 282–287.

ARBOR AND TRELLIS PLANTINGS

The vine-covered arbor or trellis makes a cool garden wall, curtained in green and decorated with dappled sunlight and fragrant flowers. The privacy and shade it offers rival those of a tree, but in a half season instead of a decade and in a width as narrow as a single foot.

The secret to enjoying vines, instead of fighting them, is to understand their individual traits, then match the right vines to your needs—whether that be cottage garden fragrance, a formal feeling, spring bloom, fall color, fruit production, or to frame a view or screen it. Keep in mind a vine's soil preference, hardiness, and sun or shade requirements, too.

Most vines grow fast, but annuals such as morning-glory take until mid- to late summer to provide much shade. Perennial vines have roots and wood in place and give shade by late spring. A combination of the two often works well.

Some vines run rampant and need frequent pruning; most provide dense shade. Where you want filtered screening or delicate holding, as on a screened porch, choose clematis, the choice honeysuckles, mandevilla, or Virginia creeper.

■ Climbing

Vines can be divided into three basic groups, depending on how they climb.

Twining vines need at least a finger-thin means of support to climb a flat surface. They climb in only one direction: bittersweet and kiwi counterclockwise, honeysuckle and Japanese wisteria clockwise. For ease of work when painting or making repairs near these vines, simply take down their supports.

Some vines climb by winding tendrils or modified leaf stalks around whatever they can. Clematis, grape, melon, pea, passion vines, and creepers all climb this way.

Vines like Boston ivy cling by attaching small, rootlike grips, usually to a wall. These vines should not be planted on frame houses because the holdfasts may penetrate and damage the siding. They also are difficult to tear away when the house needs paint or repairs. Vines with holdfasts are ideal for brick or stone.

▲ Start a vine up a trellis by winding its outside branches around the trellis support loosely, allowing them to choose their preferred direction, unless you're aware of it. Weave inside branches between the supports.

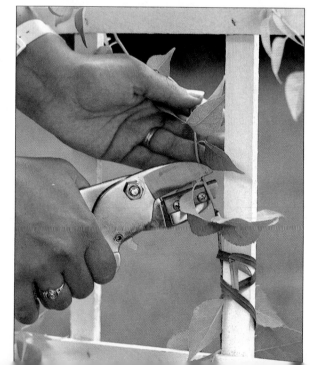

▶ To encourage branching, pinch or snip just above a bud. Tie branches loosely to the trellis if needed. Select the growth you want and remove all the rest.

▲ *To start a vine up an arbor, wind or attach one or two stems. Prune off all side growth until the stems reach the top. Then allow desired side branching to develop.*

▼*On an overhead structure, loosely weave the vine's branches in and out as needed. Do not tie them. Be sure to leave room for the growth to come.*

VINE SUGGESTIONS

Grapes *are deciduous, woody, and easy to grow. They need full sun and strong support. Foliage is rather coarse and flowers are inconspicuous, but fruit hangs all season and ripens in the fall.*

Hardy kiwi *is a deciduous vine with fragrant cream-colored blossoms in May, lush foliage, and fruit in fall on female or self-fertile vines. Needs strong support and full sun.*

Rose *varieties, like this 'Lutea' or Lady Bank's rose, are outstanding for fragrance and flowers. They need full sun, good air circulation, and fertile soil. Fruits—called hips—are edible.*

Wisteria *has long, deciduous leaflets and, in spring, hanging clusters of white or lavender fragrant flowers. It needs strong support, slightly acid soil, and nearly full sun.*

All of the above are perennial. See pages 109, 111, 166, and 314–316 for other vine recommendations. Ivy and winter creeper are evergreen; many other vines keep their leaves year-round in the South, but lose them in winter in northern gardens.

For basic information on plants and planting, see pages 292–299.

107

CHOOSING PLANTS TO PROVIDE DENSE SHADE

TREES

CRAB APPLE
Malus species and hybrids

Type: Deciduous
Height: 15–25 feet
Zones: 3–8
Soil: Rich, well drained; tolerant
Light: Full sun

Comments: Crab apples, with their profusion of fragrant spring flowers and fall fruit, are among the best of trees. Much fruit stays on the trees throughout winter, providing food for birds and a nice decoration when crowned with snow. Some is good for jams and jellies. Crab apples need regular spraying, pruning, and borer control. 'Transcendent' and 'Dolgo' are best for eating. May bear more fruit every other year.

DOGWOOD
Cornus florida

Type: Deciduous
Height: 15–30 feet
Zones: 5–9
Soil: Rich, slightly acid, moist
Light: Prefers some shade

Comments: One of the most beautiful and useful flowering trees, the dogwood offers spring bloom, good summer foliage, dark red autumn color, berries, and, with its horizontal branches and crownlike buds, winter interest. Red and pink varieties are available. Japanese dogwood (*Cornus kousa*) blooms later with pointed bracts. The other dogwoods all are good ornamentals with attractive foliage and berries, but inconspicuous flowers.

MAPLE
Acer species

Type: Deciduous
Height: To 80 feet and more
Zones: 3–8
Soil: Any good; prefers moist
Light: Full sun or light shade

Comments: Ninety species of maple vary in habit, rate of growth, and size and color of leaves. Spring and summer foliage can be maroon-red or many shades of green with white, yellow, or pink markings, or silver undersides. The fiery autumn color of New England is largely from maples in brilliant red, yellow, and orange. Easily grown; few serious pest or disease problems. Sugar maple and several others give syrup.

OAK
Quercus species

Type: Mostly deciduous
Height: 50 feet to much higher
Zones: 4–9
Soil: Acid, moist, well drained
Light: Sun or light shade

Comments: Oaks make excellent shade and specimen trees, especially where they have plenty of room. The many species vary greatly in leaves, color, and acorns, which are good for wildlife. Valued for their sturdy growth and wide-spreading branches at maturity, some have brilliant autumn color and some are evergreen. Many keep their leaves long into winter. Difficult to transplant; some disease threat.

Most trees will develop as much width as height if given room. You can get columnar varieties of maple, oak, and plane trees for narrow spaces. Low trees—such as hawthorn and maples like amur—will give shade and still stay in bounds under electric wires. Other excellent shade trees include evergreen hemlock, some pines, arborvitae, and deciduous trees like katsura tree, sweet gum, and linden. For quick-growing temporary trees, use silver maple, catalpa, silk oak, and willow. See pages 301–306 for more tree suggestions.

SPRUCE
Picea species

Type: Coniferous evergreen
Height: Most 100 feet or more
Zones: 2–9
Soil: Prefers cool, moist
Light: Full sun

Comments: Spruces are stiff, formal trees with cones that hang down. They eventually grow to great heights and can grow out of scale. Blue spruces are greatly prized for their color. Older spruces often lose their lower branches, changing their shape, but opening up the yard to traffic, views, and more air circulation. Red and black spruces are less choice. Can have spruce gall and aphids.

TULIP TREE
Liriodendron tulipifera

Type: Deciduous
Height: 75 feet or more
Zones: 5–9
Soil: Deep, rich, acid, moist
Light: Full sun or light shade

Comments: Tulip trees are fast growing. They have a pyramidal shape, green leaves like squared-off maple leaves, yellow autumn color, and tulip-shaped green flowers with a band of yellow and orange in late spring. The flowers hide among the foliage but are beautiful from a treetop deck or upstairs window. Seedpods dry in tulip shape for winter. Can drop sooty mold or honeydew from aphids; use away from patios or driveways.

SHRUBS

ANDROMEDA
Pieris species

Type: Broad-leaved evergreen
Height: 2–9 feet
Zones: 4–8
Soil: Sandy, acid, moist
Light: Sun to partial shade

Comments: An excellent shrub, andromeda has lustrous, dark green foliage with much bronze in the new leaves. Buds are showy all winter. Nodding clusters of lily-of-the-valley-like flowers, white to pinkish, cover the shrub in the spring. Floribunda is hardier than japonica. Plant both in more sheltered spots in the North. Fine entrance or accent plants. Few problems. Will produce more flowers in sun than in shade.

Other dense shrubs include camellia, clethra, privet, deciduous viburnums, and evergreens like juniper, yew, and mountain laurel.

Or plant edibles like elderberry or blueberry for both shade and food. See pages 82–83 and 307–313 for more shrub recommendations.

VINES

SILVER-LACE VINE
Polygonum auberti

Type: Woody perennial
Length: 25 feet
Zones: 4–8
Soil: Average; tolerates dry
Light: Full sun best

Comments: Rapid growing, silver-lace vine has fragrant, greenish white flowers in long erect or drooping clusters in late summer and early fall when few woody plants are blooming. Good, dense, bright green foliage. A member of the knotweed family, it climbs by twining. Prune severely in late winter to control vigorous growth. Easy to grow from seeds, root divisions, or ripe wood cuttings. Also called fleece vine.

CHOOSING PLANTS TO PROVIDE FILTERED SHADE

TREES

BIRCH
Betula species

Type: Deciduous
Height: 25–90 feet
Zones: 2–10
Soil: Moist
Light: Full sun to light shade

Comments: Birches are widely planted, often in clumps, for their interesting gray, white, black, or reddish brown bark that splits and hangs like wrapping paper. The weeping birch is valued for its shape. All have early catkin blooms that herald spring and leaves that turn yellow in autumn. All are short-lived and subject to many pests. River birch needs more moisture but resists problems better. 'Heritage' is an improved cultivar.

CHERRY, PLUM, PEACH
Prunus species

Type: Deciduous
Height: Mostly 20–25 feet
Zones: 2–10
Soil: Well drained
Light: Full sun

Comments: The prunus group, with more than 400 species, includes all the stone fruits, from chokecherry to cherry laurel. Many of these are excellent choices for edible landscaping. If you don't want fruit, use purely ornamental kinds. Most are low growing and decorative, with clouds of spring flowers, single or double, in white, pink, or rose. Some have bronze foliage or glossy red bark; a few are evergreen. Shade density varies.

GINKGO
Ginkgo biloba

Type: Deciduous
Height: 50–80 feet
Zones: 5–10
Soil: Deep, loose
Light: Full sun to part shade

Comments: Hardy and slow growing, ginkgo trees are one of the oldest plants in cultivation. They are ideal as lawn or street trees because they're pest free, widely adaptable, and tolerant of smoke and pollution. Provide extra watering after planting. The male tree is neater; berries have a rancid odor when crushed. Fan-shaped leaves turn golden yellow in autumn and all fall at once, making raking a one-time affair.

PINE
Pinus species

Type: Coniferous evergreen
Height: 30–100 feet
Zones: 3–9
Soil: Well drained, low fertility
Light: Full sun to timber shade

Comments: The pine group of needled evergreens contains few shrubs, mostly tall trees. They vary in height, hardiness, and shape. Prune for thicker growth by snapping tender candles of new growth in half in spring. Select best varieties for your area and landscape mood. Scotch pine has open shape and red bark; white pine has fine-textured needles. Austrian pine has stiff foliage, spreading habit, and round top.

Other good open trees are honey locust, Carolina silver-bell, golden larch, lace-bark pine, Canary Island pine, black locust, sassafras, mountain ash, laburnum or golden-chain tree, jacaranda, Japanese tree lilac, and bald cypress. Trees that have edible nuts or fruits and that provide less dense shade include hickory, pecan, and apricot. See pages 301–306 for more tree recommendations. (Any tree, shrub, or vine can be espaliered for controlled growth on an open frame to provide filtered shade.)

SHRUBS

FORSYTHIA
Forsythia species

Type: Deciduous
Height: 2–12 feet
Zones: 4–8
Soil: Any, except very dry
Light: Full sun

Comments: Forsythia's early-spring golden showers on arching or upright branches make it hard to resist. The plant is much hardier than the buds. Give it plenty of room; plant 8 to 10 feet from walk or patio. Never prune until after bloom. Then remove unwanted canes at the ground. Forsythia can claim more room than its limited season merits. Extra-hardy varieties are 'Northern Sun' and 'Ottawa.'

LILAC
Syringa species

Type: Deciduous
Height: 3–20 feet
Zones: 2–9
Soil: Well drained, rich
Light: Full sun

Comments: Lilac's fabulous clusters of fragrant flowers in shades of white, pink, blue, purple, and rose in mid-spring make it popular despite its limited season of interest. Prune seedpods after bloom and limit shoots coming from the crown. Good near front entry, sunny patio, open windows, and as background hedge or accent plant. Lengthen season of bloom by choosing several different species.

Good shrubs for filtered shade include tall cotoneasters, smokebush, redvein enkianthus, mock orange, and rhododendron. Pruning dense-foliaged shrubs can let in more light. See pages 82–83 and 307–313 for more shrub recommendations.

VINES

CLEMATIS
Clematis species and hybrids

Type: Perennial
Length: 5–30 feet
Zones: 4–9
Soil: Sandy, slightly alkaline
Light: Full sun to light shade

Comments: Beautiful plants, clematis species and hybrids vary widely in bloom type, color, fragrance, and season. The large, star-shaped flowers of the hybrids are spectacular in early summer. Sweet autumn clematis has fragrant flowers in fall with feathery seedpods. Plant in humus-rich soil with a little lime, and mulch well to keep the soil cool and moist. Shade the roots. Needs little pruning; wait until it leafs out completely.

MORNING-GLORY
Ipomea purpurea

Type: Mostly annual
Length: 8–10 feet
Zones: 4–10
Soil: Not too high in nitrogen
Light: Full sun

Comments: One of the most loved and easily grown vines, morning-glory blooms from early summer until frost. Soak seeds overnight or notch before sowing; sow after danger of frost passes. Train on strings against a wall or on a fence. Plant improved varieties like 'Heavenly Blue,' 'Pearly Gates,' and 'Scarlet Star.' Though fast growing, morning-glory is best combined with a perennial or woody vine for shade.

Most vines have dense, vigorous growth that requires much pruning to achieve a filtered-shade effect. Among the exceptions are runner and 'Royalty' beans and the vines mentioned on page 106. Their less dense nature yields dappled lighting.

GALLERY OF SUN AND SHADE IDEAS

▼*Even a small yard is doubly interesting with some sun and some shade. This overhead structure keeps both patio and house cooler, while leaving the garden bright enough for vegetables.*

◄*Open, airy, and inviting, this trellis shades not only the brick patio and its hanging swing, but also French doors leading to the living room. A bonus: The trellis improved the dignified but blank face of the old farmhouse, softening its severe lines.*

▲ *With wood that complements the patio, fence, and mood of the garden, this overhead structure offers the best of sun and shade. Climbing vines deepen the shade in summer and let the sun warm the adjoining house in winter.*

►*Just 16 feet of trellised wisteria between the deck and the fence give this narrow backyard shade, privacy, and character. With potted annuals added for portable seasonal color, the setting makes a delightful retreat despite the nearness of neighbors.*

◄ *This attractive overhead sunshade covers a deck divided into two separate, intimate settings, both with an open view. Vines will grow over the top to give more shade, and cover the center structure for added privacy.*

▼ *A soft mauve acrylic canvas undulates across a trellis to provide more or less shade as desired. The mauve was chosen to blend with room colors inside and to bounce warm light indoors.*

113

Mature trees frame the setting, adding a vertical dimension and a sense of permanence. Tall back-yard trees peek over the roof of the multistoried house, softening its lines and its mass.

This front-yard design demonstrates well the principles of balance, rhythm, emphasis, unity, and simplicity. Wall, lamppost, and plants combine for a pleasing scene. The driveway on the right is balanced by the porch and tree at left.

The entrance is enticing and clearly defined. A first-time visitor would instinctively start up the steps and along the walk. Long before reaching the front door, the caller would decide that this setting is enchanting.

The shrubs make the house seem a natural part of the site. They include plants that have interest and color in all seasons. Best of all, they are in scale and will not overgrow the walk or block the windows.

CHAPTER SIX

FRONT YARDS

The importance of the front yard to your landscape design cannot be overstated. Each day, it welcomes you home and makes that all-important first impression on passersby. Its design should fit the neighborhood, yet be distinctive. It should enhance your house, tie it to the landscape, and indicate to the visitor where to park and knock. Though every house cannot have a high tree above an open gate, even a town house can have a dooryard garden that says, "Welcome!"

CREATING AN ATTRACTIVE FRONT

Every house facade and site has visual assets and liabilities. The well-done front yard highlights the pleasing points and masks the poor ones.

All the elements of good design come into play as you arrange your component parts for the ideal front yard. But don't be put off by the aesthetic terms—balance, scale, unity, and the like—used by designers. All are largely a matter of common sense. If a scene pleases your eye, then it's probably well designed.

If your house needs or will adapt to your desire for a special theme garden like colonial, cottage, Oriental, or Spanish, the look must begin in the front yard. Themes are successful only if you unify all the garden aspects carefully.

You'll also need to determine if your preference is for, and your site demands, a formal or informal landscape. Formal settings include strong geometric lines and architectural features, clipped hedges, and uniformly shaped plants and beds. Informal designs are marked by free-flowing, natural-looking elements. Generally, informal home styles and sloping land require less rigid landscapes. Formal houses and flat land can be treated either way.

To achieve balance in a landscape, try to position elements so they give equal weight—through size, color, texture, or other aspects—to each side of a scene. How formal this weighting should be again is dictated by style of house and personal preference. Symmetrical houses often look best when each feature and plant is duplicated on the opposite side of a front walk (as long as the walk isn't too long or too narrow). Most houses, though, are asymmetrical, since they have only one garage or drive. In this case, balance is more subtle. Perhaps a tall tree belongs on the side opposite the driveway.

Achieving pleasant scale—or, keeping elements in proportion to each other—also is subtle, since plants must grow before you can be sure. Choose plants that will complement your home's size at maturity, as well as some plants that will grow fast enough to quickly make a mark. Don't let anything dwarf your house.

The design principles of unity and simplicity often go together. Several plants of the same color and kind have more effect and give greater pleasure in a landscape than one each of several types. Use only enough variety for sustaining bloom and adding visual interest.

If you want more types of plants, say for continual harvests of many kinds of fruit, try combining plants with similar or at least compatible shapes, textures, and foliage or bloom colors.

■ Trees for impact
Trees (and larger shrubs) are the first components to consider in front-yard design.

Because a framed view often is much more attractive than a view that's completely revealed, give serious thought to planting taller trees on either side and at least one behind your house. Trees in these spots give the yard and house a look of permanence, and soften the second story or roofline against the sky. If you can afford only one or two more-mature trees, this is the place for them.

Besides providing framing, trees and larger shrubs, along with the buildings, make up the masses in the landscape. Choose and place them for interest of outline, texture, and color in all seasons and for shade and energy control (see pages 96–113 and 301–313). Harmonize the shapes of the plants—round, pyramidal, weeping—with each other and the structures. Give visual relief by judiciously varying leaf size and shape and the textures of structural materials.

Trees and shrubs also are good for marking boundaries and separating functional areas.

■ Accent trees
To add beauty and perhaps additional shade to a front yard, carefully situate a very choice—or accent—tree between the street and the house. Accent trees make such a lasting impression, you may well identify certain houses by the dogwood or Japanese maple in the front yard. When selecting accent—also called specimen or ornamental—trees, use reliable native types with good habits and few pest problems.

(continued on page 120)

▶ *Charm and character result when landscape and home are carefully matched, as they are here. Trees and fence frame, soften, and accent the view, and the open gate invites. Window boxes, shutters, and porch railing accent.*

CREATING AN ATTRACTIVE FRONT *(continued)*

▶ *Standard plantings for a one-story house often lack design. Here, the small shrubs make the house look drab and out of place. The tall evergreen blocks the view and offers no shade. The scene is broken into discordant thirds.*

PLAIN

▶ *Here, shorter shrubs, a planter, and better-placed trees frame the facade, soften its lines, and wed the house to the site. Decorative railings set off the entryway, and a run of ground cover defines the driveway and controls the slope.*

BETTER

If you'd like a pair or row of trees to line the street in front of your house, choose carefully. Check with your city for any ordinances on street plantings. These regulations might govern both the kinds of plantings and planting distances. Find out who will be responsible for maintaining the trees.

Determine the location of water and sewer lines. If there are any plans for widening the street, plant far enough back. Look up to check overhead wires, and plant only small trees beneath (see pages 108 and 301–302).

In the inner city, only a few trees—including maple, ash, hawthorn, ginkgo, smoke tree, amur oak, Austrian or Scotch pine, littleleaf linden, and plane tree—survive the pollution and limited soil surface.

In the suburbs, growing conditions are better, making plant selection easier, but avoid trees that might drop staining fruit or petals on nearby cars.

No tree should be planted closer to the curb than 3½ feet. Given the best distance between curb and sidewalk—at least 12 feet—plant closer to the sidewalk. It usually is better to plant a tree that will be small at maturity. Smaller plants adapt more easily to adverse conditions and are less expensive to maintain later. Streetside is not the place to crowd trees.

■ Foundation plantings

In the past, plants were set where house meets ground to hide foundations and first-floor basements. Today, these so-called foundation plantings often are inappropriate and widely abused. Builders put in plants with enough size but little character, and they can soon outgrow their usefulness. Many houses come with a surrounding cloud or a border of stiffly spotted evergreens that does nothing but destroy a house's style.

Plants near the house are essential only to soften its angles and help it blend in with its surroundings. Concentrate on the complete setting, not just the foundation line. Your plantings here should be simple and dignified. They should be in careful scale so they enhance rather than hide the house. You won't see these plants from inside except for perhaps a little by the windowsill, so don't waste your beauties here.

■ Planters

Raised planting beds often are used instead of or together with foundation plantings. Build them deep enough to provide ample soil for root growth and bottomless so the bedding soil mixes with the soil below.

Because soil in raised beds dries out more quickly than it does in the ground (and because few plants can withstand full sun plus the heat reflected from house walls), place beds in spots that receive shade for part of the day.

Plants here have star billing. Be sure they are hardy, are of appropriate ultimate size, and have neat, season-long appearance. Choose dwarf evergreens, flowering shrubs, fruit trees, perennials, or bulbs. For the most profusion and longest season of bloom, rely on annuals. Cascading petunia, vinca, and asparagus fern are lovely hanging over a bed's edges. Leave some edges clear, though, for sit-down gardening or just plain sitting down.

■ Front-yard gardens

The old rule that the front yard is for the public and the backyard is for fun and family is sometimes better broken. Is your front yard the sunniest in a cool climate? The coolest in summer? On the south side where tender plants and fruit can best survive the cold? The largest part of your yard? Then reclaim some or all of it for private family use. A wall, fence, or sometimes only a small screen can give you the privacy you need. (See Chapter 4, "Privacy and Security," pages 78–95.)

PLAIN

◄ *This typical two-story house has the usual shrubs and tree. The entry is too plain, the front too busy. Though not terrible, the landscape lacks unity and makes the house appear lopsided and uninteresting.*

BETTER

◄ *Here, the tree in front frames rather than interrupts the scene, is in better scale, and makes the house seem farther from the street. The fence and vines define the driveway, protect the entryway, and help tie house and site.*

BUILDING WALKS AND PATHS

Constructing a walk or path offers an excellent introduction to the basics of garden paving. Unlike the bigger jobs of pouring a patio (pages 158–161) or building a driveway (pages 242–245), you needn't move a lot of earth, prepare extensive footings, or wrestle with large volumes of tricky materials. Best of all—even for a project as rigorous as the exposed-aggregate walk shown at right—you can work at your own pace, completing several sections one weekend, more the next.

Note, too, that here we show only two of the myriad possibilities for walkway paving materials. For others, see pages 124–125, 130, and 162–163. And if you already have a concrete walk that's sound but drab looking, consider veneering it with tile, flagstones, brick, or other materials, as detailed on pages 164–165.

■ Exposing aggregate

To achieve the rustic, skidproof texture of an exposed-aggregate walk, use one of two methods. You can either pour concrete with the aggregate mixed in it, then, after the concrete begins to set, scrub some of it away. This is the method we used at right. Or, you can seed aggregate on top of a just-poured slab, screed the stone into the concrete, and then scrub.

Masonry dealers offer a variety of aggregates that vary by region. We used pea gravel uniform in size, but you might prefer the look of river pebbles, granite chips, or another option.

As with any concrete project, timing plays a critical role in the outcome of an exposed-aggregate finish. Don't try to scrape away the concrete until the aggregate holds firm. If weather conditions are right, this stage should occur in about 1½ hours, but it could take up to six hours. To test, lay a board on the surface and kneel on the board; if the board leaves marks, allow more time. If any aggregate dislodges when you start brushing, stop and let the concrete set some more.

Finally, slow curing is what gives concrete its strength, so wait a week or so before walking on it. Also, dampen the concrete daily as it cures.

EXPOSED-AGGREGATE WALK

1 Excavate, build 2x4 forms, pour sand, and lay reinforcing mesh (see pages 158–160). If you plan to leave the forms as decorative dividers, apply sealer, then cover them with duct tape so they won't be damaged during the pour. Pour concrete with aggregate mixed into it (or, if seeding, pour plain concrete) in only a few form frames at a time. Strike off the concrete.

3 If a module hardens too quickly, scrub concrete from aggregate with a 1:10 solution of muriatic acid and water. Wear goggles and other protective clothing. Once aggregate is sufficiently exposed, rinse well with water.

2 If seeding, after striking off concrete, evenly sprinkle wet aggregate onto surface; carefully push it into the concrete with a trowel until it is thinly covered. For either method, after the concrete firms up, scrape with a brush or broom to expose aggregate. Spray water over surface; brush again. Repeat spraying and brushing until exposure is uniform and water runs clear.

4 To give the surface a lacquerlike sheen and protect the walk from rain damage, wait at least a week for the concrete to thoroughly cure, then brush on waterproofing solution. Remove tape strips from the decorative forms.

STEPPING-STONES

1 Lay out the path with stakes and string, then strip the sod (save it and reuse it elsewhere, if desired). Spray the exposed path with vegetation killer to keep weeds down. Add a thin sand base to allow for drainage, wet it, then tamp it well.

2 Space concrete rounds or stones at a normal walking stride. Stake edging along the sides (see page 128). Fill around the masonry units with bark mulch, gravel, or other natural materials.

For basic information on working with concrete, see pages 282–287.

BUILDING STEPS

Properly constructed garden steps not only take a walk or path into another dimension, they also serve as a retaining wall, holding back soil erosion. This means you need to plan carefully, and securely anchor them into the slope they ascend.

Select materials to match or contrast with the walkways at top and bottom. Besides the brick and timber versions shown here, you can build steps entirely of concrete (just dispense with the bricks), set bricks or concrete slabs into a sand base, mix stone or concrete treads with brick risers, or terrace the slope with timber risers and surface the treads with gravel, wood chips, or other loose fill.

■ **Laying out**

Whatever materials you choose, you first must decide how many steps you will need, how deep each horizontal *tread* will be, and how high to make each vertical *riser*. Here's a useful rule: The tread dimension plus the riser dimension should equal about 17 inches. Try to make your riser dimension no more than 7 inches and no less than 4 inches. No matter how you juggle the figures, just be sure all treads and risers will be exactly the same depth and height: Changes break a person's stride and cause stumbles. Also, be sure to take into account the depth of tread-finishing materials and mortar, if any, when planning a concrete foundation.

Use stakes and a level string or board to determine the total *rise* your steps will ascend and the total *run* they will traverse (see page 39). To determine how many steps you will need, divide these measurements by combinations of tread and riser sizes until you come out with equal-size steps.

A caution: Building codes usually place limits on tread and riser sizes and other stairway dimensions, so check with local authorities before finalizing your plans. Codes also mandate handrails in some situations. More about these on page 127.

BRICK STEPS

1 Mark the dimensions of each step with string, then cut carefully into the slope, digging deeper under the bottom tread for an integral footing. Mark and dig the space for each tread a couple of inches longer than the tread will be so the forms can overlap as shown in step 2.

2 Construct forms so the front edge of each tread will be double thickness. Pour gravel into the forms, then add reinforcing mesh. Suspend horizontal rerod at the points where treads and risers will meet; tie the bottom tread to its footing with vertical rerod.

3 Shovel or pour wet concrete into the forms. Poke the mix periodically with a piece of rerod to remove air pockets. Lift the mesh midway into the concrete's thickness. Strike off and trowel. Let the concrete cure for about a week, then remove the forms.

4 Once the concrete is cured, spread a ½-inch-thick bed of mortar over the riser and tread of one step. Screed the bed, then press the bricks into place. A level string line serves as a reference point for keeping bricks at a uniform height.

5 If a brick is too high, tap it with the handle of a hammer or trowel. If it's too low, lift it out and trowel on more mortar to the bottom. Use ½-inch spacers to maintain even gaps between bricks.

6 Pack grout between bricks; tool with a joint strike or piece of pipe. When grouting is almost dry, clean bricks with water and sponge. To keep from loosening bricks, do not walk on the steps for a week.

For basic information on working with concrete and mortar, see pages 282–287.

TIMBER STEPS

1 Cut carefully into the slope, making room for the desired tread and riser dimensions. Steps of two 8-inch timbers work well if they overlap by 4 inches. Lay the timbers, pound into place with a sledge, and check for level.

2 Using an electrician's extension bit, bore holes at the front edge of each timber into the one below it, then pound in rerod to tie them together. Also bore horizontal holes to secure each timber to the one behind it.

125

BUILDING RAMPS

A ramp makes a gentle transition from one level to another, smoothing the path for everything from tricycles to wheelbarrows to—most especially—wheelchairs. If your family includes someone who relies on a wheelchair for mobility, you'll most certainly need a ramp to one or more of your home's entrances, and maybe to outdoor living areas as well.

We poured concrete for the ramp at right, but you can use a variety of other materials, including wood, or even earth topped with fine gravel. Whatever material you use, make sure the surface the chair will ride on is nonskid. Textured rubber toppings (see page 185) and textured concrete (see opposite) work well.

■ Ramp basics

Safety and ease of use are the prime considerations for any ramp. Appearance, though, plays a part, too, especially for a ramp visible from the street.

Regardless of the design you come up with, certain norms apply. Slope a wheelchair ramp at a rise of no more than 1 foot per 12 feet of run. This standard can make for some incredibly long ramps—a total rise of 2 feet, for example, requires a total length of at least 24 feet. But a gentle grade is essential for a ramp to be useful to the people who need it most.

Even if your ramp won't be used by anyone in a wheelchair, slope it no more than about 1 foot for every 7 feet of run.

For wheelchair use, include handrails on both sides of your ramp (see opposite), and make the ramp wide enough so the distance between the handrails is at least 36 inches. Also, any incline longer than 30 feet needs a landing where a wheelchair user can rest and maneuver the chair. Whether your plan calls for an L-shaped, switchback, or broken straight-run ramp, all landings must measure at least 5x5 feet. Where doors open outward, the adjacent landing must be at least 5x6½ feet; this gives wheelchair users room to move back when the door is opened.

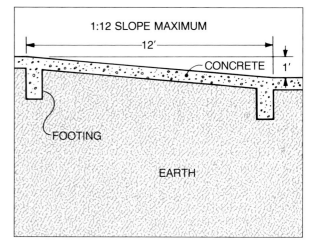

1 *For wheelchair use, plan a ramp that slopes no more than 1 foot in 12, with 5-foot-square landings top and bottom. A concrete ramp must tie into the slope with footings on either side of each landing. Dig the footings to the frost line in your area (check local codes). Make your concrete ramp at least 4 inches thick.*

3 *Pour concrete. Use a slightly stiffer mix than you would for a level slab so the concrete will hold the incline. Strike off. Float with a darby float. Define edges with an edging trowel, then tool control joints every few feet. (See pages 160–161 for more about these steps.)*

2 *We extended our ramp down from an existing slab, which we fitted with a piece of expansion strip. Cut and fill earth as necessary. Construct forms with 2x4 lumber. Double-check that the forms do not slope more than desired. Add gravel and reinforcing mesh. Tie in each footing with horizontal and vertical rerod.*

4 *To make your ramp skidproof, pull a damp broom across the surface of the just-troweled concrete. For a fine texture, use a soft-bristled broom; for a coarser one, use a stiffer bristle. (For details on other special concrete textures, see pages 162–163.)*

INSTALLING HANDRAILS

If you're building a ramp, outfit both sides of it with handrails to allow wheelchair users to pull themselves up the ramp. For steps, put a rail on one side.

Handrails for ramps should be about 32 inches high. If people in wheelchairs will use your ramp, install rails that have a grip width of about 1½ inches. Along stairways, set handrails about 30 inches high; at stairway landings, 34 inches high.

Below, we show a metal railing being attached to a concrete curb that runs alongside a ramp. To attach wooden railings to a wooden ramp, see the instructions for deck railings on pages 176–181. Particularly important is that balusters be securely attached to a wood ramp's structure, not its surface.

Similarly, for concrete steps, attach rail brackets to the treads. But for wood steps, attach the balusters to the structure.

For metal railing brackets, drill holes into the ramp's surface (or into an adjacent curb, as we did here). Install brackets with lead masonry anchors and screws. Slip vertical balusters into the brackets; tighten set screws. Install rails top and bottom and assemble intermediate balusters.

For basic information on working with concrete, see pages 282–287.

INSTALLING WALK EDGINGS

Looking for a way to dress up a plain-Jane path, provide crisp lines between paving and landscaping materials, or hold masonry units in line?

Edging can do all these jobs—and more—for only a modest investment of time and money. In most cases, you simply decide on the material you'd like to use, excavate shallow trenches on either side of the walk, and stake or set the edging in place. (One exception is the integral concrete edging, shown opposite. It's installed at the same time as a new walk.)

■ Mowing strips

Edging materials are every bit as various as the pavings they border. Choose from concrete, brick, stone, tile, wood, and vinyl. Edging styles, however, fall into just two broad categories. A *raised edging* puts a lip at each side of a walk or path. A *mowing strip* installs flush with the walk so you can run one wheel of a mower along it.

Make mowing strips 6 to 12 inches wide. Concrete, brick, tile, and other smooth-surface masonry materials are best for mowing strips. You can use timbers, but be warned that these are easily nicked by the mower blade.

■ Raised edgings

A raised edging keeps aggressive ground cover from overgrowing a walk, channels water run-off, and makes a clean break between differing surfaces. If you're planning a path of gravel, mulch, or other loose-fill material, a raised edging is the only way to go.

Keep a raised edging low, ½ inch or so, or make it 3 or more inches high. Anything in between poses a tripping hazard. The photos at right and opposite show how to install two popular types of raised edgings; page 131 shows several alternatives.

Give thought, too, to the type of plantings you select for alongside a walk or path. The box on the opposite page shows four good choices that are easy to keep in bounds.

WOOD EDGING

1 Dig a trench alongside the walk. Make it about 3½ inches deep, enough to accommodate ½ inch of gravel and all but ½ inch of a 2x4 (which, despite its name, is 3½ inches wide). The gravel bed should be about 10 inches wide for adequate drainage.

2 Lay the gravel bed, then stake 2x4s in place. Miter-cut end-to-end joints to make them less conspicuous. Drive in nails for the stakes so their tops will be about 1 inch below the top edges of the 2x4s.

3 Backfill with enough topsoil to cover the stakes. Compact the soil, then cover with sod or mulch. Or plant a path-side garden with any good edging plant, including those pictured on the opposite page.

INTEGRAL CONCRETE EDGING

1 *Construct plywood forms at the edge of your planned walk. For a 3½-inch-thick walk, leave a 3½-inch gap between the gravel bed and inside board. Temporarily nail short pieces of wood between the inside and outside boards. Stake forms every few feet.*

2 *Lay reinforcing mesh, bending it so its tips stick up into the curb forms. These tie the walk and edging into an integral unit that will ride out settlement and frost heave. When you pour the concrete, pull mesh into middle of slab and curb with a claw hammer or rake.*

3 *Pour concrete into edging forms first, then into walk area, pulling wood spacers as you pour. Strike off and trowel. Let concrete cure for a week, then remove stakes and forms.*

For basic information on working with wood and concrete, and on plants and planting, see pages 276–287 and 292–299.

WALK PLANTINGS

Ajuga *is a perennial ground cover with low rosettes of beautifully colored foliage and, in spring, blue blooms. Tolerates sun or shade. Divide crowns for quick spreading.*

Alyssum *is a low annual with clouds of dainty white or pink blooms. It needs to be sheared back whenever it gets seedy. It prefers cool weather and full sun or partial shade.*

Impatiens *vary in height and color of flower and foliage. Most need some shade; a few take full sun. All bloom neatly from summer to frost. Easy to start from seeds or cuttings.*

Lily-of-the-valley *is a favorite perennial with bright green foliage. Springtime stalks of delicate bells have delightful fragrance. It prefers shade and moist, fertile soil.*

Other good perennials for edgings include pachysandra and vinca (see page 67); ivy, thyme, speedwell, and lamium (pages 260–261). Spring bulbs and summer annuals also make good edge plants (pages 320–323).

CHOOSING WALK AND EDGING MATERIALS

WALK MATERIALS

LOOSE FILL

Description: Aggregate (shown), pebbles, crushed rock, sand, shredded bark, nutshells, seashells, and pine straw go directly on the surface you want to cover.
Effect: Organic loose fills add a rustic look and interesting texture to lightly used areas. Mineral ones have a more formal appearance.

Cost: Among the most economical walk materials, but because loose fill is prone to erosion and tends to overflow its boundaries, it needs replenishing periodically.
Comments: Drains well, conforms to contours, and is easily installed over compacted sand (see page 123). To keep fill from spreading, confine with edging.

WOOD PLANKS

Description: Docklike strips of decking you can lay on a sand or gravel base or atop an existing masonry walk.
Effect: Warm, rustic, and an especially good choice if you want to extend an on-grade or raised deck out into your yard.

Cost: Less than brick, stone, or tile; more than concrete or loose fill.
Comments: Use pressure-treated lumber or naturally rot-resistant redwood, cedar, or cypress. Keep out of contact with vegetation. Leave drainage spaces between boards. Construct as for on-grade deck shown on pages 172–175, but omit posts and footings.

WOOD ROUNDS OR BLOCKS

Description: Slices of logs or timbers set in a bed of sand or loose fill, or simply cut into sod and surrounded by grass.
Effect: Similar to stepping-stones, but even more organic in appearance. An ideal choice for a romantic country garden or a meandering forest path.

Cost: Very cheap, if you have wood and a chain saw, and set rounds or blocks in sand. Otherwise, a little more than cost of loose fill.
Comments: Rounds or blocks, when used with loose fill, aren't a good choice for heavily traveled paths, especially any that lead directly to your home: Fill materials can stick to shoes and travel indoors.

BRICK

Description: Any of a vast variety of clay-based materials set in sand or mortared to a concrete base.
Effect: With bricks you can create almost any look you want, from an arrow-straight front entry walk to a serpentine cobblestone path through clumps of wildflowers.

Cost: Relatively expensive but very durable.
Comments: For an idea of how versatile brick garden paving can be, check the pattern possibilities on the opposite page. For more design interest, consider using two or more colors. To learn about working with brick, see pages 124–125 and 154–157. Bricks set in sand may need leveling every so often.

The above are far from the only materials you might choose for walks, paths, and steps. Flagstones, set in sand or atop concrete, are another good choice, as are ceramic and quarry tiles and concrete paver blocks *(see page 157). One more possibility, asphalt, may seem better suited for driveways, but also works well for paths and service areas (see page 234).*

EDGING MATERIALS

VINYL

Description: Flexible strips of solid or metal-capped plastic that can be set into the ground with or without staking.
Effect: Because it's so easily shaped, vinyl edging negotiates curves with ease. Comes in a limited range of colors, but harmonizes with just about any surfacing material.

Cost: Moderate, especially when you consider that vinyl lasts practically forever.
Comments: The easiest edging to install. Simply slice cuts next to paving with a spade and press or stake the vinyl in place. Keep the mower away from this material.

BRICK

Description: Paving bricks set on edge, on end, or at an angle for a sawtooth effect.
Effect: Probably the most popular edging material, brick makes an excellent border for concrete, loose fill, and, of course, brick paving. Choose colors that match or contrast with the walk's surface.

Cost: Moderate to expensive, depending on the type you select. If you're willing to take time to chip mortar off them, you can save some money with used bricks.
Comments: Set bricks in sand (see pages 154–157) or mortar them to a concrete base (see pages 124–125).

Two other possibilities for edging materials are redwood bender board and metal. Like vinyl, bender board can be shaped into curves. It must be secured to stakes with brass or galvanized screws. Metal is the most expensive and permanent material, but don't use it next to concrete; rusting causes stains.

BRICK PATTERNS

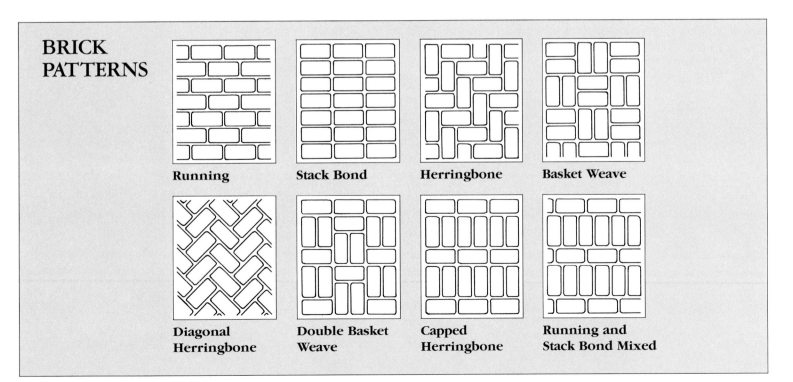

Running Stack Bond Herringbone Basket Weave

Diagonal Herringbone Double Basket Weave Capped Herringbone Running and Stack Bond Mixed

GALLERY OF FRONT-YARD IDEAS

▶ *This entry marries the house to a sloping site. The wide steps and brick walk preserve just a bit of formality, and mature trees provide shade and setting. Despite its youth, the accent tree already adds interest.*

▼ *A wall and broad gate separate the front yard of a ranch-style home from the parking area for more privacy and family use. The gate helps define the entry and frames the slate walkway leading to the door.*

▲ *Plain formality became an elegant entry with a widened front door and an extra-wide angled walkway and wall. This dramatic welcome complements the style of the house.*

▶ *A curved walkway gently tempers the basic boxiness of this house. Railings and plantings give privacy to the porch, and details add a touch of whimsy. The shade-loving plants pick up the trim colors.*

◄ A canopy of elm and maple trees frames and shelters this inviting entry. The stone path softens the setting and leads the eye—and the step—to the front porch and door. Mulched hostas, ferns, begonias, and impatiens thrive in the shade.

▲ Simple, dignified landscaping accents this old house. Columnar evergreens frame the door without blocking windows. Deciduous trees give summer shade and privacy to the porch. The low wall and taller hedges make the lawn seem larger.

GALLERY *(continued)*

◀ *Brick walkway, broad landing, and gabled porch gently guide guests to this front door. Colorful potted plants mark the way, too. The overhang protects visitors from inclement weather while they knock.*

▶ *A jogged wood path and slightly raised entry deck heighten the sense of mystery and promise in this simple but unique entry. The paper birch, bright annual flowers, and corner shrub are quiet accents.*

▶ *Before the addition of the flared brick path and curving plantings of trees and ground cover, this front yard did nothing to entice visitors to the lovely porch. Notice the lighting by the steps for safety.*

◄*Annual and perennial flowers combine with flowering shrubs to give this entry a warm, inviting atmosphere. The wooden walkway and deck bring out the rustic, cottage-garden feeling of the house and the wooded setting.*

► *Guests who make their way to this front entry take a trip to the Orient. Well-placed stones, understated plantings, and a rustic stone path all combine to give this garden the desired Japanese feeling—formal and gracious.*

▲ *A small, sloping front yard need not be bare or unattractive. Here, a series of brick-and-landscape-timber steps set in sand tame the hillside. The fence gives privacy and framing, and the arbor adds more plus shade. Well-chosen plants soften, brighten, and unify all.*

135

These tall shrubs hide anything less than two stories high, while softening the view of bigger structures. They also deter wind, reduce noise, and block car lights to add privacy to this graceful outdoor living room.

The lovely Victorian privacy screen becomes every visitor's fixation in this formal garden. The screen's sides give a feeling of safe enclosure, and its open center hints of interest beyond.

The white screen reflects sunlight into the yard during the day, and helps brighten it at night. A flowering tree and potted daffodils pick up and repeat the white accent color for harmony.

Lacy vines loosely grow against the screen, making it seem to emerge from the landscape. The vines, shrubs, and lawn in front of the screen are kept short and simple so as not to compete with the setting or make it seem busy.

CHAPTER SEVEN

CONTROLLING THE VIEW

The scenery you look at is yours to choose when you plan your landscape carefully. You can open and accent a distant horizon, be it city lights or mountain peaks. Or you can create a close-by focal point of beauty and interest: a blooming tree or winding walk. Or perhaps your need is to cover less-lovely sights: the trash cans in your yard, the busy driveway in your neighbor's. Deliberately, you want to spotlight the beautiful and desired, hide the ugly and unwanted.

137

SCREENING UNWANTED VIEWS WITH PLANTINGS

Planting carefully selected trees and shrubs is the most natural, inexpensive, and subtle way to maximize or minimize the scenery in your yard or the world beyond. A neighbor who might resent a fence can hardly object to an evergreen or flowering shrub. A single planting, well situated, can make the old car next door all but vanish as far as you're concerned.

To wall out even more, plant a hedge or group of shrubs and small trees. You can buy quite mature plants for the price of fencing. Do not stint here. You are buying instant relief. But choose plants that will not grow too big or need more pruning than you are willing to do.

Deciduous shrubs grow tall in just a few seasons. Plant them around areas you don't use in winter, such as decks. Plant evergreens for year-round screening of unpleasant views from your most-used windows and walks. A bonus: Since most summer breezes blow opposite to winter winds, evergreens can save on heating bills, yet not block cool winds in summer.

Small and large deciduous trees will hide tall neighboring buildings eventually, and soften their nearness in the meantime. Choose or prune for open or dense seclusion. And be sure plants do not grow over important views like the stop for the school bus, the mailbox flag, or the swing set.

Vines on arbors, fences, or trellises offer screening in very little time or space. Annuals take until late summer to make a good screen; combine grapes or kiwi with morning-glories for a lacy curtain from early spring.

For plant suggestions, see pages 301–323, plus the charts sprinkled throughout the book.

▶ *The arborvitae hedge at the back of this wide perennial border will eventually hide even the tall house beyond. For now, the eye wanders there, then quickly settles back to the profusion of foreground flowers.*

▲ *Looking into the yard or windows of a nearby house can take the relaxation right out of a hot-tub soak. Tall, lacy foliage here feels open and airy, but quite effectively screens soakers from the outside world.*

▶ *The trees here gave a good start toward screening, but it's the raised bed that enhances dining on this deck. Flowers at higher levels are easier to enjoy. Here, they both limit and frame the view.*

SCREENING UNWANTED VIEWS WITH STRUCTURES

There is no quicker or more definite way to reduce a view than to block it with a fence, screen, wall, gate, or building. Nor are there many landscaping options that offer as much room for creativity.

Some structures may be built specifically for screening views. Others may serve several purposes. If you are going to build a playhouse or potting shed in any case, situate it to obstruct an unpleasant view rather than shut off a view you cherish. Make the side that shows enchanting, the side that serves convenient.

Because structures are permanent, evaluate your needs and plan carefully before you build. First check building codes and any restrictions written into your deed. Be sure to verify property lines; even then it is best to stay slightly within in case of error.

If a pool or spa is in your plans, consider fencing regulations, as well as access to the area. Be sure what you build now will not be wasted or destroyed by future landscaping endeavors.

Choose materials that will complement existing structures, the house, and the mood of the garden, as well as the budget. To hire a project done usually doubles the price of doing it yourself. Keep future maintenance in mind. Painting or staining can be costly and time consuming.

■ Simple solutions

Often a simple screen, series of panels, or arbor well within the property can make an amazing difference when blocking views. Work these into pleasing patterns that fit into the complete landscaping plan. Don't let them look like isolated attempts to correct eyesores.

A combination of open and solid fencing will save money and let you select your outside views. You may want a solid section to block the next yard but an open one to accent a panoramic view of meadows, rooftops, or hills beyond.

Where slopes are involved, it is better for fences or walls to definitely jog or slope at the top than to slant slightly.

◄An eye-catching oval moon archway separates front and side yards into two outdoor rooms. It gives a focal point to both, and frames the view from one to the other. The archway also adds mystique to the surroundings.

◄An impressive gate like this is both attractive and functional as it blocks the view of the driveway from the patio and surrounding gardens. The nylon netting to the right protects windows and plants from out-of-bounds basketballs.

◄The vine-covered, latticed gazebo, opposite, hides the neighbor's garage, the owners' vegetable garden, and the compost pile that makes the yard so lush. A cozy getaway, it also makes the property seem larger than it is.

141

CREATING DESIRABLE VIEWS WITH PLANTINGS

O nce you have enclosed the world of your yard, the real delight comes from filling it with your favorite forms, fragrances, flowers, and fruits. Plan just one wide garden area or connect several separate outdoor areas with shrubbery and pathways.

Your view can be serene and peaceful with minimal maintenance, or bold and exciting with bright flowers. Combine ornamentals with edible plants for delightful blooms and tasty meals.

Plan carefully for maximum season of interest. Lilacs perfume the air for a few precious days in the spring. Dogwoods offer spring flowers and excellent autumn color, as well as interesting winter shape. Viburnums and crab apples have showy flowers and fruit that attracts birds. Smoke trees bloom for months.

Flowering shrubs, trees, and ground covers give form, color, and interest for decades with very little work. Yet many gardeners find that flowers, herbs, and vegetables are always worth the extra effort.

Either in your mind's eye or on paper, plan your plantings so colors will combine harmoniously and continue at every season of the year. Perennials and spring bulbs can be the backbone of such plantings, but annuals are the color champions that will bloom from spring until frost. Keep heights, colors, and times of bloom in mind for a view that tantalizes onlookers all season. Large drifts of the same flower and clumps of three or more of the same small shrub will make a more definite statement than too much of a mixture.

Some plants, like the first crocus and early magnolia, should be near the house and entryways so you can see them close. Others—such as butterfly-attracting tithonia—are better seen from afar where their coarseness is obscured by their other virtues.

Remember that blues, purples, and dark colors fade in the distance. White accents and stands out. Bright colors light up dark corners and bring them into focus.

See pages 301–323, plus the charts sprinkled throughout the book, for plant suggestions.

◀ *A shaded, sloping garden path in May leads between drifts of white candytuft and golden alyssum to the house and patio above. Colors and flowers change with the season, but the interest created by the view is continuous.*

◀ *Fameuse apple trees grow, bloom, and fruit against a wall in an intricate espalier pattern called Belgian fence. Espalier is a fascinating art, but it requires diligent pruning.*

▶ *Garden paths through luxuriant plantings promise the beholder new delights and discoveries around every corner. This one winds through a planting of herbs, perennials, and roses to form an ever-changing tapestry of fragrance, color, and texture.*

CREATING DESIRABLE VIEWS WITH STRUCTURES

While plants create subtle views that change with the seasons, structures bring decisive design, framing, or focus to the picture. These structures include anything you may build or add to the garden: arches, arbors, gates, walkways, steps, birdbaths, benches, and raised beds, as well as decks, patios, pools, screened rooms, walls, and fences.

All of these can be softened and enhanced with plants, but their size, materials, and location definitely determine the style and mood of a garden setting. Even your choice of edgings—wood, brick, or stone—makes an important contribution to the overall picture.

As you select larger investments, balance family needs and desires with the garden vista you're trying to achieve. If your children want a playhouse, for example, do you want to create an elaborate structure that will turn heads, or keep it simple to downplay its presence? Do you need a place to keep the lawn mower? A handsome shed can be the center of attention. A homely structure, however, may require relegation to behind the garage.

Also consider a structure's purpose when determining its importance in your garden scene. A bench or garden swing can become a focal point, or it can be a hideaway that you want to keep isolated from the house.

The route of your garden paths will influence garden design and its structures, and vice versa. Let your natural footsteps serve as a guide, but add surprises, too. Grass pathways limit your garden walks to dry times. More functional paths can have a hard surface (flagstones, for example), a soft surface (such as gravel), or a combination of the two.

Patios and decks are perhaps the most popular and useful garden structures. For detailed information about them, see Chapter 8, "Patios and Decks," pages 148–189. For details on planning and building fences and screens, see Chapter 4, "Privacy and Security," pages 78–95. For arbors, see pages 104–107, and for walks and edgings, see pages 114–135. For information on gazebos, garden pools, swimming pools, and play structures, see Chapter 9, "Beyond the Basics," beginning on page 190.

◀ *Pools usually seize the focus in garden settings—as does this serene example. Its shimmering surface of silver changes constantly as it reflects the trees, sky, and clouds above it, and the colorful rhododendrons close by.*

▶ *Would you believe this is a potting shed? The workbench and storage cabinet, surrounded with lattice and roses, sit smack in the center of a rather formal garden. Handy and pleasant, it sets off surrounding color, too.*

▲ *This attention-grabbing poolside shelter, with a white frame that mimics the nearby home, stands in striking contrast to the forest green background.*

145

CREATING DESIRABLE VIEWS FROM WITHIN

You don't have to be out in your yard to appreciate its many charms and changes. In fact, we all look at our gardens from our windows much more often than we actually go out into them, particularly when the weather turns bad. Because of this, the best landscape designs take into account the views we see from inside our homes.

Begin by marking on your landscape plan the location of every window. Note the windows you look out most often and the angle from which you usually look out of them. Make bettering these views first and most important in your scheme of landscape projects.

Arrange plants, structures, or a combination of the two to create scenes that, when framed by the windows, look like well-composed photographs, with a background, middle ground, foreground, and focal point. Important paths and structures should be in view from indoors whenever possible.

Be sure to put special plants where you can see them from inside. This is especially true for plants that bloom in spring, when the weather often is wild. You may miss the crocus altogether if they are under a window instead of visible through it.

Rotating the rows in the vegetable garden to follow the line of sight instead of crossing it will let you watch the details of growth much more closely. On the other hand, lines of hanging clothes that dominate the scene when crossing the view almost disappear when parallel.

Parts of most yards cannot be seen from indoors at all. Put the compost pile in one of those concealed spots.

◄ *This charming court is perhaps even lovelier viewed from an upstairs window than from one of its benches because the overall paving and design need distance for full appreciation.*

► *Even the grayest days are a cozy delight because of the spectacle outside this oversize window. Rainfall, snow, swelling buds, autumn leaves, birds, and wildlife all are part of the warm kitchen atmosphere.*

► *Open windows in good weather, the changing drama in bad allow the people who live here to be part of nature when eating or working in the kitchen, as well as when they are in the yard.*

CHAPTER EIGHT

PATIOS AND DECKS

One of the best ways to civilize your yard is to add a patio or deck. With the addition of either, you'll soon be escaping to the great outdoors at every possible chance. As a bonus, you'll find that a patio or deck enriches life within the home, too. The new inside-looking-out views will visually expand crowded indoor rooms, plus help assuage fits of cabin fever by stirring memories of pleasant moments spent outside.

Shrubbery and existing trees are both protected and used to full advantage. The green pockets soften the wooden structures and give shade and substance to the sitting areas. Pachysandra flourishes at the base of the tree.

The multilevel deck turns this sloping yard into useful, separate outdoor rooms, each designed for a different function—cooking, dining, or conversing—and each graced with different degrees of sunshine and seclusion.

Decks and steps wind around the corner of the house to a shady back patio of brick on sand, creating a perfect transition from the decks to the yard. The deck-and-patio combination affords outdoor access from each indoor level.

Containers of petunias and geraniums in repeated colors brighten the scene. The pots can be rotated from sun to shade as needed.

CREATING THE ULTIMATE PATIO

Build the perfect patio and your summers will be filled with breezy afternoons, outdoor suppers, and gentle evenings with children chasing fireflies while adults relax and watch.

This ideal patio is visible indoors from doorways and windows, gently inviting you to go outside, if only for stolen moments. It is so easily reached from the kitchen and family room that it becomes an extension of both.

It has enough privacy and comfortable, practical furniture to make it as cozy as the den. Yet it also has space for a breath of fresh air and for entertaining a crowd with special flair.

The surface drains and dries quickly after a rain, though certain flagstones, when wet, give off a lovely reflection that amplifies the garden's appeal. Most important, the surface must be safe, nonskidding, and comfortable underfoot. Softer materials will do for paths, but more-solid surfaces are better for feet mostly at rest.

The perfect patio is a focal point of beauty for both house and garden. The choicest plants grow around it, so you can pull weeds, plant seeds, or pull off spent flowers from your chair if you wish. You are close enough to notice the butterflies on the marigolds and to water easily at the first sign of wilting.

While you have the hose out, you can whisk away any dirt or debris. Patio work should be mostly pleasant puttering.

Children can play here safely. You can watch them from indoors or out without squelching their imaginary worlds or caring how rowdy or rambunctious they get.

The ultimate patio blends the beauty of the garden with the comfort of the house. Blooming flowers and visiting birds at feeders or birdbaths entice even the most indoor person to venture out.

The ideal patio has a natural feeling of being part of a magnificent landscape, as if it grew there, and the owners simply were wise enough to make the most of such a pleasurable site.

► *This all-brick outdoor area with latticed gate elegantly enhances the adjoining house. Retaining walls enclose the patio, and wide steps lead to the grassy slope and the pleasantly elevated garden beyond.*

BUILDING SAND-BASE PATIOS

Laying bricks, flagstones, or other paving materials on a sand base, then packing more sand between them, creates a surprisingly durable patio surface—one that's flexible enough to ride out all but the severest frost heave and settlement.

Laying a sand-base patio is easy, too, because you need only excavate deep enough to make room for a thin layer of crushed rock, about 2 inches of sand, and the bricks themselves. Best of all, you needn't mix and pour one cubic inch of concrete. Contrast this with the much more arduous process of constructing a concrete patio detailed on pages 158–161.

■ Panoply of choices
Patio bricks come in a myriad of sizes, shapes, and colors—and you can lay them in a variety of patterns (see page 131). If you live in a northern climate, order SW (severe weathering) bricks. For milder zones not subject to freeze-thaw cycles, buy MW (moderate weathering) grade. No matter where you live, however, don't use NW (no weathering) bricks outdoors; they won't stand up to the elements.

How many bricks will you need? Compute the area of your new patio in square feet and take this measurement, along with your patio plan, to the brickyard. Dealers have tables that tell how many bricks of a given size you'll need per square foot.

■ Other materials
Brick isn't the only topping you can lay over a sand base. Stone comes in three main types: rubble (round rocks), flagstone (irregular-size flat pieces), and ashlar (dimension-cut stone sliced into uniform pieces). The box on page 157 depicts several other possibilities for a sand-base patio. Installation procedures are the same, except that in some cases you may want to fill spaces between masonry units with mortar, as explained on page 157.

1 To save cutting bricks, lay out a few in the desired pattern to gauge their most-efficient use. Cut ¼-inch spacers to maintain even distance between the paving bricks. The edging brick at lower right has been marked to assure that the depth of the trench, fill, and paving bricks does not exceed the brick's height.

4 For the edging bricks, pour a small amount of sand into the trench and set the bricks on end. Check to be sure each brick is level. If one is too high, tap it with the handle of a trowel or remove sand from underneath; adjust low bricks by adding sand. Backfill as you work.

2 Mark the patio's perimeter with strings, batter boards, and powdered chalk (see pages 58–59). Remove sod and dig trenches for the edging bricks. (If you like, mark the inside edges of the trenches with string while you dig them.) Excavate the patio area to the necessary depth. Tamp the soil to firm it.

3 Thoroughly spray the patio bed with preemergent weed killer or a vegetation killer. This prevents weeds or grass from growing up between bricks. Spraying also helps settle the soil.

5 After you've installed all the edging bricks, roll out plastic sheeting as further insurance against weeds. Overlap each sheet an inch or more as you work across the patio area. For drainage, cut 1-inch-diameter holes spaced about a foot apart into the plastic.

6 Now spread an inch-deep layer of crushed stone over the plastic. This layer of stone helps drainage and provides a sound base for the sand and bricks.

(continued on page 156)

For basic information on working with brick, see pages 282–287.

BUILDING SAND-BASE PATIOS *(continued)*

7 Pour sand to a depth of 2 inches. Level the bed with a rake and shovel, then spray with water to compact it. If the sand begins to dry out as you work, spray it again.

8 Improvise a screed board like the one shown to assure a uniform depth of sand. Screed one area, lay bricks, then move on to another. Our screed consists of a 2x6 notched at the ends; you also can make a screed by nailing together lengths of different-dimension lumber.

10 After laying a 4- or 5-foot-square section, check the surface with a level and adjust the height of any brick too high or too low. As you work, kneel in the sand, not on the bricks. They will wobble until you fill the spaces between them.

11 When all the bricks are laid, sprinkle dry sand over them. With a stiff broom, gently sweep back and forth to work sand into the joints. Sweep at an angle so you don't dislodge sand from the cracks.

9 Stretch a level line across the patio and press bricks into the sand, checking their tops against the line. Use more sand to raise bricks; dig sand away to lower them. Move the line and spacers as you proceed.

12 After all the joints are filled, flush away excess sand. As the sand settles, sweep in more and wet again. You may need to repeat this process several times over a few weeks.

OTHER PATIO SURFACES

Concrete paver blocks *come precast and in several sizes; or build simple forms and pour your own. Install them like bricks or leave a wider, ½-inch space between the units.*

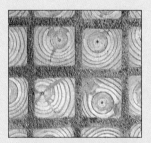

Wood blocks *or rounds provide a slightly resilient surface. We made these by slicing 4x4s with a circular saw. Use only redwood or cedar heartwood, or pressure-treated lumber.*

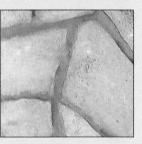

Flagstones *can be set in sand, then grouted with sand, as we did with the bricks. Or grout them with mortar by sweeping dry mix into the joints and sprinkling with water.*

Cobblestones *have an irregular texture. Grout between them with sand or mortar mix. Cobblestone streets, set in sand, have lasted for many centuries.*

You also can lay a variety of other paving materials in sand, including loose aggregate and wood planks (see page 130), ceramic tile, and quarry tile. These last two are best grouted with mortar mix.

BUILDING CONCRETE PATIOS

Compared to the task of laying bricks or other paving materials on a sand base, constructing a concrete patio is a more demanding project. First, you must excavate and build forms to contain the concrete. Then you must pour the concrete, strike off the excess, level, and trowel a smooth surface—all within the several hours it takes for concrete to set up. For all your pains, however, you'll be rewarded with an absolutely flat, durable surface that will last for decades with little or no maintenance.

■ Tools for concrete work

Besides ordinary carpentry and garden tools, you will need to improvise, rent, or purchase several specialized items: a *tamper* for compacting earth, a *darby* or *bull float* to smooth wet concrete, an *edging trowel* to round off edges and separate them from the forms, a *jointer* to groove control joints into the slab, and a rectangular concrete *trowel* to finish the surface.

Once concrete starts to flow, it's too late to alter the forms, run for tools, or look for more help. So, before you start mixing or the ready-mix truck arrives, make extra sure you have everything and everyone you need on hand.

■ Building forms

Patio slabs typically measure 4 inches thick, so construct forms with smooth, straight 2x4s, setting their tops about an inch above lawn level. Wet concrete exerts tremendous pressure, so brace forms well. If you're in doubt about whether your forms are rigid enough, drive a few extra stakes and install added braces.

For proper drainage, slope your patio ¼ inch per foot away from the house.

If you want to edge your patio with wood, construct permanent forms with redwood, cedar, or pressure-treated lumber. Apply a coat of sealer to further enhance the wood's natural rot resistance, then put masking or duct tape on the top edges to keep cement from staining or scratching the wood. (See pages 122–123.)

1 *Use stakes, string, and powdered chalk to mark your patio's outline, as explained on pages 58–59. Be sure to place strings about 3 inches outside the slab's perimeter to allow for forms. To mark curves, wind garden hose between stakes. Strip sod; excavate. Tamp the ground well, then saturate with vegetation killer.*

3 *Adjust strings to reflect proper slope. To begin building forms, pound stakes until their tops are at the same level as the planned top level of the forms. Pound stakes every 3 to 4 feet. If you like, pound stakes at any height, attach form boards at proper level, then saw stake tops.*

2 *Install asphalt-impregnated expansion strips wherever the patio will abut a foundation, wall, or other structure. Expansion joints accommodate expansion and contraction caused by temperature changes.*

4 *Using the stakes as guides, hold form boards at correct level, then nail through stakes into boards with doubleheaded nails. Leave strings up during this step, if you prefer, so you can easily double-check the level of the form boards.*

POURING SUNSHADE FOOTINGS

1 *If you plan to build an overhead sunshade over your patio, dig holes for footings wherever posts will rest on the patio surface. Several-inch-deep footings are necessary to keep the concrete from cracking under the weight of the sunshade posts.*

2 *After pouring the concrete and letting it stiffen a bit, position anchor bolts or post anchors above the footings. Let the concrete cure, then attach posts to anchors. See pages 100–103 for details on sunshade construction.*

(continued on page 160)

For basic information on working with concrete, see pages 282–287.

BUILDING CONCRETE PATIOS *(continued)*

5 Make a bed for the concrete by spreading gravel, cinders, or crushed rock. The bed's thickness will depend on how well the soil drains. If drainage is poor, provide 3 to 4 inches; if soil drains well, 1 to 2 inches will be sufficient.

6 Roll out wire reinforcing mesh, then flatten. Slip rocks or other shims under the mesh, lifting the mesh so it will be suspended about midpoint in the slab's thickness. If you like, skip the shimming and plan to pull the mesh up with a rake during pouring.

9 After the water disappears from the surface, begin edging the slab. Hold the edger flat on the surface with its front tilted up slightly when moving ahead with it. Raise the rear slightly when moving backward. Repeat the edging process after each of the other finishing tasks.

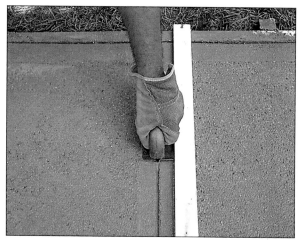

10 To control cracking, tool grooves (control joints) at distances equal to the slab's width. For patios wider than 10 feet, also run a joint down the center. Control joints should have a depth equal to one-fourth of the slab's thickness. Use a straight board as a guide.

7 *Pour the concrete; then, with help from a friend, strike it off with a straight 2x4 long enough to ride atop forms on two sides. Begin striking as soon as you've poured the first 3 or 4 feet; this will show whether you're putting in enough material.*

8 *When you're done pouring and striking the concrete, use bull and darby floats (the darby float is shown) to further smooth the surface and embed aggregate beneath it. Stop floating when water starts to bleed onto the surface of the slab.*

11 *Trowel and finish the patio surface. Two passes with a wood trowel leave a rough, skidproof surface; for a slick finish (not advised for patios), make three passes with a metal trowel. For additional information about finishes, see pages 162–163.*

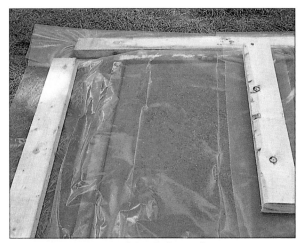

12 *Once you've achieved the surface texture you want, cover the slab with sheets of polyethylene to hold in moisture. This retards the curing process, allowing the concrete time to bond properly. After a week, remove the plastic and forms, then backfill against the patio's edges.*

CHOOSING A SPECIAL CONCRETE SURFACE

(Far left) Swirl texture onto a drab expanse of concrete by working a wood or metal trowel over the surface in arclike motions. The rougher the trowel, the coarser the finish will be.

(Near left) Broom a surface by pulling a push broom across a slab of just-troweled concrete. The depth of the texture depends on the stiffness of the broom's bristles.

(Far left) For a checkerboard pattern, divide a patio into squares with permanent forms or control joints, then float the sections in alternating directions.

(Near left) Tool concrete with a mason's joint strike to create geometric shapes or patterns that resemble flagstones. Score the concrete soon after floating and again each time you do other finishing operations.

(Far left) Produce a wavy broom finish by brooming intersecting curves into the surface. For subtle texture, use a nylon-bristled broom.

(Near left) For a keystone finish, broom a coarse texture into the surface, then spatter on ridges of soft mortar made of pigmented white cement and sand (mixed in a 1:2 ratio). As the mortar hardens, trowel to make it smooth.

(Far left) Broom and trowel alternating squares for design variety. Separate the squares by cutting grooves between them with an edger or jointer.

(Near left) Stamping concrete with special rubber molds can create a look that resembles brick, cobblestone, slate, even rough-hewn wood. This is a job for a contractor experienced at stamping and coloring concrete.

WEATHERPROOFING PATIOS

Water is the natural enemy of all masonry materials. Moisture finds its way into tiny crevices, then freezes, turning the cracks into open wounds. Water also weakens masonry by dissolving salts and leaching out binders. A good paint or clear sealer will keep out water and maintain the strength of your new patio.

When painting your patio, choose an alkyd masonry paint. Water-thinned latex masonry paints perform well on vertical masonry surfaces, but alkyds stand up better to the normal wear and abrasion a patio is subjected to.

Clear sealants go on fast and protect masonry through the rainiest season. Apply the clear sealer of your choice annually, and your patio will maintain its youth almost indefinitely.

If weather or stains have already taken a toll on a patio at your house, revive it by scrubbing with a 5-percent solution of muriatic acid. Wear gloves and protective clothing, and rinse well. Wait a week or so, then apply paint or a clear sealer.

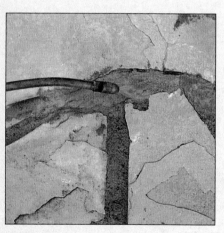

Spray sealer onto coarse surfaces like flagstone. Most sealants are thin enough to be atomized by a garden sprayer. Spray thoroughly, paying particular attention to grouted joints or other areas that could trap water.

On smoother surfaces like brick and ceramic tile, apply sealant with a paintbrush, paint roller, paint pad, or squeegee. The sealant will flow on fast, but take your time to assure complete coverage.

SURFACING EXISTING CONCRETE PATIOS

Looking for a way to dress up a boring slab of concrete? Consider veneering it with flagstones, slate, or ceramic, mosaic, quarry, or paver tiles. You simply clean the concrete, spread a thin layer of mortar onto the slab, set stones or tiles into the mortar, then fill spaces between them with mortar or grout.

■ Surface choices

Unlike indoor tiles, outdoor versions are unglazed and stand up to the elements much better. Ceramic tiles (the kind we used here) typically measure 6 inches square by ¼ inch thick. Mosaic tiles are 1 or 2 inches square, ¼ inch thick, and come mounted in groups on large pieces of paper or mesh. Quarry and paver tiles are 6 or 8 inches on a side by ⅜ or ½ inch thick. Pavers have slightly rounded edges; edges of quarry tiles consist of crisp right angles.

Besides tiles, you can veneer a walk with flagstones or rough-cut slate. These materials aren't uniformly thick, so you need to set them in a thicker mortar bed.

■ Preparing the base

To start, patch any cracks in the existing surface with patching cement (see pages 268–269). To check for low spots, roll a length of pipe across the concrete and mark any spots where you can see light under the pipe. Fill these with patching cement and level with a straightedge. To ensure proper adhesion for the mortar, scrub the entire patio with a 5-percent solution of muriatic acid. Rinse well before applying mortar.

■ Grip

To improve adhesion, mix latex bonding cement into the mortar or brush bonding cement onto the acid-cleaned patio as directed.

The secret to successfully working with mortar is to keep everything wet. Very slow evaporation during the curing process gives mortar its strength. Spray concrete well before applying mortar. Soak tiles in water before setting them. Periodically sprinkle water over everything as you work.

1 Cut a trench for a temporary wood edging, then stake wood in place. The edging must be absolutely parallel with the slab's surface, and the stakes must be below the top of the edging so you can screed the mortar bed.

4 Align edges and gently press tiles into the mortar, using spacers to keep grout lines uniform. After you've laid several courses of tiles, check that they lie flat and even by laying a long, straight board over them. To seat any tiles too high, tap the board over the wayward tiles with a hammer.

2 *Mortar sets quickly, so spread and screed only about 15 to 20 square feet at a time. For ceramic tiles, make the bed ¼ inch thick; paver and quarry tiles go over a ½-inch-thick mortar bed; flagstones require a 1-inch bed.*

3 *Screed the mortar with a 2x4 notched to fit over the edging at either side of the patio. You'll need a helper for this job. Fill any low spots with additional mortar. Remember to work only small areas at a time.*

5 *Let the mortar set for a day, then use a soft wooden or rubber (not metal) trowel to grout between tiles. Spread soupy mortar or grout mix over the tiles and force it into the cracks with diagonal swipes. Make the joints slightly concave by packing and smoothing them with a piece of ½-inch dowel.*

6 *When the mortar or grout is nearly dry, wipe off excess with a damp sponge and fine spray of water. Don't wipe or spray so hard you dislodge mortar from joints. Finally, spray lightly with more water, then cover with polyethylene. Let the project cure for a week.*

For basic information on working with mortar, see pages 282–287.

PATIO PLANTINGS

Patios offer ideal conditions for plants. Typically, these areas are protected from winter winds and summer sun, and nearby structures often reflect springtime warmth and sunshine.

Still, you'll want to choose what you grow near your patio carefully, because nowhere are plants more the focus of attention.

Select only tidy, long-blooming plants that grow to size quickly, then stay in scale without constant pruning. Relegate plants that have a short season of interest, a season of excess seediness, or a coarse appearance to more-distant parts of the yard.

All of the principles of design assume greater importance near a patio. Color clashes you could live with in a border at the back of your yard will dizzy you if they appear at the edge of your patio. Form and texture, too, are accentuated, especially when the plants are brought closer to eye level in raised beds.

Fragrances, which often go undetected away from the house, are easily sniffed around the patio. Especially good choices are the fragrant plants—like moonflower vine, evening primrose, and angel's-trumpet—that open widest in the evening, when you're most likely to be using your patio.

To add a dramatic accent to your patio, select a spot nearby to espalier a tree, arrange a vine in tracery shape, or grow a rose or shrub in standard form. For a delightful evening show, surround your patio with white-bloomed plants.

■ The nitty-gritty
Lawns and planting beds around patios should be an inch or more below the level of the paving to allow for digging and stirring in soil amendments without having soil wash onto the paving. Planting beds above the patio level need to be held back with some sort of retaining wall. Good drainage in either case is vital.

Set plantings far enough from patios so that their growth won't encroach on the paved space. To avoid cracked concrete later on, select trees with small root systems.

PATIO PLEASERS
Spiff up your patio with small plants between paving sections or cascading plants to surround them. Choose fast-growing vines for quick shade and privacy.

Between pavings	Cascading plants	Fast-growing vines
Ajuga or bugleweed	Asparagus fern	Clematis
Corsican mint	Cotoneaster	Grape
Corsican sandwort	Cucumber	Hydrangea, climbing
Pearlwort	Geranium,	Ivy, English
Sedum, creeping	ivy leaved	Kiwi
Sempervivum,	Pachysandra	Morning-glory
creeping	Petunia	Nasturtium, climbing
Speedwell	Strawberry	Rose
Thyme	Vinca	Winter creeper

See also pages 186–187 and 301–323.

◄ *Small plantings allow intricate designs that would be difficult—and expensive—on a large scale. This pattern features boxwood clumps coupled with low hedges of trimmed germander. Begonias add color and contrast.*

► *A neat boxwood hedge here screens a retaining wall that turned a steep slope into a planting bed. Fern, azalea, rhododendron, and Japanese iris set the pattern, and geranium, marigold, and viola add splashes of color.*

▲ *For ease of care plus different tones and textures of green around their patio, these homeowners turned to small trees, low-growing shrubs that need little pruning, and ground-cover plantings.*

▶ *This dense row of arborvitae is routinely sheared for a uniform appearance. Azalea mix with annuals for both spring and summer color, and containers add spots of interest. The shorter plantings accent the curved patio border.*

▲ *Wildflowers and a woodland setting envelop this pleasant patio. Fern and hosta heighten the serenity of the scene, while bright begonia and coleus capture the splashes of sunlight.*

167

GALLERY OF PATIO IDEAS

◄*A patio and retaining wall wind around three sides of this cottage, here connecting the detached garage to the kitchen. The concrete paver blocks complement the stone chimney and wall, harmonizing the setting.*

▶ *To capitalize on the great view offered by this narrow strip, a stamped-concrete patio follows the contours up to a seating area. Pea gravel and large boulders sit among oleander, agapanthus, and naked-lady lily.*

▶ *A deck and sunken patio team up to transform a flat, narrow lot into separate outdoor rooms. The patio's low profile and the floating platforms on the right provide needed privacy.*

◄*This semicircular brick patio and central platform seem to radiate from the house's bay window, repeating its arcing lines. Wide steps amplify the expansive feeling of the surroundings.*

▲ *With its stark simplicity, monochromatic tile, and sturdy wood furniture, this patio continues the mission style set by the house. Overlooking a canyon, the patio provides an appealing extension of the living room.*

◀ *Tucked into secluded space between garage and house, this patio and its surrounding plantings turn a once-exposed corner lot into a private family retreat. Forsythia and crab apple trees form a dense screen.*

169

CREATING THE ULTIMATE DECK

The best decks make outdoor living so like indoor comfort that they become extra rooms, with the added advantages of easy care and natural surroundings.

The well-designed deck starts at the floor level of the adjacent indoor room, enabling users to step out without stepping up or down. And, since we tend to look up and away rather than down and around when we move from indoors out, the well-placed deck takes maximum advantage of any treetop views or distant vistas.

For the function and feeling of separate rooms, decks often are built with varying levels. At right, a cooking area lies only three steps above the main level, yet seems quite removed. Decks and steps can be combined in any number of ways to lead to all of a yard's attractions.

Privacy is crucial, for few people are comfortable on stage. Screens can provide needed sanctuary. If made of lattice—and perhaps entwined with vines of fragrant flowers or clusters of grapes—they impart a romantic effect.

■ Design counts

Although decks seem simple, their design is important. Unimaginative planning can result in a deck that looks like a large box. To avoid this and to add interest, alter the square or rectangle—even the slightest bit—by cutting off a corner diagonally or adding a point or a half circle. Repeat architectural elements from your house.

Railings or surrounding benches or planters can set the mood of this outdoor room, too, while adding comfort, storage, and safety. Be sure that lazing adults or monkeyshining children won't have to worry about falling over the edge, even if this would be only a foot or two.

Though you are less likely to garden from a deck than you are from a patio, bright blooming containers are a necessary accessory. Where arbors, screens, or overhanging tree branches offer anchorage, hanging pots are appropriate. Use ground covers, flowers, and shrubs, too, to tie your deck to its site.

For do-it-yourselfers, on-grade decks are easy to build. The higher your raised deck, the more likely you are to need professional advice.

▶ *This hexagonal deck offers roominess and seclusion. The privacy wall combines gray clapboards, white lattice, and a peak that mimics the one on the house. Roses and impatiens camouflage the structure's underside, plus add desired charm.*

BUILDING GRADE-LEVEL DECKS

A grade-level deck, which stands on its own just a few inches above the ground, is considerably easier to build than its elevated cousin, the raised deck. The simple design of a grade-level deck spares you the intricacies of constructing the stairs, railings, and structural bracing required for even the most-basic raised deck. And with a freestanding, grade-level deck you needn't worry about securely attaching the structure to your house.

You can situate a grade-level deck just about anywhere: adjacent to the house or, if you'd rather, in a shady corner of the yard. Build one over an existing, too-small patio, or stair-step two or three of them down a gentle slope. And, just because a deck is grade level doesn't mean it has to be only a plain-Jane platform. Dress one up with a distinctive decking pattern, railing style, or built-in bench (see pages 180–183).

Use the project we get off the ground on the next three pages as an introduction to the de-

lights of deck building. Once you see how everything goes together, you might be tempted to take on the bigger challenge of a raised deck (detailed on pages 176–179).

■ Getting started
A sturdy deck begins with a sound plan and high-quality lumber. After you've sketched out the platform you'd like to build, consult the span table on page 185 to determine the dimensions and amounts of lumber and other components you will need, adding 10 percent for waste. Then refer to the descriptions of deck materials on pages 184–185 to decide what kind of wood to use for your deck.

As you select lumber at the yard or as it comes off the truck, examine each piece and reject any that are split or badly twisted. Don't worry about boards with minor warping and cupping, though; nailing these in place will straighten them out for you.

(Near right) For a grade-level deck, a series of posts, resting on footings or piers, support beams around the deck's perimeter. Metal hangers connect joists to the beams. Decking boards nail to the joists; skirts add a decorative finish.

(Far right) With a raised deck, taller posts support the end and sides; a ledger fastens the deck to the house. Codes require that any deck higher than a few feet off the ground must be equipped with railings.

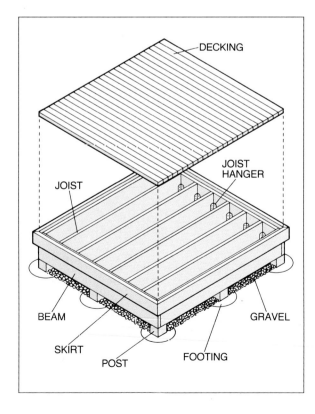

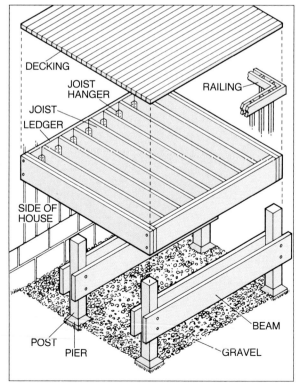

1 *For a preview of how your deck will look, test-assemble a section on a patio, drive, or other open space. This also gives you a chance to identify your straightest lumber. Cut scraps of ½- or ¾-inch plywood to serve as spacers between boards.*

2 *Lay out the site with stakes and string (see pages 58–59). Here we're marking the location of an intermediate post. Measure diagonals to assure that corners are square and fix them by erecting batter boards.*

3 *Excavate deep enough so that the deck will sit just a little above grade level. We used a marked board to check depth. The dotted line at the top indicates the combined height of the deck materials. The middle line shows the sod level. The bottom line indicates how high the posts will be above the ground in the excavated area.*

4 *Dig postholes to below the frost line, pour a few inches of gravel or crushed rock into the bottom, then set posts in place. Plumb and brace each post in two directions, then shovel concrete around it. Bevel the top of the concrete down toward the outer edges so water drains away from the post. (See page 60 for more details.)*

For basic information on working with wood, see pages 276–281. For working with concrete, see pages 282–287.

(continued on page 174)

BUILDING GRADE-LEVEL DECKS *(continued)*

5 Let the concrete cure for a day or two. Then mark the tops of posts and cut them off with a chain saw, making them all a level height. To help you make straight cuts, mark all four faces on each post.

6 Saturate the excavated area with vegetation killer; then, to further inhibit vegetation growth, spread polyethylene on the area the deck will cover. Top this with crushed rocks or gravel.

9 Cut joists to length. Before installing them, sight along each and determine which edge has a hump or crown. Nail joists in place crown side up; the weight of the decking will flatten them out.

10 Also nail decking boards to the joists crown side up. Drive at least two nails into each joist, maintaining uniform gaps between boards with plywood spacers. For strength, stagger end-to-end joints.

7 *Construct beams by nailing two 2x8s together. Lay the beams atop posts, check to be sure they are level, and attach with galvanized metal straps (shown) or special saddle brackets.*

8 *Position joists according to the span table on page 185. Use a scrap of lumber to adjust joist hangers so the joist tops will fit flush with the beam tops. Nail hangers to the beams.*

11 *Don't worry about trimming deck boards to fit until you've installed all of them. Then snap a chalk line along the deck's edge, tack down a strip to serve as a guide for the circular saw's table, and cut the boards flush.*

12 *A skirt board covers ends and adds a decorative touch. We shaped the top edge of this one with a router, and used a saw to miter joints at corners and splices. For a snug fit at splices, attach the in-mitered board first, then the out-mitered one, as shown here.*

BUILDING RAISED DECKS

Though more formidable than a grade-level deck, constructing a raised deck is still possible for a do-it-yourselfer equipped with a hammer, circular saw, electric drill, and socket wrench set. The wrenches are for tightening lag screws and bolts, which provide more strength than nails and are used at critical junctures.

One of these critical points is the ledger that fastens the deck to your house and serves as its starting point. This board must be absolutely level and securely fastened to your home's floor framing with 5½-inch lag screws spaced 24 inches apart. To attach a ledger to a masonry wall, drill holes with a masonry bit and drive lag screws into expansion shields. Check your local building code before finalizing structural details. Some require 2x8 ledgers, others 2x10s.

■ Stairs and railings

Most codes also mandate a step or steps for outdoor access from any deck more than 8 inches above grade. If the deck is more than 30 inches high, you also must provide railings at least 3 feet high, with no more than 9 inches between horizontal rails or vertical balusters.

When you lay out a stairway, familiarize yourself with the *rise* and *run* information shown on page 179 and juggle figures until you come out with steps that are exactly equal in height; one that's higher or lower than the others could cause a serious stumbling accident.

For attaching railings, either extend the posts above the decking or bolt verticals to the deck beams as we did on page 179. (To learn more about railing styles, see page 181.)

■ Selecting materials

Pages 184–185 present your materials options. No law says you must use the same grade or species of wood throughout a project. For economy, we used pressure-treated lumber for all the structural members of our raised deck. For appearance' sake, we used redwood for the decking, skirting, railings, and stairs.

Finish your raised deck by laying polyethylene underneath and topping it with gravel. Add wood or plastic edging to hold the rock in place.

1 First, test-assemble your deck (see page 173). Then, starting at the house, lay out the site with string, driving stakes where posts will be located. Use a tape measure and the principle of triangulation to assure the layout is square. (See pages 58–59 and 74–75 for more details.)

4 Dig postholes at stake points, sink and plumb posts, and pour concrete around them (see page 60). Build a form around the posts to raise the footing; this keeps grass and other vegetation away from the bases of the posts. Bevel the tops of footings to shed water.

2 Mark the ledger's position by measuring down from the door sill. Plan to locate the finished deck surface ¾ to 1 inch beneath the sill, so rainwater won't back up into the house. Here the upper dotted line represents the top of the decking, the lower one the top of the ledger.

3 Use a level to make markings because the house or sill may be out of level. Attach the ledger by fastening lag screws through the siding into your home's floor framing. Fit the lag screws with washers and caulk under them just before tightening down the screws.

5 To mark the tops of posts for cutting, extend a level board from the ledger. Use a combination square to bring the cutoff line around all four faces of each post.

6 Cut posts to size with a circular or chain saw. The face here marked with an X will be notched to catch half of the edge joist (see step 9, page 178).

For basic information on working with wood, see pages 276–281. For working with concrete, see pages 282–287.

(continued on page 178)

BUILDING RAISED DECKS *(continued)*

7 Now use bolts to attach beams to each side of posts. We drilled holes and ran the bolts all the way through the post and both beams.

8 Space the joist hangers along ledger (see joist-span table on page 185) and nail the joists in place. We chose to toenail the joists to the beam tops, but you also can attach the joists with metal saddle anchors or use joist hangers and make the joists flush with beams.

9 Double joists at edges and ends. We notched the posts to carry the outer joists and toenailed the inner ones between ledger and post and between post and post. As an alternative to notching, extend the beam beyond the post, rest joists on it, then nail to the post.

12 Assemble the staircase by nailing spacer boards between top and bottom of stringers. Nail treads to all but the top step; wait until you've installed the decking before nailing the final tread. You'll need to pour a concrete footing for the base of the stairway or bolt it to a precast pad.

13 Drill holes, then use bolts to fasten the top stair spacer to the edge joist. You also can attach stairs with metal stairway hangers; or use lag screws to attach the stringers to the ends of joists.

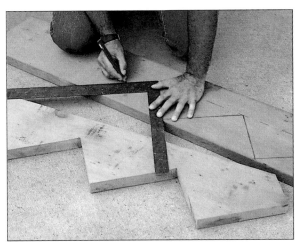

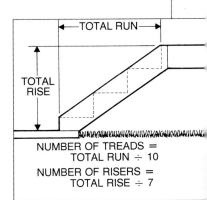

10 *Build and install stairs before attaching decking boards. If you're not restricted in the total length (run) of your staircase, measure its height (rise) and multiply by 1⅓ to determine the run. For more on planning stairs, see page 176 and the illustration at far right.*

11 *Purchase precut stair stringers or lay out your own with a square. Cut one stringer with a circular saw, then use it as a pattern for laying out the second. Be sure to subtract the thickness of a tread from the bottom riser so steps will come out equal in height.*

TOTAL RUN

TOTAL RISE

NUMBER OF TREADS = TOTAL RUN ÷ 10
NUMBER OF RISERS = TOTAL RISE ÷ 7

Generally, each step should have a depth (run) of about 10 inches and a height (rise) of about 7 inches. Adjust the total run until you come out with even-size steps that are near these dimensions.

14 *Install decking, starting at the house to ensure a snug fit under the sill. Lay decking with the crown (humped) side up. Hold spacers between boards, then drive two nails into each joist. Trim ends as shown in step 11 on page 175.*

15 *We nailed a redwood skirt to the perimeter joists, bored holes through the skirt and joists, then fastened railing balusters with bolts.*

16 *For comfort, round rail edges with a router or buy routed lumber. Drill holes; drive lag screws through balusters into the rail.*

CHOOSING A DECKING OR RAILING STYLE

DECKING STYLES

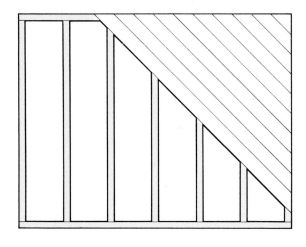

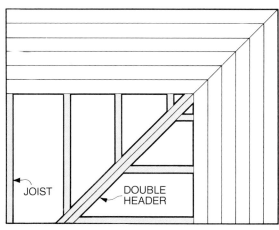

(Far left) Trim ends of decking boards at 45-degree angles and install them diagonally to your house instead of parallel. A table saw simplifies making accurate, repetitive angle cuts.

(Near left) Some decking patterns require different framing plans. In this example, butting boards at a diagonal calls for installing a double header from corner to corner.

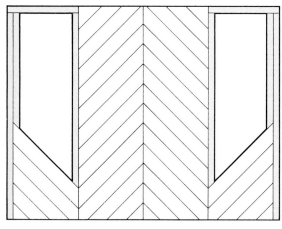

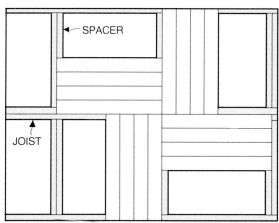

(Far left) For a herringbone pattern, double the joists and space them 2 feet apart. Cut board ends at 45-degree angles and install them in alternating directions.

(Near left) Grid-pattern decking requires spacers nailed between joists. Additional framing increases the weight—and cost—of a deck, so be sure to plan a substructure that can carry the load.

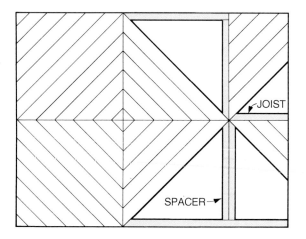

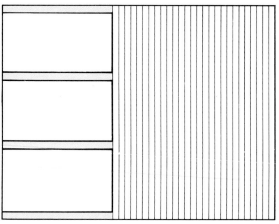

(Far left) With the same framing plan used for grid-pattern decking (see near left, above), you can create a parquet effect.

(Near left) For a superstrong deck, toenail 2x4s on edge. To calculate the number you'll need, multiply the deck's width by 6.9. Round up to the next whole number and add 5 percent for waste.

RAILING STYLES

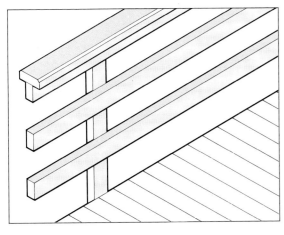

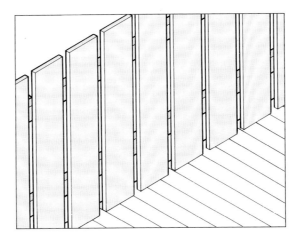

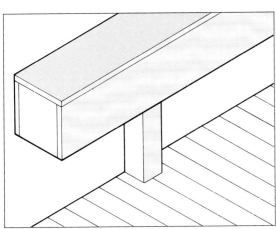

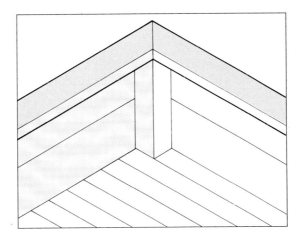

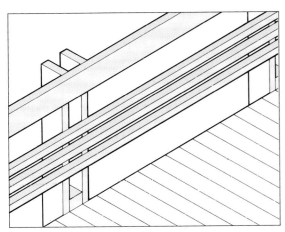

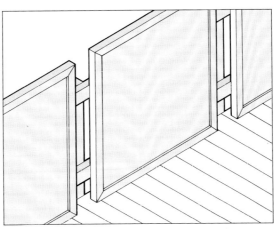

(Far left) A horizontal-rail railing can consist of three 2x4s or 2x6s capped with a 2x6 handrail. Bolt the verticals and rails; nail the handrail after chamfering its edges with a router or plane.

(Near left) For a privacy screen that lets in cooling breezes, space 1x8s 2 inches apart. Nail all boards to one side of the rails, or alternate them for design interest.

(Far left) On decks less than 2½ feet above the ground, a railing can do double-duty by serving as a bench, too. Bring the posts up through the deck and top them with an inverted box to form the simple seating.

(Near left) Or build a low, solid railing of horizontal 2x8s capped with 2x6s. Keep the solid railing less than a couple of feet high, or wind will play havoc with it.

(Far left) In lieu of extending posts to railing height, stretch them by bolting a 2x6 to each side; then nail 2x2 and 2x6 rail materials to the extensions.

(Near left) Plywood makes a good contemporary-looking railing treatment. Frame 3x3-foot panels with 1x2s; space the panels 4 inches apart.

BUILDING DECK BENCHES

Provide your deck with one or more comfortable benches and you just might end up with some of the best seats in—or out of—the house.

Orient benches so sitters take in an attractive view—or turn their backs on one that's not. To define the edge of a grade-level deck without blocking your line of sight, build a backless bench, like the one shown in the illustration opposite, top right. On a higher deck, integrate the bench and railing, as we did with the one shown going together at right.

■ Bench basics

As you plan benches, refer to the standard seating dimensions in the box at the bottom of the opposite page, allowing 30 inches of width per person. Make the backs slightly lower if you want an unimpeded view, slightly higher for privacy. Open, slatted construction lets air circulate and also discourages water from puddling.

As with railings, you can secure benches to the same posts that support the deck or fasten uprights to joists. Unlike rails, you also can attach benches to decking. For safety's sake, be sure to use bolts, not nails, at all critical structural points.

Consider, too, whether permanently anchoring your benches really is necessary. Freestanding benches, built of the same materials as the deck itself, can be easily moved around to accommodate different functions. Come winter, you can put your freestanding benches away or use them indoors. On higher decks, of course, you should butt any nonanchored benches against a firmly attached railing.

■ Beyond the bench

While you're planning your benches, think about how you might integrate benches with structures other than railings. Two benches and a table, for example, could be built diner-booth style. Add a trellis or sunscreen overhead (see pages 100–105) and create an inviting open-air spot where every summer meal will taste better.

For basic information on working with wood, see pages 276–281.

1 Taper 1x12s and attach them to both sides of each post, nailing short pieces of 2x4 between them to support the leg assemblies. To prevent rust, use hot-dipped galvanized nails for all outdoor projects.

3 For comfort, round off the front edges of 2x4 seat and back slats with a plane or router. You also can buy prerouted boards. For seating, use only good-quality, splinterless lumber, and seal it well.

2 *For the legs, assemble three-sided 2x4 boxes. Slip these into the back support, and nail to the cross braces and deck. Also nail through the 1x12s into the 2x4 boxes. Check that everything is plumb, level, and square.*

4 *Nail back slats to each 1x12. Nail seat slats to the 2x4 legs. Countersink nailheads so they don't snag clothing. Cap the back with a 1x6 or 2x6 to protect cut ends from moisture that could cause rot.*

OTHER BENCH STYLES

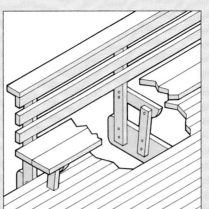

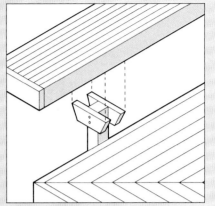

Begin this bench before laying all the decking. Bolt slightly slanted back and seat supports to the joists, then notch decking around them. Joists can protrude from the deck, as shown, or be cut flush with it. Finish off with 2x4 horizontal railings, a 2x6 cap, and 2x8 seating boards.

For a strong, handsome, backless bench that also can provide a platform for potted plants, extend posts above the deck surface and bolt 2x4 wood saddles to them. Build the seats by laying 2x4s on edge, then nailing them together with ¼-inch spacers between them. Nail seats to saddles and posts.

STANDARD BENCH DIMENSIONS

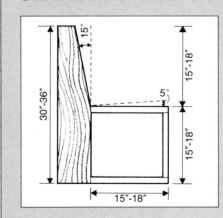

Incorporate the dimensions of the bench we built at left into any that you design. For comfort, cant the back of a bench about 15 degrees and lift the front edge of the seat about 5 degrees. Allow 30 inches of width for each person.

CHOOSING DECK MATERIALS

REDWOOD
Description: Handsome and naturally rot resistant. Use common-grade redwood for framing members, decking, and railings; use construction- or clear-heart for posts and for near-ground structural members.
Appearance: Redwood's distinctive red hue weathers to a brown-gray. Preserve original color by applying sealer every other year.

Cost: The most expensive way to go. To save money you might want to use redwood only for parts that show, as we did with the raised deck on pages 176–179.
Comments: Redwood boards go down flat and stay flat, and because they contain little or no pitch or resin, they are easier to saw, drill, and shape than treated lumber.

PRESSURE-TREATED LUMBER
Description: Fir, pine, and other softwoods saturated with chromated copper arsenate. Above ground, use wood treated to .25 pounds per cubic foot (pcf). Posts and other ground-level members need .40 pcf wood.
Appearance: Some comes prestained to resemble redwood or cedar. Most has a greenish cast that weathers to a silvery gray.

Cost: About 30 percent less than redwood.
Comments: The densest lumber you can buy, which makes it heavier and stronger than any of the others. Treated lumber poses no danger to plants or groundwater, but it contains a toxic chemical, so saw outside, wear a mask over your mouth, and do not burn scraps.

CEDAR
Description: Naturally rot-resistant wood noted for its strength, light weight, straight grain, and freedom from knots. Use common-grade cedar above ground, heartwood for ledgers, posts, and near-ground members.
Appearance: Cedar weathers from tan to silvery gray; use a sealer if you want to prevent the weathering.

Cost: About 10 to 20 percent less than redwood, depending on local availability. A good alternative to redwood, especially in regions far from the South and West Coast.
Comments: Because of its greater density, cedar is somewhat stronger than redwood. Compared with treated lumber, however, its shock resistance is quite low.

CYPRESS
Description: Naturally rot-resistant lumber that is logged in the Southeast, where cypress is a popular alternative to cedar. As with redwood and cedar, use common-grade above ground and heartwood for elements where rot could set in.
Appearance: Slightly lighter than cedar; has a strong grain pattern. Weathers to a pale gray.

Cost: Slightly less than cedar in the South, slightly more elsewhere. Not distributed in every region.
Comments: Lightweight, soft, and easily worked. As with redwood, consider using cypress for appearance items and pressure-treated wood where strength counts.

TOPPINGS

Description: Skid-resistant polymer or plastic coatings that are applied with a trowel or roller to plywood decking. Also rolls of textured rubber, in various widths, that are glued to plywood with a special adhesive.

Appearance: Polymer and rubber toppings come in several colors. Neutral-shaded polymer coating can be tinted.

Cost: $1 to $4 a square foot.

Comments: Use where slipperiness could be a problem. Because it's self-flashing, polymer coating can make a deck waterproof. Solvent-weld the seams of rubber rolls to turn your raised deck into what amounts to a roof—the perfect topper for a patio below. Pitch plywood ¼ inch per foot for drainage. Use ¾-inch exterior- or marine-grade plywood.

FASTENERS

Decks seem to eat nails. For every 40 square feet of deck, you'll need 1 pound of 16-penny common nails (for joists) and 2 pounds of 12-penny common nails (for decking). Use only hot-dipped, stainless-steel, or aluminum nails; ordinary steel rusts and stains the lumber.

Galvanized nails cost the least. Aluminum nails resist rust better, but they cost more and bend easily. Stainless-steel nails are the most costly and resist rust best. Spiral-shank or coated nails grip better than ordinary types.

Bolts, nuts, washers, and screws also should be galvanized. Bolts should be as long as the total thickness of the materials being joined, plus ¾ inch. Screws should be long enough so that two-thirds of their length goes into the member you're fastening to.

For more details, see pages 273–275.

JOIST AND BEAM SPANS

Joist size	Distance between joists		
	16 in.	24 in.	32 in.
2x6	8 ft.	6 ft.	5 ft.
2x8	10 ft.	8 ft.	7 ft.
2x10	13 ft.	10 ft.	8 ft.

Beam size	Maximum distance between posts
4x6	6 ft.
4x8	8 ft.
4x10	10 ft.
4x12	12 ft.

These spans will carry 40 pounds per square foot, a typical code requirement. Use 4x4s for posts up to 8 feet high, 6x6s above that.

DECK PLANTINGS

Deck plantings, like their patio counterparts (see pages 166–167), assume great importance in a landscaping scheme. The trees, shrubs, and flowers immediately surrounding a deck should offer the greatest interest for the longest season while having the fewest faults possible. Although maintenance is convenient in an area so close to the water source, give low-maintenance deck plantings prime consideration. After all, you shouldn't feel obliged to toil when you are working hard at relaxing.

■ What to consider
Before choosing plantings for your deck area, keep in mind the landscaping role they will play. Edging plants, for example, are especially important to tie a deck to its surroundings. Around a grade-level deck, plant neat ground covers or low flowers or shrubs. Use ground-hugging evergreens for textural variety. Around a raised deck, take advantage of the bird's-eye view and plant flowers, shrubs, and small trees that will look good from above.

The underside of your deck may need shrubs of appropriate height to screen from view the void or storage space below. For a low deck, try dwarf winged euonymus, barberry, viburnum, floribunda rose, dwarf pfitzer juniper, spreading yew, or azalea. For a high deck, try upright juniper and yew, or rhododendron. Where the ground slopes steeply, the plants also must check erosion (see pages 66–67).

Container plants often are called upon to bring needed color to decks (see box at upper right). Use soil substitutes that have less weight and more water retention so you can move the containers as desired. Remember, too, that the smaller a pot is or the brighter the sunshine it receives, the more often you will need to water the plant. Containers in full sun on hot days may need to be checked twice a day. Large pots in shade may need checking only twice a week.

Herbs are ideal on decks. Many release lovely odors when you barely brush against them.

See pages 301–323, plus the charts sprinkled throughout the book, for more plant ideas.

CONTAINER PLANTS FOR DECKS
Container plants are likely to play an integral part in your deck's landscaping. Try some of these in your pots and baskets.

Hanging baskets	Standards	Potted flowers
Achimenes	Abelia	Begonia
Browallia	Andromeda	Browallia
Campanula	Azalea	Caladium
Dianthus	Benjamin fig	Calendula
Fuchsia	Bougainvillea	Celosia
Geranium	Boxwood	Chrysanthemum
Herbs	Butterfly bush	Geranium
Hoya	Fuchsia	Impatiens
Lantana	Holly	Marigold
Nasturtium	Lantana	Nicotiana
Petunia	Magnolia	Sea lavender
Portulaca	Rose	Spring bulbs
Torenia	Wisteria, standard	Tuberose

◄ The richness of colorful plants adds beauty to any deck. Here, an intersecting group of angled planters overflows with purple-leaved plum, geranium, begonia, and, for year-round greenery, creeping juniper.

◄Background trees and shrubs create a cove of greenery around this deck and wraparound bench. Geranium, petunia, and taller zinnia add cascading color. Built-in planters bring the beauty closer to the eyes of beholders.

◄Evergreens outline this series of redwood decks for all-season neatness. Attractive containers display flowers at different levels and in lush abundance. As whim strikes or as needed, these can be replaced or replanted.

187

GALLERY OF DECK IDEAS

▶ *This porchlike deck features traditional railings and columns but has an arbor overhead. Deciduous vines let in the spring and winter sun, while providing ample summer shade. The arbor adds to a feeling of privacy yet retains a sense of space.*

▲ *Two levels, angled steps, and a cutoff corner add charm to this deck. So do the lattice panels between levels. Because the yard backs to a greenbelt, privacy is no problem, and the view of woods, wildlife, and sunset is left open.*

▶ *Planters under the eave soften this home's lengthy facade and tie the house to the decking. Diagonal steps add interest, too. For added space, benches box in an existing tree. Under all of this is an old step-down patio.*

▲ This octagonal treetop dining area is part of a series of decks that wrap around and between chosen trees. The steep slope made the untreated yard almost useless. Builders used sturdy steel posts for the tall support system.

◄ This smart-looking deck has something for all ages. The sandbox is safely bordered by built-in benches. A hinged cover of cedar decking folds open for playtime and closes when more room is needed for entertaining.

189

The most whimsical of outdoor rooms lies within the gazebo. Here, a yesteryear light fixture and ribbon detail on the cupola and posts form an old-fashioned sitting area where the weary can rest and watch others play.

A swimming pool is an ambitious outdoor project, but also one with the most appeal to most people. This free-form pool includes a spa and, at right, a waterfall that meanders through a rock formation.

If you've forgotten how to have fun, a water slide like this will bring it all back in one high-spirited glide. The boulders in the pool make both a stepping-stone bridge and a statement about the realm of design possibilities.

CHAPTER NINE

BEYOND THE BASICS

To many families, a yard needs more than just a patio or deck to be useful for outdoor living. They like to relax in a graceful gazebo, refresh near a still garden pond, or recreate in a swimming pool or play area. The options for creating the right outdoor living scheme are limitless. Most important is to select those features that satisfy both family needs and site conditions.

CREATING THE ULTIMATE GAZEBO

From the footings below to the cupola on top, a gazebo's design and use can vary greatly from yard to yard.

Yours could be an Oriental teahouse, a Victorian summer room, or a geodesic dome. It could be round, square, hexagonal, octagonal, or almost any other shape. (Octagonals are the most popular; squares, the easiest to build.)

A gazebo can be a rather substantial structure—with timbers or brick—or, more typically, a light and whimsical one—with lattice rails and scrollwork under the eaves. A variety of designs is available in precut kits; or, for a challenge, design your own. Choose the design that matches the mood of your garden and the structure's intended use. Consider borrowing elements from your house's architecture.

Provide a minimum diameter of 10 feet if you plan to use the gazebo for entertaining. Make the floors and benches nonskidding and quick drying. Choose the floor material that best fits your gazebo's style. Choices include wood, gravel, flagstone, tile, concrete, slate, and brick.

The roof can be slatted to protect from the sun only, or solid—with shakes, shingles, thatch, tile, or tin—to protect from the rain. The gazebo itself can be open, screened, or glazed. A barbecue, spa, or storage nook can be built in.

■ Location

Because a gazebo provides such a strong focal point in any landscape setting, its location is as important as its design.

Gazebos ordinarily are set some distance from the house; if you plan to use yours as an outdoor dining room, however, make sure it is near, or easily accessible to, the kitchen. Consider, too, wind direction, sun and shade patterns, nearness to neighbors, and the views of the garden each side of the gazebo will frame.

Usually a gazebo is freestanding, but it also can adjoin a patio, deck, or possibly a fence. It doesn't need much planting around it; it's decorative enough in itself. A freestanding gazebo does need to be connected with the house and garden by an easy and inviting path.

▶ *The slatted, bell-shaped roof on this redwood gazebo lets the sun in without scorching those seated beneath. Its eight sides were left open to frame eight views of the garden. For those entering the yard, the gazebo diverts attention from a nearby house.*

◀ *Tucked near the top of a wooded knoll, this white gazebo sits on a brick foundation. Assembled by two people in just a few hours, it came unpainted in a kit that included screws and even drill bits.*

◀ *To make use of a wooded floodplain, and create a focal point, the owners of this yard built a square gazebo on piers. The Chippendale lattice of the bridge railings is repeated in the gazebo sides, forming an open enclosure large enough for two rocking chairs.*

193

BUILDING GAZEBOS

To construct a bell-roofed, eight-sided Victorian gazebo like the one at right, you can: A) Painstakingly compute, cut, and assemble a hundred or so complicated angle joints; or B) Let a prefab manufacturer do the intricate geometry for you, allowing you to put the whole thing together in just a few enjoyable hours.

We opted for the second course of action.

The kit you see us putting together on this page and the next three came from Vintage Wood Works in Quinlan, Texas. Kits, of course, vary greatly in design, but our experience can give you a general idea of the work involved.

Our kit consisted of eight preassembled side panels, eight triangular roof panels, a finialed octagonal king post for the point where the roof panels converge, miscellaneous trim pieces, plus all the bolts and other hardware needed to fasten the components to each other.

Tools? We managed the entire job with an automotive-type socket wrench set, stepladder, framing square, mason's line, tape measure, pliers, hammer, C-clamp, and electric drill.

■ Anchors

We bolted our gazebo's posts to 6x6 pressure-treated wood piers. You also could use precast concrete piers, pour concrete footings (see page 60), or screw mobile-home soil anchors into the ground. Whatever anchoring system you decide on, you'll need eight anchors, leveled as explained on pages 74–75. Step 2 on the opposite page shows how to lay out the footings.

If your kit has a roof overhang, be sure it won't collide with trees, buildings, or other potential obstructions.

■ Personal design

If you're a dedicated woodworker, blessed with an abundance of power tools and patience, you might prefer to design and construct your own gazebo. To simplify figuring the angles, consider scaling back from eight sides to six. If you'd like your gazebo to have a wood floor, build it like a deck (see pages 172–189) with extra-tall posts and a roof.

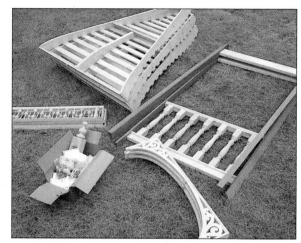

1 Start by unpacking the kit and taking an inventory of its pieces. Make sure each component is intact and hasn't been damaged in shipping. If you plan to stain or paint the wood, now is a good time to do it.

4 After erecting three side panels, install the two doorway sections, which are usually positioned opposite each other. Again, leave bolts only finger tight. Now put up the remaining three side panels.

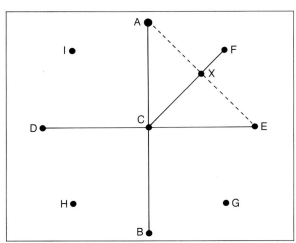

For basic information on working with wood, see pages 276–281.

2 To site post footings, drive stakes at points A and B; tie a line between them. Drive stake C at their center point. Using line and a framing square, locate D and E. For other posts, tie line to stake C and, centering it between two adjacent points, determine F, G, H, and I. Install footings (see options listed opposite).

3 Stand two side panels atop footings, align outer edges of post halves, then tap carriage bolts through predrilled holes. Do not put bolts in top holes of posts at this time. Add washers, then thread on nuts finger tight. Later, after roof sections are installed, go back and snug up side-panel bolts with a wrench.

5 Once all eight sections are bolted together, measure diagonally from alternate door frames. If these measurements differ by more than an inch, slightly shift panels in or out to square up the structure.

6 Once everything is square, attach posts to their footings. We drilled pilot holes, then drove lag screws through angles into each post and pier. Make these screws wrench tight.

(continued on page 196)

7 *Remove the finial from the bottom of the king post; lag-screw the first roof panel to the king post. Don't tighten the last ½ inch. With our kit, predrilled holes in the king post slant up toward the center when the king post is in the right position.*

8 *Now, with one person inside the gazebo and another outside the gazebo, lift the first roof panel into place from the outside in. Support the king post with a pole supplied by the manufacturer. The pole has a pin that fits into the hole for the bottom finial. Slip rafters into slots at tops of posts, but don't bolt here yet.*

11 *After all panels are in place, align corners where fascia boards meet and tighten rafter end bolts. Insert carriage bolts through holes at tops of posts and tighten securely.*

12 *Snug up all king post screws, remove the support pole, and screw the bottom finial back in place. Nail shingles or shakes to the slats on the gazebo roof, if desired.*

9 Next, lift the opposite roof panel into place and lag-screw it to the king post. Again, don't tighten all the way. As before, slip the rafters into the slots at the tops of posts.

10 Raise the third panel in place beside the second one. C-clamp rafters together, lag-screw the third panel to the king post (within ½ inch), and bolt rafter ends. Finger-tighten these bolts. Raise and attach remaining roof panels to the king post, working alternately side to side.

13 Place bolts in remaining holes along rafters; snug them up. Then tighten all side-panel bolts. The weight of the roof panels should have moved side panels into place; if not, make minor adjustments.

14 Finally, install gingerbread panels. Ours feature lacy brackets topped with ball and dowel spindles, a design copied from Victorian pattern books.

CREATING THE ULTIMATE GARDEN POOL

▶ *Centered in a secluded garden, this classically inspired pool presents a pleasing profile regardless of a viewer's vantage point. The pool's black interior creates an illusion of depth and mystery, and the splashing of fountain waters contributes to the garden's sense of serenity.*

The shimmering surface of the ideal garden pool should reflect peace and tranquillity, as well as the surrounding foliage, flowers, sky, clouds, and sunsets. Sound too visionary? Well, water features are adaptable to more garden situations than most people ever consider.

And despite the new realms of plant, fish, and wildlife pleasures offered by these pools, they need not require great time or money. You can learn enough to begin the venture in just one evening with a catalog. And the typical water garden requires no more work and little more cost than the standard flower border.

■ Design
Pages 18–19 discuss many of the elements that make a garden pool ideal. To test your ideas, shape a garden hose on your lawn.

To keep fish, a pool needs to be at least as large as a bathtub; a surface area of 50 or more square feet—a 7-foot square, an 8-foot-diameter circle, or a 5x10-foot rectangle—is best. Smaller ponds get too hot in summer, which can lead to algae problems. A depth of 1½ to 2 feet works for most goldfish. Japanese koi need 3 feet.

■ Maintenance
Most pools can be filled with a hose and emptied by siphon or bucket. Where winters are severe, transfer fish and tender plants indoors. In mild climates or with added heat, fish will live under a foot of ice as long as an air hole is kept open. Don't do this by smashing the surface, however; the concussion could damage or kill the fish. A floating deicer will do the job. Wherever ice forms, put a log in the pool in winter to absorb the thrust of the ice.

Every few years, drain and clean your pool in the spring. If algae builds up, ask at your pet store for algae-killing chemicals that will not harm fish. Use them and add more plants. Refilling to take care of algae is seldom advisable.

▶ *This backyard fishpond was built by the owners in less than two weekends using a PVC pool liner. The first weekend they dug the hole, put down the liner, and filled the pond. The next, they added the border trim, the plants, and the fish.*

BUILDING GARDEN POOLS

Basically, a garden pool is a hole filled with water; but when it comes to choosing what to interpose between the water and the earth underneath, you have a number of options. Let's look at the pros and cons of each.

Preformed pools usually are made of plastic reinforced with fiberglass. They're easy to install, and sturdy ones needn't be sunk entirely into the ground. Shapes are limited, though—usually kidney, square, or round—and smaller preformed pools are algae prone.

Polyvinyl chloride (PVC) liners mold themselves to any shape, and you can buy them in just about any size. To install a PVC liner, simply dig a hole, lay the liner in position, weight its edges, and fill the pool with water. Later, however, after the liner has settled, you must cover its edges, usually by building a stone or brick coping around the pool's perimeter.

Galvanized livestock tanks are inexpensive and easy to install. Buy one at least 2 feet deep. Paint the outside with roofing tar to protect against rust, and line the interior with heavy black plastic. Stock tanks come in even fewer shapes than preformed pools.

Concrete pools have been around for centuries and are still a favorite with landscapers. Though a bit more work to install than the other types, concrete is inexpensive and as versatile as any of the other materials. The photos at right take you through the steps of building a concrete pool.

■ Pool particulars

All pools, regardless of type, must have a 1- to 2-inch-high rim around the edges so groundwater can't flood the pool during heavy rains.

Because water seeks its own level, you needn't worry about keeping the bottom of a pool absolutely flat, but its rim must be even from end to end and side to side.

A pump to recirculate water usually isn't necessary, unless you want a fountain or waterfall. See page 202 for more details.

As for all construction projects, check local codes first. Even a shallow pool poses a safety hazard for a small child.

1 *Excavate, then compact earth, particularly on sides. Dig to the depth you want the pool to be, plus 4 inches for concrete. Cut back sod to make room for a rim. If your plans include a pump (see page 202), make provisions now for the electrical cord, including laying any necessary conduit. For a waterfall or remote fountain, make plans for a water-return line.*

4 *After all concrete has been poured and smoothed, cover the pond with polyethylene. This further slows the curing process and keeps rain- or surface water out of the pool until the concrete has completely hardened.*

2 *Contour reinforcing mesh into the hole, then drive stakes to hold the mesh about 2 inches above the ground. The stakes also can guide you in keeping the concrete a uniform 4 inches thick.*

3 *Pour the concrete into one portion of the pool at a time, then pack it into the mesh with a trowel. After you reach a 4-inch thickness, pull the stakes or drive them into the ground, fill the stake holes with concrete, and pour the next portion. Work quickly. Dampen the concrete periodically to retard the curing process.*

5 *Wait a week for the concrete to completely cure, then mortar a brick or cut stone coping to provide a lip around the pool. Check the coping with a level and adjust the bricks or stones if necessary.*

6 *Fill pool, let water stand at least 24 hours, then drain. Scour concrete to remove cement residues; rinse well. You can seal the surface with pool paint or a plaster made from white marble powder and cement, if you like.*

For basic information on working with concrete and mortar, see pages 282–287.

INSTALLING PUMPS, FOUNTAINS, AND WATERFALLS

Want a pond that stirs silently beneath the surface, with scarcely a ripple above? A dramatic fountain that arcs a jet of water above your pool or even from a remote location? A waterfall that burbles down a steep slope into a lily-speckled catch basin below? With a submersible recirculating pump, you can put your pool's water into motion in a variety of ways.

A submersible pump pulls in water through a screen that snags leaves and debris, and expels a steady stream through its outlet. To gently move water and keep it from stagnating (usually not a necessity), just set the pump a few inches above the pool bottom (perhaps on a brick or two) and connect it to a source of electricity. For an in-pool fountain, attach any of several nozzles to the outlet (see illustration, below, top). To pump water from the pool to a waterfall or re-mote fountain, run flexible vinyl tubing from the outlet to wherever you want the water to go (see illustration, below, bottom).

To help you choose a pump, your dealer will need to know the height at which you want the water to discharge and the volume of water in your pool.

■ Safety musts

Check with an electrician or consult your local community's electrical codes before bringing power to a submersible pump. Most codes require that a pump be plugged into a weatherproof receptacle located within 6 feet of the pump and 18 inches above the ground. This receptacle should be protected by a ground-fault circuit interupter (GFCI); a GFCI shuts down the circuit instantaneously should a potentially dangerous malfunction occur.

Check the code, too, to learn the components required for underground wiring in your area. Most call for underground feeder (UF) cable, rigid conduit, or a combination of both—conduit above ground, UF cable below. Codes also specify how deep cable and conduit must be buried. Neglect these regulations at your peril: electricity and water can be a lethal combination, especially outdoors.

For more information about working with electrical wires underground, see pages 92–93 and 288–291.

▶ *For an in-pool fountain that creates a misty spray, attach an elbow fitting, a length of pipe, and a spreader nozzle to the pump's outlet. Any of a wide variety of precast and prefab fountains can be attached to pool pumps.*

BRICK COPING
WATER
FOUNTAIN ATTACHMENT
SUBMERSIBLE PUMP
EARTH
CONCRETE, PVC LINER, OR OTHER MATERIAL
BRICK OR STONE
ELECTRICAL CORD

▶ *For a waterfall, run tubing from the submersible pump's outlet to a remote, and higher, site. Use concrete or PVC liner and stones or other material to construct the waterway. Each level of a stair-stepped waterfall should have a vertical drop of 6 to 12 inches.*

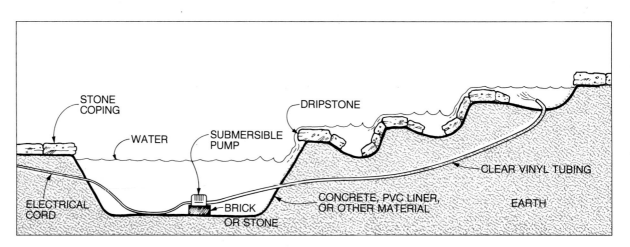

STONE COPING
WATER
SUBMERSIBLE PUMP
DRIPSTONE
CLEAR VINYL TUBING
ELECTRICAL CORD
BRICK OR STONE
CONCRETE, PVC LINER, OR OTHER MATERIAL
EARTH

CREATING WATER GARDENS

Plant your water garden after the weather warms in spring. You can plant in bottom mud, but containers allow flexibility in depth and position and make cleaning easier. Use a mix of garden loam and aquatic plant fertilizer. Do not use swamp muck, compost, peat moss, or dry manure.

First, add submerged oxygenating plants: water milfoil, waterweed, underwater grasses. Fill several 5-inch pots or shallow containers with soil, topping off the uppermost inch with sand. Root several oxygenators per pot by pushing them a third of the way into the soil.

Plant only one water lily per 20-inch pot; pygmy varieties need only 8-inch containers. Plant hardy varieties at an angle against the pot side; in harsh winter climates, store them indoors during the cold months.

Plant tropical water lilies only after the nights grow warm. Set each tuber in the center of a pot with the crown at the soil line. Sink pots 6 to 8 inches below the water surface. Treat these plants as annuals and order new roots each year.

Edibles like lotus, water chestnut, and watercress can grow in a pool; cranberry, natal plum, banana, citrus, clump bamboo, sorrel, and many herbs do well on the moist banks. Lotus can be invasive.

■ Fish facts

Add one fish per 2 square feet of pond surface. You can choose from many colorful goldfish, such as calicoes, comets, black moors, and fantails. If your pool is large and at least 3 feet deep, you can add Japanese koi.

Do not let the bags the fish come in get hot in the sun. Before freeing fish, float the bags in the pond for a half hour to equalize temperatures.

Feed pet store food every one to three days. Remove any food left after five to 10 minutes. Give extra protein food in the fall and none from November until March, a natural resting period for the fish.

Welcome any snails, frogs, toads, or turtles that come. You also can buy these. With the fish, they help control insects and algae growth.

WATER-GARDEN PLANTS

Hostas *are fine plants for shady edges. They come in a wide variety of sizes, colors, and foliage patterns. Some have fragrant spikes of flowers as well.*

Siberian iris *are edging plants that produce up to 50 blooms per clump in white, blue, or purple above 2- to 4-foot-tall swordlike leaves. Grow these flowers in full sun to partial shade.*

Sword fern *is one of many ferns that thrive on moist banks in full sun to partial shade. This fern is hardy and easy to grow. It spreads by spores or by division.*

Water lilies *come in many colors and sizes. They do best with their roots in containers on the pool floor. Some are fragrant. Most bloom freely all season long.*

Floating plants like water lettuce, floating heart, or water hyacinth need no soil. When these spread too far, scoop out the excess. (No more than half of your pool's surface should be covered by plants.) Other poolside plants are primrose, lily, daylily, forget-me-not, water snowflake, grasses, and reeds. Buttonbush and sweet pepperbush are good for larger masses of foliage.

CREATING THE ULTIMATE SWIMMING POOL

A personal swimming pool offers the ultimate in backyard recreation. It can accommodate a brisk before-breakfast dip or a few healthful laps at lunchtime—all without requiring a long trip to the local swimming hole.

And for those of us who wouldn't be caught dead at a crowded beach, a home-based pool allows family swim time, an enjoyment that would go unexperienced otherwise.

There was a time when even baths were public facilities. Now, the swimming pool has made the transition to private grounds. The trend started in the Sunbelt. Still, Southerners seldom swim before May or much after September, except in heated pools. Summers in South Dakota get just as hot, and a swimming pool there can add just as much pleasure to outdoor living.

To be ideal, a pool should be integrated into the landscape. Patios, decks, and nearby plantings should be carefully planned to enhance the scene's beauty and enjoyment, yielding an adjoining space for sunbathing and a shaded area where nonswimmers can relax and avoid splashes. A drinking fountain and door to a bathroom or shower add great convenience.

Many in-ground pools are designed to be the focal point of view from both indoor and outdoor rooms; some are visible through a foyer from the front door, adding to the grandeur of the entryway. Even during winter, these pools can give visual refreshment and reflection.

Some homeowners, however, prefer not to see their pool in the dead of winter; if you agree, plan your pool's location accordingly. Or use plantings or surrounding materials to make the winter scene as pleasant as possible.

Some pools, especially in yards with overhanging trees, are enclosed with screen to keep out falling leaves, insects, and blowing debris. Screening also cuts down somewhat on the sun's intensity, a benefit in summer. But the water will be colder in spring and fall.

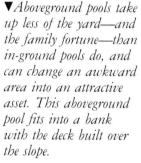

▼*Aboveground pools take up less of the yard—and the family fortune—than in-ground pools do, and can change an awkward area into an attractive asset. This aboveground pool fits into a bank with the deck built over the slope.*

▲ Green and white
plants accent and add
serenity to this half-circle
pool. Clever planning
and planting achieved
privacy plus a sense of
an established garden in
a small space.

◄ The surrounding deck
and plantings give this
aboveground pool all the
aesthetic advantages of
an in-ground one. The
deck also allows for easy
access to pool plumbing
and handy storage of
equipment underneath.

ASSESSING SWIMMING-POOL OPTIONS

The addition of a swimming pool to your yard is a big decision. Read pages 16–17, as well as this section, and consider all of the options. Also, talk with people who have pools, trying to learn all you can about what kind, shape, and size of pool might be best for you.

A pool will provide years of summer fun, sun, exercise, and relaxation; and, with the right decisions, it will increase dramatically your yard's beauty, value, and use.

If you decide that a pool isn't right for you now but may be in the future, plan present use of the space for easy changeover: a lawn or flower garden, not a patio or clump of trees. Also, remember to leave access for heavy machinery. In areas where swimming pools are the norm—if not almost mandatory—lack of access for pool construction could be a serious drawback to would-be buyers someday.

Pools today can be installed quickly—by professionals, that is; as you research the work required to build a pool, you'll quickly realize that this is not a do-it-yourself project.

■ Safety and cost

A pool can be as safe or as dangerous as the family car, but it isn't as essential. You can postpone building a pool until the children are old enough to ease the worry (though at no age should you allow them to swim or play in the pool unsupervised). Begin planning and saving now, and you'll enjoy your pool all the more later on.

The cost of the pool itself represents only from 50 to 60 percent of the total outlay; the fencing, decking, and surrounding plantings that will transform the pool from the visual appearance of a raw wound to that of a luxurious landscape constitute the remaining expenses.

This cost comes into better perspective, though, if you realize that, when you sell your home, you can largely recover the money spent on a professionally built pool if the pool does not exceed 10 percent of property value.

Besides cost, consider, too, the maintenance demands a pool will put on you (see pages 210–211). Time spent maintaining water quality and equipment will seem minimal as long as you and your family enjoy the pool. If your leisure interests turn elsewhere, however, maintenance can become a major pain.

■ Site

There isn't a great deal of choice in most yards for where to put something as big as a swimming pool. But if you do have a choice of sites, consider these points.

■ Will the foundation of existing buildings be weakened by the excavation? Will the slope and grade accommodate the pool? Often the grade can be built up around the pool, thus reducing the hole's depth and the cost of carting off soil.

■ How about the soil type and the drainage? The soil has to bear the weight of pool materials and water, and it must drain well enough so that the pool won't float out of the ground.

■ What about sun and wind patterns? These affect both warmth and cleaning. Too much sun could promote algae growth. If possible, the prevailing wind should drive all floating debris toward the skimmers. A strong wind against the flow decreases efficiency. You can build wind baffles and screens, if necessary.

■ Do you prefer to swim in the morning or evening, in sun or shade? If possible, choose your site accordingly.

■ Will the pool be far enough from trees, flowering shrubs, and hedges to avoid leaf drop and birds overhead? Don't let the lawn come too close either; otherwise, grass cuttings will blow or get tracked into the water.

■ Is there access to electrical and water lines, and proper drainage for overflow. Filters are best kept as near to the deep end of the pool as possible so suction pipes are short.

■ How do relevant zoning and fencing regulations affect your plans? Often, self-latching gates are required.

■ Finally, for safety's sake, will the pool be visible from the house?

■ Types

Pools are installed either in the ground or above it. Your site selection may determine which is better for you (see photo, page 204). Above-ground pools may not seem as luxurious as in-ground pools, but they offer certain advantages.

■ They are less expensive. True, they take some landscaping to fit, but an in-ground pool usually requires more.

■ They are not as permanent. If you change your mind, you can move or get rid of an above-ground pool. If you are not so sure that you want a pool, you can afford to try an above-ground one while you decide.

■ They can be safer, because very small children usually must climb before they can fall into the water. Some quite attractive decking and fencing right around the pool can add to its safety, as well as to its enjoyment and visual appeal.

In-ground pools, on the other hand, should be considered major investments. Planning for them is more important than it is for above-ground pools because they are not only permanent but also prominent.

■ Shapes and materials

Swimming pools today come in just about any shape, from free-form to kidney, oval, L, and coffin. Rectangular is the most economical.

Your site selection and choice of pool material may help decide your pool shape. Fiberglass pools—perhaps the least expensive—are limited to preformed shapes. So are vinyl-lined pools. Gunite or concrete pools can be built in any shape and generally are more durable.

Knowing how you'll use the pool will help determine its shape, too. Lap pools should be long and narrow; often they are shallow. Diving pools take more room and depth where divers enter the water. Rectangular shapes work best for pools used mainly for recreational games such as water volleyball.

(continued on page 208)

Trees can provide shade, serve as windbreaks, and frame and soften the scene. To avoid overhang and debris, however, keep a good distance between all trees and the pool. Or screen the pool area.

Pick a pool design that fits both function and feel of yard and house. Siting, material, and intended use can influence the design. Simple shapes often work better than fanciful ones.

The necessary fencing and equipment storage area should be designed to fit the scene. The surrounding decking also can add greatly to a pool's look and use. Make room for sitting.

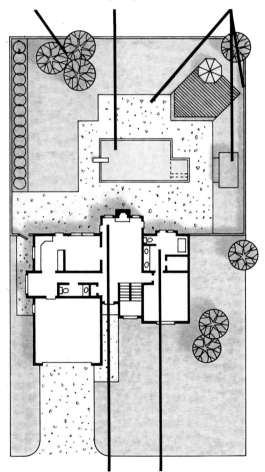

Consider the view from inside the house and during every season of the year. Pools are safer if they are in full view. With proper planning, the scene can be pleasant even in winter.

Access to dressing area and bathroom should be direct and over a drip-absorbing surface easy on bare feet. Pool use, climate, and age of swimmers will largely dictate the extras.

ASSESSING SWIMMING-POOL OPTIONS *(continued)*

Once you've decided on the site and shape of your pool (see pages 206–207), consider carefully its size. Some families are happy to have the pool dominate the landscape. They plan the surrounding deck and plantings to eliminate lawn mowing altogether. Others prefer the pool to be secondary in size and importance to other aspects of the garden. Often, however, pool size will be determined by the available space and by budget.

As a rule of thumb, allow 100 square feet of pool surface for each diver, 24 to 36 square feet for each swimmer, and 10 square feet for each splashing child. If you intend to use your pool for a variety of activities, plan on one that's at least 16x32 feet. Remember, though, the smaller your pool, the lower the maintenance costs.

Families may want a shallow section for waders. Underwater benches around the edge of a pool can add to the relaxation and provide footing for visiting babies.

■ Pool lights
You will want both exterior and underwater lights for your pool to extend the enjoyment and the beauty into warm summer nights. Such lights are good safety and security features, too.

Choose both light and location to avoid glare in a diver's face or into the house.

Underwater lighting, like garden lighting (see pages 92–93 and 212–215), can be either the regular 120-volt or the lower 12-volt system. The latter is safe, even if it should short, and thus is recommended.

Underwater lamps can be in either *wet* or *dry* niches. A wet assembly is sealed and can be changed underwater. A dry niche requires that the water level of the pool be dropped to change the lamp.

As a general rule, use one lamp for every 24 to 30 linear feet of pool side. In a 16x32-foot pool, for example, you might have three lamps: one on each side and one under the diving board. Put one of the side lights near the ladder or steps.

You also can buy a portable underwater light that is safe, runs on low voltage, and operates up to six hours on its own rechargeable battery. If you have a pool without lighting that's less than 20x30 feet in size, one of these portable lights can yield lovely nighttime effects.

Decorative floating lights and candles are striking when people are gathered around but not in a pool.

Other pool components to consider buying are ladders, steps, grab rails, diving and jumping equipment, floating ropes to mark off the deep end, floats for both relaxation and safety, and in-pool play equipment for basketball, volleyball, or the like.

■ Decking
The solid surface surrounding your pool requires both careful planning and its share of expense. It can add or detract from the eye appeal and enjoyment of the pool.

The width of the solid surface should be a minimum of 3 feet; 6 to 8 feet is much better. More activity will occur around the shallow end of the pool, so if there is to be a wider area of surrounding decking, make it there.

Concrete decking is used most often. It is both practical and economical. Exposed aggregate (see pages 122–123) can add nonskid, nonglare safety and comfort, as well as a richness of color and texture. Both concrete and aggregate can get hot from the searing sun, though; a troweled-on cooling surface that costs more but saves soles is available.

Other pool decking possibilities include modular paving tiles, blocks, bricks, stones like bluestone, and granite.

Wood decking works well where the grade level around a pool changes. Use wood along with concrete for a pleasant contrast.

The material and prominence of the coping that immediately surrounds the pool are largely matters of personal preference. The coping can be a definite, dominating line, or the decking can extend right up to the pool's edge.

Proper drainage of the decking area is vital. Puddles can cause falls in summer and freezing and cracking in winter. Runoff of treated water into adjacent plant beds could cause trouble.

■ Pool plantings

Plants near pools should be of the low-care, high-drama variety. For the most part, plantings should be somewhat separated from the pool itself. But placing a few plants so they cast a reflection on the water will relieve the flat surface and increase the effect. A raised bed or two right at the water's edge will do this nicely.

Trees and shrubs can be fairly distant from the pool and still cast interesting shadows and reflections. If planted on the north or west side, these also can reduce chilling breezes without blocking the sun's warmth.

Avoid trees with extensive or invasive root systems. Don't plant trees with leaves so tiny that they escape skimmers, nor plants with slippery fruit or small litter; pine needles and bottle-brush stamens can clog filters.

Most plants thrive in the increased humidity near a pool, but some are much more sensitive to chemical splashes than others. Fragrance is lovely wafting across the pool, but don't plant bee-bringers nearby. The bees probably would be harmless enough, but could cause panic.

Avoid plants that are fussy in any way, that need spraying, or that drop messy leaves, blossoms, or fruits. Among the limited edible choices, bamboo, natal plum, and some herbs are especially good.

Container plants can be moved in or out as their condition and the occasion requires.

■ Professional help

When building a pool, most homeowners work with a pool contractor and perhaps an architect, landscape architect, or landscape designer. The person you hire will depend on your budget, the person's background, and your yard.

Interview and get bids from several recommended professionals. Ask to see their previous work and talk with their clients. Make sure that the professional you hire has liability insurance and worker's compensation, and check with your own insurance company to see if you need added coverage while work is under way.

Draw up a contract that says who is responsible for zoning compliance and building permits. The contract should include a drawn-to-scale plan of the location, shape, and dimensions of the pool and its support system. Have an attorney check for specifications such as work to be done, materials to be used, equipment to be installed, and dates to start and finish, as well as the cost of relocating utility lines, clearing access to the site, final grading, and cleaning up.

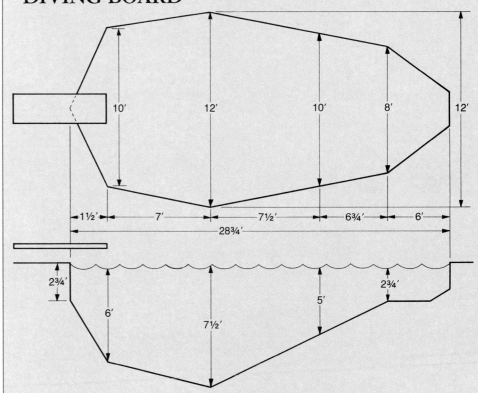

MINIMUM DIMENSIONS FOR POOL WITH DIVING BOARD

Maximum length of board for this pool is 6 feet and maximum height of board from surface of water is 20 inches.

EQUIPPING AND MAINTAINING YOUR POOL

Pool water is seldom drained. Rather it is maintained in healthful cleanliness by circulation through a system of skimmers, filter, heater (if there is one), lint trap, pump motor, piping, and valves. All of the water in your pool should so circulate at least once every eight to 12 hours.

To accomplish this, both the pump and the filter need to be of the proper size for the volume of water in your pool. Oversized, they waste money and electricity. Undersized, they won't do the job and eventually will burn out.

To be safe from puddling and easily accessible for draining, the pump and filter need to be 24 inches above ground level. To save on plumbing and piping costs, place them close to the pool. Include ventilation in any housing you provide for the equipment.

All pools must have at least one skimmer. More are required for odd-shaped pools than for simple rectangular ones. Maintain the water level at the middle mark of the skimmer.

■ Filter options

Three types of filters are available, all of which clean by straining the water through a tank containing material that catches dirt and debris.

Diatomaceous earth (D.E.) filters remove particles as small as a half micron. They require the addition of powder. Cartridge filters remove particles of 20 microns and larger. They must be cleaned or replaced. Sand filters remove particles only as small as 40 microns. Some of the dirt is recycled. To clean these, you must flip a valve to backwash water through the sand and out into a drainage system.

The kind of water you have may dictate your choice of filter. Hard water, for example, often clogs a D.E. filter.

Hoses are used only on aboveground pools (all in-ground pools have hard plumbing). These hoses should be changed yearly whether they need it or not. Usually, people wait until their hose springs a leak. But at that point, their pool is half empty, and water is everywhere.

ELECTRICAL NEEDS

A swimming pool requires electricity for the water circulation system, for lighting, and possibly for heating and nearby outdoor power outlets. For maximum economy and efficiency, think of your electrical needs and wants thoroughly when planning your pool.

Strictly follow code requirements for the wiring and grounding of all equipment associated with a swimming pool, and the bonding and grounding of all metallic additions. Power outlets must be at least 18 inches above the level of the pool apron and fully protected. The electrical service to the pool must have its own circuit; so must the pump and filter. An electrician or your pool contractor can check your current amperage capacity to ensure it's adequate for your pump.

■ Pool heaters

Three methods are most commonly used for heating pool water: solar heating, conventional heating, and solar covers.

Solar heating requires that the water be circulated through solar-collector panels that face south or just east of south.

A solar heater works only with ample sunshine. If typically more than half of the days in your area are cloudy (check with your local weather bureau), you may need a backup heater. Some systems will switch automatically.

Conventional heaters include gas- and oil-fired heaters and heat pumps.

Solar covers or blankets can raise pool-water temperature by 10 degrees or more, at a fraction of the cost of other heating methods. The covers also lessen the amount of water lost through evaporation. Because they help keep debris out of the pool, they reduce the wear and tear on filters and save on chemicals.

Covers—whether solar or not—can be made to blend in fairly well with pool decor. They also can be installed on tracks for easy removal. Some pool blankets—with properly restrained edges—can support several adults and possibly save a small child from drowning. If a person falls on a free-floating cover, however, it could add to the danger of drowning by wrapping around and pulling the person under.

Special chemicals also are available to help cut heating costs. These chemicals increase the surface tension of the water and form a thin, invisible layer that reduces heat loss and evaporation.

■ Other needs

To keep your pool clean, you will need a net for skimming the occasional leaf or dead bug from the surface.

A must, too, is some type of vacuum cleaner to remove any debris that escapes the filter and settles to the bottom. These vary in price and use from a simple brush and hose attachment for the filter to a separate robot that crawls around the pool bottom.

■ Winter

Pool winterizing chores vary by climate. Where pool water freezes, lower its level to 2 to 3 inches below the bottom skimmer face plate in an in-ground pool. In an aboveground pool, lower the water surface to 24 inches below its usual level.

Clean and treat the water. Drain pipes and place winter plugs in the suction and return fittings. Remove and store ladders, slides, and such. Put an empty barrel in the water to help protect walls against the expansion of freezing.

Covers will prevent evaporation and help keep dirt and leaves out. Water out of sight, however, often is neglected. In the South, pull back the cover at least every month and treat the water as needed.

When removing a cover, take care not to let the accumulated gunk and untreated water that collects on top of the cover get into the pool.

POOL CHEMICALS

You can have pool experts come weekly to check and add pool chemicals, or you can do it yourself with the aid of a simple test kit.

Chlorine—in the form of powders, tablets, or other stabilized types—is added to pools on a day-to-day basis to meet regular needs. It's also added at intervals—after heavy rains, for example—in *shock* form.

Such shock treatments work better if you check and adjust the pH level first (see below). That way, the chlorine immediately attacks and destroys bacteria and algae, and is quickly expended or exhausted in the process.

Shock your water after, not immediately before, swimming. Besides following heavy rains, apply the treatment after heavy use or whenever the color of the pool water begins to turn green or brown, an indication of algae growth. If the water does not return to its clear, clean color, you may need to add an algicide.

Milder sanitizing chemicals that take longer to work but have a less irritating effect on the skin and eyes of extra-sensitive people are available.

Also test weekly the balance of the pH levels in the pool. Do this more often in very hot weather or with heavy use. If the reading is below 7.2 or above 7.6, add the needed chemicals.

Total alkalinity in the water is the measure of carbonates and bicarbonates. This measure should range from 60 to 100 ppm for best chlorine effectiveness and scale control, minimum eye and skin irritation, and least corrosion.

CREATING THE ULTIMATE LIGHTING SCHEME

When Louis XVI strolled with his courtiers through the gardens of Versailles, thousands of torches lit the way. Today, you don't have to be royalty to enjoy the wonder of the garden at night. After sunset, even the most modest of gardens can assume a regal enchantment, thanks to skillfully used lighting.

Most outdoor settings, however, remain basically dark when the sun goes down. Sometimes, they even lack enough lighting to satisfy safety and security requirements (see pages 92–93).

The benefits of the right decorative lighting scheme are numerous. With today's busy schedules, people do most of their relaxing and entertaining after nightfall. Garden lighting can stretch the hours of outdoor living, as well as the seasons of garden enjoyment. Few activities are more exciting for children or adults than to go out in the first snowfall of the season or to step outdoors after supper on an unusually warm evening in February.

When done well, garden lighting also creates a living mural beyond your windows, which you can enjoy without venturing outdoors in rain, ice, or cold. Well-placed and -chosen fixtures can create dramatic pools of light near plants or structures and direct the patterns of shadows. Interesting textures and forms—whether of foliage or branches—can be played up.

New or evolving gardens sometimes benefit the most from lighting. Fixtures can be placed to illuminate the garden's outstanding features and cast the rest into darkness.

Even if you cherish the peace darkness brings, you can enjoy the diffused, perimeter lighting of garden features. A wide variety of fixtures is available that offer glow without glare.

Best of all, today's low-voltage kits let you install energy-efficient garden lights quickly with minimal expense, no electrician, and complete safety. See the next two pages for more on selecting, placing, and installing outdoor lights.

▶ *Small lights around the cupola and ceiling of this gazebo invite long evenings of pleasant visiting. A spotlight accentuates the tree at right, while mushroom lights make the walk and steps safer, softer looking, and more interesting.*

◀ *Low-voltage light fixtures along this garden path bestow a warm glow to plantings and invite nighttime strolls. Such subtle and diffused lighting often makes gardens look better than ever while also creating magical moods.*

213

ASSESSING LIGHTING OPTIONS

Wide-spreading lights accent the patio plantings and the rock garden. Illuminating one area or both at the same time shifts the focal point— and feel—of the garden at night.

Diffused lights wash the fence and hedge to create a soft backdrop for the yard. The lighting visually spreads out rather than closes in the space, yet forms a frame for the setting.

Pole lights around the gazebo and low-level patio lights near the house emit enough illumination for outdoor living, without glaring or intruding on the peace of the evening.

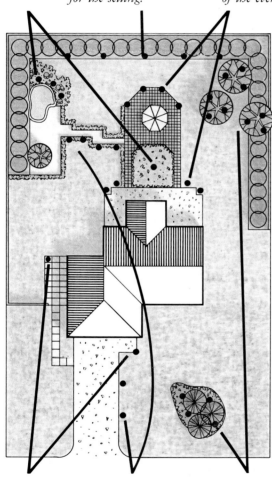

Bright post lights near the entry and the service area enable people to come and go, work on the car, or unload groceries after dusk. Additionally, they provide security.

At the front of the house, low-level drive and walk lights extend a sense of welcome or safe return. In back, they connect the patio and rock garden, encouraging evening garden walks.

Lights hung in or directed up into the trees move the eye up from the ground to give that all-important third dimension to the night garden. They highlight patterns and textures.

Study the exciting possibilities for outdoor lights carefully before you buy the first bulb. Decide what effect will add the most enjoyment—both visual and recreational—to each area of your yard.

To begin, go outside at dusk and again after dark with a strong flashlight or a trouble light on a long extension cord. Shine the light different directions, trying to play up moods. Don't simulate daylight.

Lights pointing down can give a broad, natural highlight to interesting features of the yard. Upward lights can give a glow to leaves. Backlighting can accent the drama of a tree or structure, particularly if the lighted object is in front of a plain surface.

Lights diffused with translucent screens can shine down subtly from high in a tree or the side of a house, mimicking moonlight. Lights that graze or wash across an interesting architectural surface, like a fence or chimney, can be striking.

The height and brightness of a light, as well as the direction of its reflector, will change the effect. Avoid glare in a stroller's eyes or on nearby properties, especially into windows.

■ Drawing a plan

Once you've developed your lighting ideas, lay tracing paper over your landscape plan and mark which light types you want placed where. Try to visualize the overall look. The goal of the plan at left was to highlight certain use areas and visual elements in the landscape, while at the same time provide a low level of light throughout so that the site has warmth and charm.

If your house is in the planning stage, let the electrician who wires the house install major fixtures like door lights, floodlights, and post lights. These will be bright-burning lights that operate on the same 120-volt system as your house. If your house and yard are established, hire an electrician; tackle simpler 120-volt installations yourself, if local code allows (see pages 92–93 and 288–291), or work with easy-to-install, but less versatile 12-volt lighting systems (more details on the next page).

Put switches indoors, if at all possible. That way, you can enjoy the sight of your garden long hours later or in weather when you really don't want to go outside to turn lights on and off. Also, consider whether you want a central switch to command all lights, several so you can use them separately, or an automatic timer. If you have a 120-volt system and only one central switch, be prepared for some high electric bills.

■ **Low-voltage lowdown**

Low-voltage fixtures let you light up the night without burning out the budget—either for installation or operation. Their secret is the transformer or power pack. It reduces to 12 volts the 120-volt current from any grounded outlet.

Few code restrictions apply, so you usually can set up these lamps without an electrician. The wiring is so safe that it need not always be buried, and it never needs encasing in conduit.

There are drawbacks. The transformers usually can handle only five or six fixtures, with bulbs no brighter than 75 watts. Also, the longer the run of wire, the dimmer the light.

To install, just securely mount the transformer near an outlet. Put it as close to the fixtures as possible. If the kit includes a photosensitive control that turns lights on at dusk and off at dawn, be sure to position the sensor so it's exposed to daylight but not to artificial light at night.

After hanging the transformer, lay the cable where desired, then snap the fixtures to it. Spike each fixture into the ground.

Before burying the cable or covering it with mulch, turn the system on to check if the fixtures cast light the way you want. If not, just snap them elsewhere on the cable.

Bury the cable with enough soil or mulch to hide it and prevent tripping. In turf, dig out a V-shaped wedge of sod, place the cable beneath, then replace the sod. Under shrubbery, the cable can lie on the ground or under mulch.

To minimize the effects of frost heave, fill around the fixtures with gravel. Raise or lower the bulb to expand or reduce the circle of light. For best illumination, keep foliage trimmed.

FIXTURES

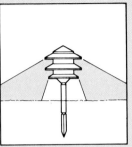 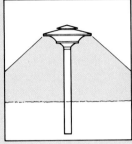 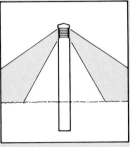

Accent lights *give garden features more prominence at night. Remove this fixture's cap and center louvers to change the direction of the light and create different effects.*

Mushroom lights *with large shades direct a subtle shine downward on walks, steps, or plants. Shade or height changes alter the width and intensity of the circle of light.*

Post lights *like this one have adjustable louver settings for subtle or bright illumination, depending on the desired effect. These can be cut to specified heights for patio or gazebo.*

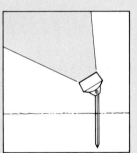 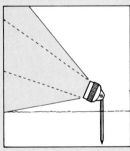 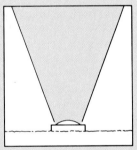

Floodlights *can provide dramatic silhouettes, as well as security. Mount them on walls or in trees. Or, for even greater vertical emphasis, install them in the ground and point them skyward.*

Variable-focus floodlights, *often used to dramatize foliage, fences, or walls, offer great lighting flexibility. Rotating the focus ring gives a spotlight or a broad wash.*

Well lights *achieve dramatic uplighting effects on interesting tree shapes, shrub foliage, architectural features, or statuary. For added romance or intrigue, use colored lenses.*

Garden lights come in many other interesting shapes, from long, sparkling sticks to round stepping-stones that have low-voltage bulbs in grooves around the edges. Some hang on fences or flower boxes; some string like Christmas lights. Others provide safety lighting under deck railings or steps.

CREATING THE ULTIMATE PLAY AREA

However lovely, yards must always be primarily a place to play for family members of all ages.

The same children who drive you crazy indoors can delight you with their wonder and imaginations outside. Teenagers can spend hours shooting baskets or giggling on a distant private swing. Grown-and-gone young adults will return periodically and want a lively game of volleyball or badminton. Old cronies can pitch horseshoes or play shuffleboard, or just enjoy each other's company on a porch swing.

■ Planning
The ideal play area does not develop haphazardly. It is designed and situated so it directs kid traffic away from a potential danger, such as a busy street, to the desired avenue of escape, such as a tree house. It is fashioned so it neither violates nor dominates the rest of the landscape.

The play area should allow room to roam without fear of unplanned encounters with obstacles. That's easy, of course, in a big yard. But even the smallest outdoor space can become an ideal play area with the right planning and equipment. After all, a single swing hung from a tree branch can provide hours of entertainment.

The ideal play area also should offer children and adults special places for private retreats (though, for children, it should be somewhere they can be seen).

■ Growth and play
Because children grow quickly and adult interests change as well, the ideal play area relies more on convertible and multifunction uses and fixtures than on permanent, unchangeable installations like tennis courts.

A good play area offers something for children in a range of ages or of one age for several years. When choosing a play structure, look for one with many possible uses; it will hold children's attention longer. Once swinging is passé, the kids can slide or play house on a platform.

▶ *This playhouse perched atop a raised deck provides kids with a place of their own, plus lots of fun. Climbing across the clatter bridge is as delightful as zipping down the slide. A sea of pea gravel eliminates wet grass and mud, and cushions falls.*

◀ *This redwood structure encircles a mature cypress tree with complete safety for both children and tree. In full view from patio and family room, the play equipment blends in with its surroundings without dominating the scene.*

◀ *Here, children can climb to their hearts' content, develop their motor skills and imaginations, and come in tired enough to be peaceful people. The swings were set wide to the side for safety.*

ASSESSING PLAY-AREA OPTIONS

Locate play areas where kids have plenty of open space to run and roughhouse, and far enough from the house so you're separated from the noise. Put play structures on a level surface.

Look up and around before you make a final decision. Keep high-flying activities away from power lines, balls away from the street, and tricycle riding areas away from driveways.

Don't put play areas near gardens you want to protect. Any planting behind home plate or first base will be trampled often. Here, the gardens are deep in right field.

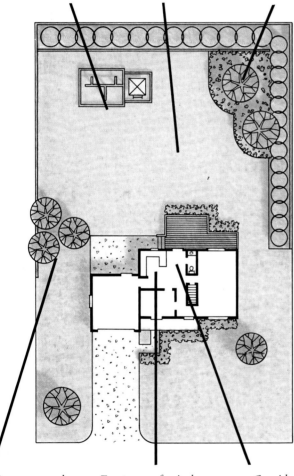

Overhanging trees and adventurous children can do each other possible damage. Plan for safety (see the top photo on page 216) or downplay the temptation with separation.

For peace of mind, position play areas within easy view from indoor rooms where you can watch your children while you work or rest, usually the kitchen or family room.

Consider easy access between the kids and the bathroom to allow for inevitable emergency runs. Make sure your path to play areas is unimpeded, too, for quick access if needed.

Location of play areas is important. They will be used more hours of the day and seasons of the year if they have some sun and some shade. A sense of seclusion and some wind protection also are important.

Few yards have as much space for play as could be desired, but games can be condensed. An area as small as 20 by 40 feet can work if you make a point not to plant a tree in the middle. You can set short pieces of tile or pipe in concrete in the ground and take down or put up poles or stakes as needed.

Concentrating plants around the edges of a yard will yield the most open play space. Be sure to surround play areas with expendable plants. If games are infrequent and space is at a premium, try putting tender plants in movable containers and planting only the most rugged ones in the ground.

Use tough grass such as tall fescue or St. Augustine where the neighborhood kids gather for football or baseball. Around play structures, a soft surface underfoot is best. This can be grass, though it will become spotted from wear and tear, feet will get wet, and mowing will be more difficult. If you use sand or mulches like pea gravel or tanbark, you may want to lay plastic underneath and make the mulch thick enough so weeds will not grow through.

As children grow older, you can emphasize to them how their strength and skill have outgrown the yard, and strongly suggest, even rule, that they must move on to the nearest park. Or you may turn the greensward into a swimming pool at that time.

■ Play structures

Design and build your own play structure, or assemble one using architect's plans or a kit. When selecting equipment, consider first the ages of your children and what will best help them develop muscular coordination, self-confidence, and creativity.

Locate play structures where they will be used and where adults can check on children often from indoor rooms. Passive supervision allows for more creative play yet fewer accidents for kids and greater peace of mind for parents.

Leave plenty of room for swing clearance and slide landing (see right). Check often for rough edges, splinters, or protruding pieces that could cut or scratch. All bolts should have smooth heads and covered ends. Firmly anchor the bases in concrete. Ask children to report any damages and involve them in frequent maintenance checks.

Check that swings, ladder rungs, and ropes are at usable heights. On many units, you can add additional features as children grow, thus keeping their interest and spreading your costs.

Equipment that is beyond little ones' capabilities should be safely out of their reach and is better out of their sight.

■ Sand castles

Sand provides great entertainment for kids of all ages, whether it's in a tractor tire, a sunken pit, or a veritable backyard beach. Provide good drainage under in-ground boxes by lining the bottom with gravel or flagstones.

A retaining edge can serve as a seat or a drying surface for sand pies—plus keep the bulk of the sand inside. Put the box far enough from the house so that the sand kids carry out of the box on their clothes has a chance to sift off. A cover is nice, especially if cats are around.

Sandboxes, which can occupy unused corners as long as they are in view from the house, are easily converted back to gardens when the time is right.

■ Private worlds

Hiding places are great for children of all ages. These can be as elaborate as tree houses and playhouses or as simple as a cubby under the deck or on the far side of a sheltering tree. Shrubs and trees, especially those with pendulous or weeping branches, are great for games of hide-and-seek. A pole tepee or little house covered with beans or flowering vines also can make an inexpensive playhouse.

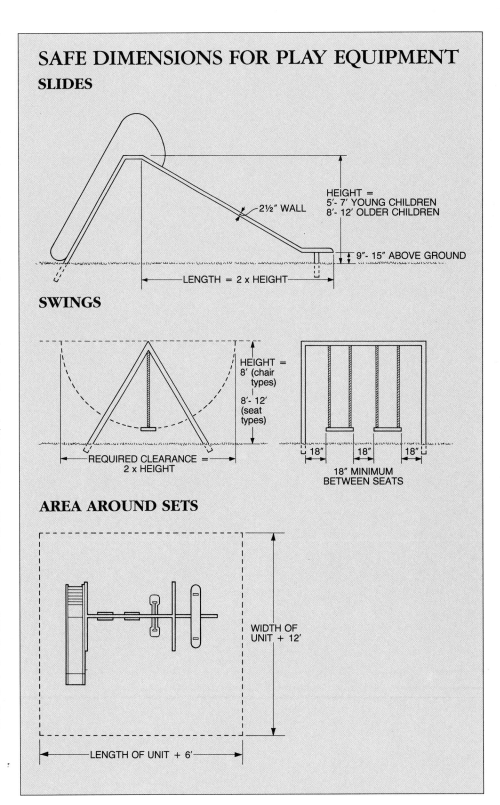

SAFE DIMENSIONS FOR PLAY EQUIPMENT

SLIDES

2½" WALL

HEIGHT =
5'- 7' YOUNG CHILDREN
8'- 12' OLDER CHILDREN

9"- 15" ABOVE GROUND

LENGTH = 2 x HEIGHT

SWINGS

HEIGHT =
8' (chair types)

8'- 12' (seat types)

REQUIRED CLEARANCE =
2 x HEIGHT

18" 18" 18"

18" MINIMUM
BETWEEN SEATS

AREA AROUND SETS

WIDTH OF
UNIT + 12'

LENGTH OF UNIT + 6'

Marigolds are among the many colorful, fragrant plants that delight people but repel various insects. The right plant in the right place can help make you more comfortable while you enjoy your landscape.

CHAPTER TEN

CONTROLLING INSECTS

Key to controlling the people-stinging pests and plant-eating bugs that can waste a landscape if their numbers grow too large is to accept that insects are a part of nature. If you appreciate and protect the good ones while working to outwit the undesirable ones, you'll preserve both peace of mind and an ecological balance.

Here, a combination of screened porch and open deck offers a choice for different moods, times of day, and seasons of the year. Screened rooms trade a bit of openness for a greater sense of seclusion.

Screened porches or outdoor rooms offer the ultimate in pest protection. They're ideal for dining and for sitting, especially at dusk when mosquitoes take to the air in search of victims.

Insects generally act as nature's cleanup crews, setting out to destroy weak and dying plants. Healthy plants—properly situated, watered, fed, and mulched—seldom are attacked.

ASSESSING INSECT-CONTROL SOLUTIONS

Many insects are great garden friends. Ladybugs and lacewings gobble up aphids and mealybugs. Ground, or carabid, beetles hide under stones and eat caterpillars and slugs. The hover fly, cousin to the sweat bee, is parasitic to many caterpillars and helps control gypsy moths. Dragonflies and damselflies dine on mosquitoes. Many other insects are harmless.

The few pesky bugs that have gained the group its nasty reputation can be separated into two classes: the ones that pester people and the vegetarians that prefer to eat our plants.

■ People pests
Although flesh-seeking bugs may outnumber us, and they may pack more punch per particle than we do, we still can outwit them.

Among the possibilities: Place your patio on a breezy hillside instead of a hollow. Shade the kitchen door. Plant herbs and shoo-fly around the deck and bee-attracting plants at a distance.

Locate service areas—trash cans and bright lights may attract insects—well away from outdoor living areas. Because a working compost pile draws fewer flies than a garbage can, compost your spoiled food instead of throwing it away. (See page 235 for more on composting.)

Clean animal pens often, working at the coolest, driest times available. Compost the wastes or spread them at a distance from the house.

Plant carefully so as not to block breezes that blow bugs away. Prune to let breezes in. Remove all sources of standing water that could offer breeding grounds for mosquitoes. Put fish in your ponds, empty the plastic wading pool, and fill tree hollows with sand.

You can fog or mist your yard with commercially available chemicals, but the relief will be temporary at best, and the chemicals may bump off friendly insects, too. Layers of clothing and possibly a shot of repellent are much preferred.

Scented coils and candles, and a variety of other products, also are available. Try to get a guarantee of satisfaction before buying.

■ Birds
Birds, because of their love for insect meals, can be among your greatest allies in the battle of the bug. If you encourage them to come to your yard with food, water, and nesting places, you can quickly and significantly best the average of only four birds per acre.

To provide the food birds need, plant berry-producing trees, shrubs, and vines; keep feeders well stocked; and grow certain annual and perennial flowers (calendula, coreopsis, grasses, and sunflower, among others). A birdbath or shallow saucer can fulfill the water needs. Just be sure to set the containers near enough to trees and shrubs so birds can quickly retreat when they sense approaching predators. And keep the containers clean and filled—even during the winter, if possible. For nesting sites, plant plenty of trees and shrubs. To attract some bird species, though, you'll need to install a birdhouse or two.

Check your library or a bookstore for specific advice on how to attract the birds that will help you the most.

Less delightful but almost as effective as a bird is a toad. Some toads eat as many as 15,000 insects a year. Provide a shallow container of water to encourage toads to stay.

■ Pest-chasing plants
Plant *Nicandra physalodes,* or shoo-fly plant, near your outdoor living area and you can reduce a fly population of hundreds to a swattable dozen. As a bonus, the plant produces little lavender flowers and forms five-sided paper-lantern seedpods. An annual that usually self-sows, shoo-fly grows as easily as its cousin, the tomato plant.

Sweet basil, pennyroyal, sassafras, garlic, mint, dill, horseradish, and rhubarb leaves, as well as nasturtium, marigold, and painted daisy, all are variously deterrent to different pests.

■ Blessed screens
One of the greatest of modern inventions is screening. Imagine not having it for windows and doors. To make an outdoor room as bug-

free as the indoors, screen in a porch or gazebo, or perhaps a walk-out patio that lies below a deck (see pages 230–231). Or, add an enclosed sun-room to your house (see pages 226–229).

You can screen in any existing porch by attaching the screening directly to the porch structure if it has vertical supports no more than 5 feet apart and enough of a knee wall for horizontal support.

Or you can frame the screening and then set it just outside the present structure. Your porch railing will not show quite as clearly from the street, but it still will add charm inside and hold pots and brief visitors.

To save money, screen only part of a larger porch or patio. If you do, you'll be able to enjoy both open outdoors and enclosed comfort.

■ Plant pests

Because healthy plants are far less likely to be damaged by bugs than weak ones, your first steps in controlling plant pests should be to improve your soil, mulch around plants, compost or bury dropped fruit, and control weeds. Supply plants with ample amounts of nutrients, water, and sunlight. And choose native plants suited to your conditions.

Select insect-resistant varieties of fruits, vegetables, and ornamentals. Where pests have been a problem, plant what they don't like. In years when beetles eat a bite of every green bean, they often leave the purple kinds whole.

Fool flower and vegetable pests with companion planting—setting chive or garlic among the roses, for example—and crop rotation.

Inspect your plants daily for predators; pick off the first few before they become a hundred. If you're squeamish, handpicking may at first seem repulsive; but that feeling will fade when you see how much more effective and less polluting it is than spraying. Wear a pair of gloves, if you like.

Keep your plantings diverse so you'll attract as many of the beneficial insects mentioned in the first paragraph on the opposite page as possible. Or, purchase them from garden catalogs. Once released in your yard, these bugs will quickly go to work.

■ When nature fails

Weather conditions and other uncontrollable situations sometimes disturb nature's balance and leave you with a burgeoning pest population that calls for drastic measures.

Zappers, traps, netting, and row covers are now available for mechanical insect control. Don't buy until you see—and hear—these in action, or get a guarantee.

Sometimes a strong mist or spray from the garden hose will dislodge and drown aphids.

Before you resort to stronger chemicals and possible poisons, see if soapy water—1 tablespoon dishwashing liquid per quart—can purge the infestation. Wash the soap off with clear water a day after the last treatment. Or, use the new insecticidal soaps.

Try a biological control; these are proving more useful as well as much safer than broad-spectrum chemicals. *Bacillus thuringiensis* (Bt)—in spray or dust form under trade names such as Dipel and Thuricide—causes a disease that kills caterpillars. *Bacillus popiliae* (milky spore disease) helps control Japanese beetle grubs. A disease called *Nosema locustae* controls grasshoppers; juvenile hormone analogues (JHAs) affect some flies, fleas, mosquitoes, scales, whiteflies, aphids, and mealybugs while remaining nontoxic to birds and animals. A new control called *neem* acts systemically—it's added to the soil and spreads through the plant—and may largely replace conventional insecticides for home use.

If you resort to chemical insecticides, choose the ones least toxic and most selective, and follow label directions to the letter. The chemicals will do less damage to beneficial insects if you use them in late afternoon or when the fewest bees are buzzing—after mowing the dandelions, not during the fruit-tree bloom.

CHOOSING AN ORGANIC OR CHEMICAL CONTROL

PEOPLE PESTS

Insect	Description and Trouble Signs	Control
Ants	Most ants are only pesky and a nuisance in food and cupboards. Tiny fire ants and large harvester ants make mounds in the yard. Their bites can hurt; can be serious to sensitive individuals.	Spread red pepper on shelves or counters; plant pennyroyal or tansy near doorways or strew leaves along ant runs. Buy ant traps or sprays for fire ants. Cover feet and legs.
Bees, wasps, hornets, bumblebees	These stinging insects—which take on many shapes—are beneficial, necessary for pollination, and non-threatening unless disturbed, stepped on accidentally, or blocked from entering their hive or nest. Study their habits and relax around them.	If one lands on you, just stand still until it flies away. Put bee-attracting plants far from outdoor living areas. Provide water in a birdbath so these bugs won't hover in thirst. Scrape stinger from sting, wash with soap, then apply ice and baking-soda paste.
Chiggers	So small they're almost invisible, these mites cling to grass, hay, and blackberry bushes. They attach themselves to animals and people. Bites aren't felt at the time, and they usually are not dangerous, but they can cause intense itching later.	Feed lawn with nitrogen. Treat lawn and shrubs once a month with 1 ounce of liquid dish detergent dissolved in 16 gallons of water. Avoid sitting on infested grass. Some repellents help some people (see gnats, below).
Fleas	Usually more bothersome to people's pets than people themselves, these insects are brown, flat, and wingless, with hard bodies and long, slender legs. They move by jumping. Sand fleas can infest an entire house.	To expel sand fleas, turn on heat briefly in summer, or apply oil of lavender. Scatter fresh or dried sprigs of pennyroyal or tansy. Use cocoa shells as bedding for pets. Spray area or bathe animals with solution of wormwood or cloves, or with alcohol. Use collars.
Flies	These pests need no description. They cling to screens and some enter each time the door opens. Although they seem to bite only in certain weather, they are always dirty and pesky, and can sometimes carry diseases.	Plant *Nicandra physalodes,* or shoo-fly, plant by doors, animal pens, and compost piles. Separate animal areas from entry areas as much as possible. Shade doors. Swat or use fly strips for mechanical control. Sprays are only temporarily effective.
Gnats, midges, blackflies, and other no-see-ums	Luckily, these tiny, mosquitolike flies are seasonal. While they are biting, apply a repellent before going out to garden. Try pure vanilla extract, certain bath oils, or mosquito spray.	If you're bitten by any bug, wash the site with soap and water and apply an antiseptic. Juice from broken aloe leaf relieves itching. Doses of aspirin or antihistamine reduce pain.
Mosquitoes	The mosquito has a round head, slender proboscis, long legs, and transparent wings. Unfortunately, its humming warning does not always precede the immediate piercing of its bite. Mosquitoes attack most often at dusk or in damp weather, and they can carry several severe diseases.	Remove or treat all standing water to prevent breeding. Attract birds, add fish to ponds, and welcome toads and lizards. Rub your skin with leaves or oil of citronella, pennyroyal, basil, castor beans, garlic, sassafras, or tansy, or with deterrents for gnats (see above). Treat bites with aloe. Thiamine or vitamin B_1 taken orally helps some people.
Ticks	Most ticks are small, round, and hard shelled creatures—not true insects—that bury their heads in the flesh, often in the scalp. Incidents are rare in most locales and usually are more frightening than harmful.	To release the hold, light a match, extinguish it, then press the hot tip against the insect body. Or apply a drop of alcohol or gasoline. To trap ticks, plant molasses grass near the edge of woodlands.

PLANT PESTS

Insect	Description and Trouble Signs	Control
Aphids	Aphids are small, soft-bodied, sap-sucking insects that can be black, green, red, or brown. They form colonies along buds and new growth, and can exude a sticky honeydew.	Use fingers, a strong spray from a hose, or soapy water to dislodge. Import predators like ladybugs or lacewings. Kill the ants that raise aphids for the honeydew. Plant nasturtium around infested plants.
Borers	The larvae of several borer species tunnel into trees, especially birch, dogwood, and fruit. A gummy substance marks their presence. Sometimes, sawdust comes from the holes. They can greatly weaken or even kill trees.	Let gum remain until you cut out or kill borers with knife or wire. Prune beneath swellings in roses. Wrap young trees with masking tape at the soil line; pull soil back in winter to give cold and birds access to the borers.
Caterpillars	Armyworms eat grass at the soil, leaving dead spots. Gypsy-moth larvae and tent caterpillars can quickly defoliate a branch or tree.	Keep lawn healthy. Spray at first sign with soapy water (see chinch bugs). Handpick or knock down from trees in evening. Use sticky band like Tanglefoot around trunk. Use Bt or carbaryl when desperate.
Chinch bugs	These tiny—1/3 inch at longest—black and white insects have red legs. They attack grasses in summer, causing patches of brown, dead lawn. To detect, press a bottomless can into the lawn and add water.	Keep the lawn well fed. Control thatch. At the first sign, spread gypsum or spray with 1 cup dish soap to 10 gallons of water. If they persist, treat lawn in June and August with Oftanol and replant bare spots.
Grubs	Grubs are thick, whitish beetle larvae that stretch up to 1½ inches long, though they're usually rolled into a C shape. Found underground, they kill grass in spring and fall. Worst damage may come from small animals that tear up the lawn to eat the grubs.	Water well, then apply diazinon or isofenphos as directed. Water thoroughly again. Do not allow runoff. Treat Japanese beetle grubs with *Bacillus popiliae,* milky spore disease.
Moles	Not an insect, but just as destructive, these small, burrowing rodents have very small eyes and ears and pointed noses. They eat earthworms, often raising a series of unsightly tunnels in lawns and undermining roots in flower and vegetable gardens.	Trapping is most effective. Castor beans will discourage moles but also are poisonous to children. Blend 2 ounces castor oil with 1 ounce detergent, then add equal volume of water. Apply 1 tablespoon mixed with 2 gallons of warm water around garden areas.
Slugs and snails	These fat, wormlike insects (snails have shells) come out at night to eat jagged holes in the leaves of flowers and vegetables, leaving a slimy trail behind.	Some gardeners now raise these for restaurants. To kill, handpick or place saucers of beer or poison bait nearby. With the latter, be sure to protect pets.
Spider mites	Almost invisible, these tiny bugs suck plant juices until leaves look tarnished or turn yellow or brown, then drop off. They like dry conditions. Look closely for webs.	Prevent with dormant oil spray. Spray severe infestations with water, soapy water, miticide, diazinon, or malathion. Avoid heavy feeding of plant. Ladybugs and lacewings will help.
Thrips	Thrips are barely visible black insects that hide among flower petals and suck juices, causing distorted buds that may not open, smaller flowers, and quicker fading. They prefer white and pastel flowers.	Cut and remove flowers at the first sign of infestation. Apply insecticidal soap, soapy water, strong water spray, or insecticide to the tops of plants like rose and gardenia.

ADDING SUN-ROOMS

Constructing a screened room can be as simple as fitting screen panels to an existing porch or as complex as adding an entire room to your home. Which route you choose depends in part, of course, on whether you already have a porch or protected patio. It also depends on whether you would like to use the room year-round or just during the warm months.

Photos here and on pages 228–229 take you through the steps involved in building an all-seasons sun-room from scratch. Pages 230–231 show how to screen in an existing porch for bug-free summer use.

■ The preliminaries

Unless you've had extensive construction experience, you'll probably want to hire a contractor to build all or part of a sun-room. And since any addition at the front, side, or back of your house will change its appearance, you may need an architect as well. You most certainly will be required to apply for a building permit and prove that your new room will satisfy setback and code stipulations.

As you plan your sun-room, pay special attention to how it will relate to the rest of your home, both in terms of appearance and convenience. Also think about how you will get into and out of the new room. For our addition, the old back door worked just fine. At your house, you may need to cut a new doorway or replace a window with a door.

■ Bundling up

When it comes time to insulate the floor, walls, and ceiling of your sun-room, aim to meet or exceed the R-factor norms for your region. Large expanses of north-, east-, or west-facing glass make a room chilly during winter.

A heating specialist can tell you whether your present heating plant has enough capacity to handle another room. If not, consider installing a wood-burning stove, through-the-wall furnace, or other independent heat source. That way, you can conserve energy during periods when you're not using your sun-room.

1 Our addition started with a series of concrete piers, fortified with lengths of ⅜-inch reinforcing rod. To guard against heaving, footings must extend to the frost line (check with local building authorities). The tops of the footings rise several inches above grade to protect the posts that will rest on the piers from moisture.

4 Because our new sun-room is large, a double 2x12 interceptor was positioned midway between the house and the porch's outer edge. Joists, supported by joist hangers, complete the floor structure.

2 Our builder fastened a 2x12 support ledger to the home's brick exterior wall. Long bolts extend completely through the wall at 2-foot intervals. The ledger also could have been attached with lead anchors and lag screws. The ledger is set high enough to allow a smooth transition from the new addition to the house.

3 Pressure-treated 4x4 posts rest atop the footings. Reinforcing rods that protrude from the piers slip into holes drilled into the bottoms of the posts, eliminating any need for post anchors. Doubled 2x12 beams are toenailed to the tops of the posts.

5 Vertical 2x6 plates fasten to the existing brick walls with lead anchors and lag screws. The lag screws are positioned so they enter mortar instead of brick. The plates provide wood surfaces to which the addition's end wall studs can be nailed.

6 Underlayment-grade plywood decking covers the floor joists. One wall features 2x6 stud construction. The two others consist of 6x6 posts notched to support 2x12 headers. The tall post at right will support the roof's ridge beam. Fiberboard sheathing is nailed to the stud wall.

(continued on page 228)

For basic information on working with wood, see pages 276–281. For working with concrete, see pages 282–287.

ADDING SUN-ROOMS *(continued)*

7 Because we wanted our sun-room to have exposed ceiling beams, the builder took special pains with post-beam connections. Notching members together takes more time than simply nailing or lag-bolting, but results in a neater appearance.

8 Doubled headers provide extra support for the heavy 2x10 rafters that were used for appearance' sake. Spacer blocks between the ends of headers and at intervals along their lengths make each two-header unit a full 5½ inches thick. A 2x6 plate on top of each pair of headers further ties them together.

12 After sheathing the roof and covering it with roofing paper, the builder trimmed its edges with redwood fascia boards. With this preliminary work done, the builder then shingled the roof.

13 To further thicken the posts, carpenters nailed a 2x6 to one side of each. To allow for maximum air flow and light, the design had the windows extend from post to post. Short 2x4 walls were built to support the long windows.

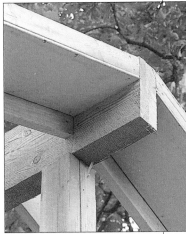

9 *To support the house end of the ridge beam, the builder chiseled a pocket opening into the brick, then inserted the beam. Rafter ends were cut at an angle determined by the roof's pitch. The rafters were toenailed to the ridge beam and the walls' top plates, again for appearance' sake. Metal hangers would have worked, too.*

10 *Our plan called for an asymmetric roofline, with one slope longer than the other. On the long side, the builder made bird's-mouth cuts so each rafter rests squarely on the top plate and still overhangs by several feet. On the short side, the rafters were cut so their ends are flush with the outer edge of the top plate.*

11 *To create a soffit for the extended rake at the ridge beam end, the builder made a framework of 2x4s. Exterior drywall sheathes the rake.*

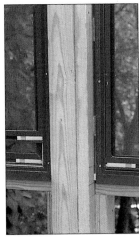

14 *Using spacers (made from thin sheets of plywood) and 1x4s, workers squared up and leveled each of the rough openings. The new framing provides a surface the windows can be screwed to.*

15 *The windows then were set in place, squared, and screwed to the 1x4s.*

16 *Siding was installed below the windows and elsewhere around the structure. After caulking around the windows, workers started putting up exterior trim. All that remained was to hang a door, insulate, and finish the interior.*

SCREENING IN A PORCH

If you already have an open porch—or a patio that's sheltered by a deck above—the best way to win the bug battle is to put up screens.

In some cases, you can simply staple screening to support members, then cover the staples with strips of lattice or a special molding—called *screen bead*—designed specifically for such uses.

Another way to put up screening is to construct framed screens and screw them in place, as we did for the under-deck patio shown on these two pages. Framed screen panels are more work, but they're easy to remove for repairs or wintertime storage.

■ Screening candidates

For the mesh, you can choose aluminum, plastic, fiberglass, copper, or bronze. Let appearance and upkeep be your guides. Aluminum is inconspicuous but subject to staining; plastic and fiberglass won't stain, but their filaments are thicker, which reduces visibility; copper and bronze must be coated with spar varnish periodically to prevent staining.

Buy 18/14 mesh or finer (the numbers refer to the quantity of horizontal and vertical wires per inch) in widths of 24, 36, 48, 60, or 72 inches. Aluminum screening comes in green, charcoal, or natural finish; plastic and fiberglass screening include these colors, plus a few more.

If your porch or under-deck patio has a southern or western exposure, consider using fiberglass solar screening. It filters out up to two-thirds of harsh sunlight, with a commensurate loss in visibility.

■ Screen door

Home centers and millwork dealers offer wooden screen doors in a variety of sizes and several different styles. Unlike a conventional door, a screen door doesn't need a jamb. You can hang it directly from a post with surface-mounted, spring-loaded hinges. Just nail a 2x4 header between posts on either side of the door. If there are no posts at the spot where you want your door, install a set with 4x4s or doubled-up 2x4s and hang the door from one of them.

1 *Sill boards go between the bottoms of the posts. Nail them to a wood floor. If the floor is concrete, rent a pneumatic nailer and drive concrete nails. Or, drill holes, insert lead anchors, and lag-screw the sill boards.*

4 *Nail the surrounds to posts, header boards, and sill boards. Check to be sure corners remain square; make adjustments, if necessary. Measure carefully and size screen frames to fit snugly into surrounds.*

2 Header boards fit between the tops of posts. A ½-inch plywood spacer between two 2x6s makes each header the same thickness as a 4x4 post. Secure the headers by nailing through perforated plates.

3 Build screen surrounds, using 2x4s for the frames and 2x2s for the stops. Miter the 2x4s; butt-join the 2x2s. Size the frames so they fit precisely between the posts, the sill boards, and the header boards.

5 For screen frames, butt-join 1x4s with galvanized screws and strap irons (see photo 6). Have a helper hold screening taut while you staple it to the frames. Trim off excess screening. Stops will conceal the staples.

6 Finally, drill pilot holes and screw screen frames to the stops. Screws make it easy to remove the panels for repairs or for storing during the winter months. A drill/driver speeds up this job.

For basic information on working with wood, see pages 276–281.

CHAPTER ELEVEN

SERVICE AREAS

Like a smash hit at the theater, an enchanting landscape relies as much on what happens behind the scenes as it does on the drama before your eyes. A yard's backstage—its service areas—should organize tools and trash, cars and compost, vegetable and cutting gardens, even places for pets, so that each gives its all to the performance.

What you don't see in this tranquil backyard setting are the support systems needed to keep it going and growing. Lattice-laced doors on an 18½-foot-long storage shed open wide for easy access to potting and gardening gear.

The shed also screens the outdoor living space from the neighboring driveway and backyard. A lattice trellis, covered with clematis, provides a gracious entry and visually connects the shed with the house.

Brick pavers set in sand wrap around the curvilinear on-grade deck, providing a transition to the yard and an easy surface for moving around wheeled equipment.

CREATING THE ULTIMATE STORAGE UNIT

Efficient, good-looking storage units don't just happen. In fact, planning one is an evolutionary process that should unfold over a period of time. First, you need to inventory the items you want to keep in it. Next, ask yourself what other jobs your storage unit might do. Then, decide where to locate it. Finally, come up with a design that will harmonize with your house and overall landscaping scheme.

■ Taking stock
Bicycles, trash cans, garden tools, patio furniture, the lawn mower, barbecue equipment, sports gear, ladders—the candidates for shelter in a storage unit could (and sometimes do) fill a two-car garage. As you list the things you'd like to get out from under foot, note the dimensions of each and add them all together for the approximate number of cubic feet your structure should contain.

Realize, too, that space alone is not enough. Organization is at least as important: Gardening, outdoor cooking and entertaining, and family activities go more smoothly when the items you need are properly stored so they're ready when you are.

Perhaps when your inventory is done, you'll realize that you don't need a full-blown storage unit at all. If so, look for tuck-away spaces under decks or benches, or in handy corners.

■ Think multipurpose
The best storage units do a lot more than just hold things. They also solve other problems, such as creating privacy or providing a protected place to nurture seedlings. The examples shown at right and on the opposite page are five cases in point.

Your shed can be freestanding or attached to a house, garage, carport, or other outbuilding. It should be sited and styled so it's not only convenient and accessibile, but also compatible with its surroundings. Keep the structure in scale with your house and yard, and develop a design that complements rather than competes with the architectural styling of your home.

▶ *Here, garbage cans hide behind a lacy, lattice-topped fence. Latched doors open for deposits and collections. The fence continues on to screen a 12x30-foot side-yard deck.*

◀ *Three posts and an overhead sunshade turned a seldom-used patio into an open-air potting shed. Tilted garbage cans under the workbench hold potting mixture, vermiculite, and sand.*

▶ *This streetside structure houses two big garbage cans, with space left over for lawn equipment. It also doubles as a privacy screen, topped with potted annuals and perennials. The planter in the foreground helps solve a drainage problem.*

▲ If your home has deep eaves, consider hanging a cupboard from them. This one holds all sorts of things up off the ground, away from possible water damage. Matching siding and paint make the unit look like part of the house.

◄ Two facing sheds, each approximately 4x8 feet, stand at the rear of a freestanding deck. A ramp between the sheds makes it easy to wheel heavy equipment in and out of storage.

BUILDING SHEDS

Constructing a shed is much like building a very small house. You sink support posts into concrete footings, build a platform floor, put up wall studs and rafters, then close it all in with siding and roofing. Once the concrete has cured, the carpentry can be accomplished in a weekend or two, depending on your level of skill and the complexity of the structure you've chosen to tackle.

For tools you'll need a hammer, portable circular saw, hand- or jigsaw, drill/driver, combination square, and—last but far from least— a level. Use this often to assure that everything comes out perfectly level and plumb.

■ Structural alternatives
The 2x4-stud system shown here works for just about any design, but there are other shapes a shed can take, as well as other ways a shed can *take* shape. One of the simplest examples of both is the A-frame. Because its roof and walls are one and the same, you need only put up a series of triangular rafters, plus stud walls front and back. Unfortunately, with an A-frame, the roof's slope limits the height of items that can be stored at the sides.

Or, consider using posts and beams instead of studs and plates. Post-and-beam construction uses fewer but thicker vertical members. For the basics of post-and-beam construction, see pages 100–103, 172–179, and 226–229.

■ Bird's-mouth cuts
Rafters for a shed roof must be notched at or near their down-slope ends so they'll fit neatly atop the wall's top plate, as shown in the photo opposite, far right. To mark these cuts, known as *bird's-mouths,* have a helper hold one rafter against the end of the wall, overlapping it by 1½ inches. Draw a vertical line for the heel of the cut and a horizontal line to the forward edge. Cut this bird's-mouth and use it as a template for the others. You might find it easiest to cut bird's-mouths with a hand- or jigsaw.

1 *Set posts (see pages 58–60 and 74–75) and nail 2x6 band joists to them. Space intermediate joists according to the span table on page 185. Install these with joist hangers, then top the framework with ¾-inch plywood.*

4 *Nail ¾-inch plywood sheathing to the rafters. For the walls, we used textured, vertical-groove plywood siding. You could substitute clapboard or other materials that match or coordinate with your home's exterior.*

2 For short walls, you'll find it easiest to prefabricate the framing on a patio, driveway, or other flat surface. Raise completed wall sections into place, then nail them to the band joists and each other.

3 Double up studs at sides of door openings and fit 2x6 headers between them as shown. Cut rafters to length, then cut bird's-mouths (see detail at right and explanation opposite). Toenail the rafters to plates top and bottom.

Bird's-mouth cuts seat rafters squarely against the wall plate at the roof's lower edge. Mark and cut these as outlined opposite. For design reasons, you might also want to make cuts at the upper ends, but these aren't required.

5 You also have a broad choice of roofing materials. Nail on roofing paper, trim roof edges with fascia boards, and install metal drip edging before roofing your new shed.

6 Construct the door with frame boards and siding. For rigidity, include a gate-style cross brace (see page 85). Make the door ½ inch smaller than the opening. Screw hinges to the door and support it at the bottom with shims, then secure the hinges to the shed.

For basic information on working with wood, see pages 276–281. For working with concrete, see pages 282–287.

CREATING THE ULTIMATE AREA FOR VEHICLES

Screen parking areas with low fences and plants. For security reasons, don't completely obscure them—and leave a clear line of sight from the car to the door you will enter at night.

A different surface material can give a driveway a whole new look. Consider surfaces that will better relate the drive to your home, or use the same material that covers a backyard patio.

Let your overall landscaping style determine the shape of a drive and connecting paths. Use curved edges with a loose, informal scheme, straight lines for a formal, symmetrical look.

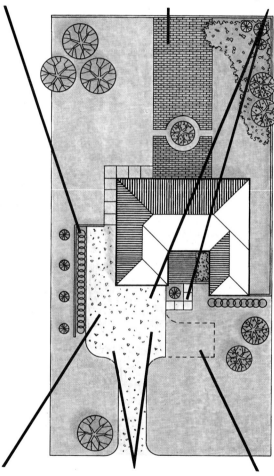

Tired of playing musical cars? Provide extra parking for visitors and deliveries. Make auxiliary parking easily accessible, but take care that it doesn't overpower your home and yard.

Drive and parking areas should be 10 to 12 feet wide, so drivers and passengers step out onto pavement, not grass or ground cover. If the drive also serves as a walkway, add 2 more feet.

If extra off-street parking is sited here, instead of alongside the garage, the space also can serve as a turnaround. Again, screen cars with plants or fencing.

At most homes, the driveway and perhaps an additional parking area are already well-ensconced parts of the landscape. Removing them and paving a different route from street to garage are expensive and often impossible propositions. None of this is to say, however, that you can't add to your driveway, resurface it with a more pleasing material, or reshape its edges.

Captions on the site plan at left identify the main points to consider when thinking about driveway and parking-area changes. Use these to prepare a traffic report about the situation at your house, and as a source of ideas for improvements that might be needed.

■ Improving an existing drive

Start with the width of your drive. Builders typically stick to absolute minimums of 6 to 8 feet, rather than the 10 to 12 feet recommended at left. If your drive doesn't measure up, you needn't widen it along the entire length, just the points at which people will be alighting.

Also, there's no rule that says you must match the driveway's current surface when you widen it. Instead, why not add a distinctive walk area to one or both sides of your driveway? Pages 122–123 show how and page 130 presents walkway material options.

Next, consider surfacing your entire driveway with a different material, especially if your drive is due for a resurfacing anyway. Loose fill could give way to concrete, perhaps tinted to pick up a hue from your home's exterior or textured to improve traction. See page 234 for a comparison of driveway surfacing materials.

Or maybe all your drive needs is a new edge treatment. Page 245 shows how to pour concrete curbing. Pages 128–129 and page 131 tell about other edging materials.

■ Building a new drive

If the only answer to your family's traffic jam is an entirely new driveway, parking area, or both, prepare yourself for a big, costly, but rewarding project. Pages 242–245 take you through the process of pouring a new concrete driveway.

◄ *Throwing a curve on this drive provided space for the owners to turn around as they backed out of the garage, a convenience if you have a long driveway or live on a busy street. The curve also softens the garage's pyramid shape and arcs gracefully to the front entryway.*

BUILDING DRIVEWAYS AND PARKING AREAS

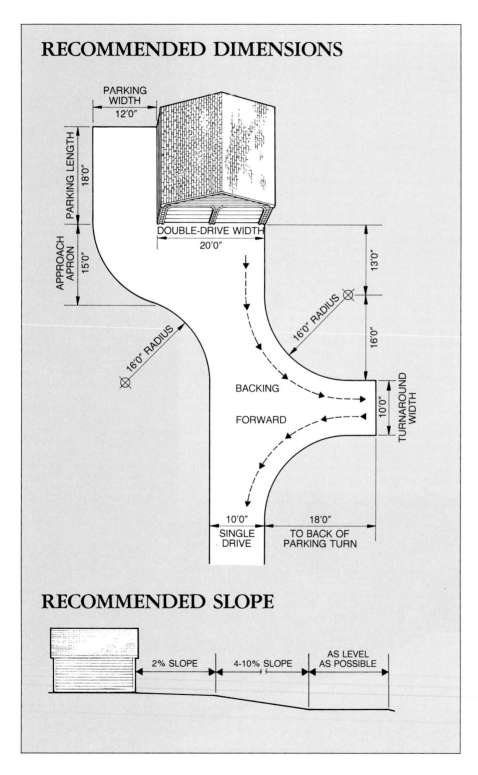

RECOMMENDED DIMENSIONS

PARKING WIDTH 12'0"

PARKING LENGTH 18'0"

APPROACH APRON 15'0"

DOUBLE-DRIVE WIDTH 20'0"

16'0" RADIUS

16'0" RADIUS

16'0" RADIUS

13'0"

16'0"

BACKING

FORWARD

TURNAROUND WIDTH 10'0"

10'0" SINGLE DRIVE

18'0" TO BACK OF PARKING TURN

RECOMMENDED SLOPE

2% SLOPE   4-10% SLOPE   AS LEVEL AS POSSIBLE

Think long and hard before deciding to construct your own driveway. Even if you don't need to move much earth, mixing, pouring, screeding, floating, and troweling that much concrete is backbreaking labor—and it can drag on for weekend after weekend while your car or cars sit out on the street.

This doesn't mean that you can't save a considerable amount of money by laying out your own drive and even building the forms for it. Here and on the three pages that follow we take you step by step through the entire process—useful information, regardless of whether you do the work or a contractor does.

■ Laying out
Consult the illustration at left for the dimensions you need to know. As noted on page 240, 10 feet is the minimum recommended width for a single-car driveway; 12 feet is better. Make the radius of any curves 16 feet, except those where the drive meets with the street. These can have a 15-foot minimum radius.

The maximum grade for a drive should not exceed 1¾ inches per foot. Any more than that and cars will bottom out on humps or drag at street level.

Also, for proper drainage, the drive must slope away from the garage, carport, or house at a rate of about ¼ inch per foot. If the terrain is flatter than this, provide your drive with a crown, as illustrated on page 245. A garage situated below street level requires a concave, gutter center and a large drain directly in front of the garage door.

■ Getting started
If the ground on which you'll place the driveway is firm and has good drainage, don't disturb the soil. Just skim off all vegetation, set the forms, lay down a bed of gravel, top with reinforcing mesh, then pour the concrete.

If the earth is not solid, you'll have to add a base—from 4 to 6 inches thick—depending on soil conditions and code requirements.

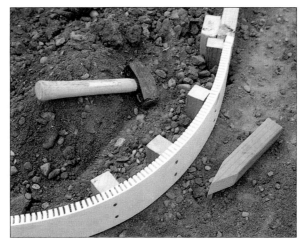

1 *Lay out the site as explained on pages 58–59. Refer, too, to the steps for pouring a concrete patio on pages 158–161. Excavate where necessary. Put up 2x4 form boards, braced from behind with stakes. Nail through boards into stakes, or hammer doubleheaded nails through the stakes into the boards.*

2 *Build curved forms with ¼-inch plywood or hardboard, or special bender board. To determine the correct radius, use a stake and string like a compass. Mark the curve with lime or spray paint. All stakes must be driven flush with the tops of forms so that the wet concrete can be leveled.*

3 *Stake every 3 to 4 feet. Every 6 to 8 feet, brace forms with outriggers like the one at upper left. Pour a gravel base. Here we just needed to compact the existing loose-fill drive.*

4 *Place a length of expansion strip between the garage slab and the new pour. If you need a drain, now is the time to run piping for it. The apron here must slope ¼ inch per foot away from the garage. Also use expansion strip at the street or any place new concrete abuts old.*

(continued on page 244)

For basic information on working with concrete, see pages 282–287.

BUILDING DRIVEWAYS AND PARKING AREAS *(continued)*

5 *Reinforce a driveway with 6x6 mesh, not the 4x4 material used for patios. Unroll the mesh. Use wire cutters to shape it around curves. Protect your hands with heavy work gloves throughout a concrete project.*

6 *Divide the forms so you can pour modules of 8 to 10 feet. This makes the job much easier and the drive much stronger. After one module sets up, replace the divider with an expansion strip and pour the next.*

8 *Use a wooden or darby float and a bull float to bring water to the surface. Once the bleed water disappears, go over the concrete surface with metal finishing floats. Afterward, apply any special textural effect you might have in mind (see pages 162–163).*

9 *Dampen the finished concrete with spray from a hose, then cover it with polyethylene so water evaporates slowly. Slow evaporation creates a strong bond. Plan to pour several modules a weekend until the project is completed.*

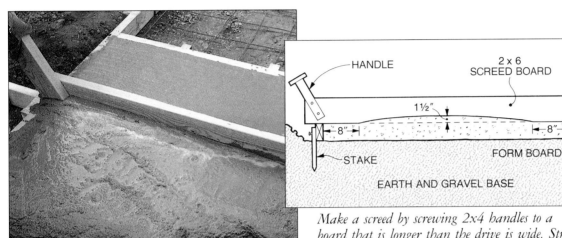

Labels within diagram:
HANDLE
2 x 6 SCREED BOARD
1½"
8"
8"
STAKE
FORM BOARD
EARTH AND GRAVEL BASE

Make a screed by screwing 2x4 handles to a board that is longer than the drive is wide. Strike off a flat drive with a straight 2x6 screed, as shown at left. To give the surface a crown, notch the 2x6 as shown above. For a concave, gutter center, use a 2x8 and invert the curve.

7 Pour concrete, then strike it off with a two-person screed, pulling the screed along the tops of the forms. The screed can shape a flat, crowned, or concave surface, as discussed and shown at right. Remember to lift the mesh midway into the concrete's thickness as you pour.

POURING A CURB

To pour a rounded curb along with the rest of the driveway, construct curb-height forms, then drive rerods into the ground where the curb will be. The tops of the rerods should be slightly lower than the tops of the forms. Pour concrete, wait until it's stiff and self-supporting, then strike off with a notched screed.

If you'd like to throw a few curbs at your driveway, try one of several methods.

First, you can form and pour integral curbing: rounded as shown at left or square as shown on page 129. (Rounded curbing is kinder to car tires and wheels.)

You also can build curbing on top of an existing drive. Just drill holes in the drive, insert lengths of rerod, build the forms, and pour the concrete. The rerods tie the new curb to the drive.

Adding curbing alongside an existing drive is a much more difficult proposition, because curbs that don't rest on top of a slab must have footings that reach below the frost line. Slabs spread their weight over a broad area and aren't affected by frost heaving. Separate curbs are, in essence, walls, which must rest on footings to ward off frost damage.

CREATING THE ULTIMATE KENNEL

If your dog has taken over your home and yard, build him or her a personal kennel that includes a fenced-in run for playful romping and a cozy house for shelter from the elements.

■ Kennel basics

Situate your kennel within barking distance of outdoor living areas, so your dog can keep in touch with family activities. Don't, however, choose a spot where he or she might annoy you while you sleep or neighbors anytime.

Try, too, to find a location that receives some sun and some shade, with good ventilation and good drainage.

The size of your kennel depends partly on the available space in your yard and partly on your dog's size and exercise needs. A 6-foot minimum width for the run is generally recommended. Make the enclosure at least 5 feet high, of a material that's not easily clawed to pieces or tunneled under.

For the house, you can buy a ready-made version, as the owners of the kennel shown at right did, or build your own, as we show on pages 250–251. Just be sure that the house is only slightly larger than the animal that will occupy it: A snug doghouse conserves body heat—and pets seem to feel more secure in one. Site a doghouse with its opening away from prevailing winds.

■ Other considerations

As you plan your kennel, consider incorporating these amenities.

■ A hose bibb in or near the kennel not only provides drinking water, but also simplifies cleanup.

■ For the kennel's surface, choose a material that's easy to clean and kind to tender paws. The example at right features pea gravel; the one we built on pages 248–251 uses concrete.

■ A storage cabinet for dog food, grooming aids, and other pet needs saves trips from doghouse to your house. (To learn about building storage units, see pages 236–239.)

▶ *Antique-iron fence panels strung between lodgepoles enclose this kennel, which a basset hound and two golden retrievers call home. More lodgepoles support a pitched, wood-shingled roof that shields their houses from the sun and the rain.*

BUILDING KENNELS

If you live in a northern climate, check with a veterinarian about your breed of dog's tolerance for cold nights. You might be surprised to learn that many breeds can safely and comfortably endure temperatures to well below freezing—provided the dog is properly sheltered from the elements. Insulate the walls, floor, and roof of a doghouse and your pooch may never need to spend the night in the basement or garage, regardless of the weather.

We insulated the house that takes shape on pages 250–251 with blankets of R-11 fiberglass. Half-inch particleboard sheathing on the interior walls and lap siding on the exterior add several more points to the overall R-value.

Our doghouse sits at one end of a rectangular concrete pad. Chain link fencing at the sides and a gate at the other end complete the enclosure.

■ Chain link

Chain link fencing enables you to close in a dog run in a matter of hours. You simply drive galvanized posts into the ground, secure them with concrete (you'll have to let the concrete cure) or special underground anchors, bolt on rails, then stretch mesh between the posts.

The job requires a few specialized tools: *fence pliers, cutters* for the mesh, a *stretcher bar* that holds the mesh while you pull it taut, and a pair of *cable jacks* to do the pulling. Many fencing dealers rent this equipment.

A dealer also can help you work up a list of the components required for the installation you have in mind. *Terminal posts* anchor the ends, corners, and gates. Slimmer *line posts,* spaced at intervals of no more than 10 feet, go in between. A variety of special fittings attach rails and mesh to the posts.

Galvanized chain link fencing is rustproof, petproof, and lasts for decades. If you don't like the plain-pipe color of galvanized fencing, you also can buy mesh and posts with a white or dark green vinyl coating.

1 Lay out the site (see pages 58–59), build forms for the slab (see pages 158–159), then pound posts into the ground. Plumb the posts, then temporarily wire them to the forms. Sink posts 24 to 30 inches.

4 Strike off and float the concrete (see pages 160–161). Round off edges with an edging trowel. Tool a control joint every 6 feet or so. To improve traction, texture the surface, as explained on pages 162–163. After the concrete cures, remove the forms.

2 *Prepare a base for the concrete with gravel and reinforcing mesh, as explained on page 160. If your dog run will have a drain, install it now. Otherwise, slope the forms ¼ inch per foot so water will run off the slab.*

3 *Pour the concrete, working it with a hoe or shovel to release entrapped air bubbles. After you've filled the form to half its depth, lift the reinforcing mesh to the surface with the tines of a rake, then pour the remainder of the concrete.*

5 *Attach rails to the posts with clamp fittings. Some chain link fences have only top rails, but a dog run should be equipped with rails at the bottom, too. Otherwise, a dog could attempt to escape by pushing against the mesh and possibly injure itself.*

6 *To hang a gate, clamp hinge pins to one post and set the gate in place. Gates come preassembled, in a variety of sizes. For extra security, you might want to install a latch that has a hasp for a padlock.*

(continued on page 250)

For basic information on working with concrete, see pages 282–287. For working with wood, see pages 276–281.

BUILDING KENNELS *(continued)*

7 Slip a tension bar through the mesh and clamp it to a terminal post. Then unroll the mesh, snug it up with rented cable jacks and a stretcher bar, and attach it to the terminal post at the other end of the run. Finally, clamp mesh to the rails and line posts.

8 We found it easiest to cut 2x4s and pre-assemble the doghouse's stud walls on a driveway, then raise the sections into place. This eliminates any need for toenailing the studs to the top and bottom plates.

11 Insulate the walls, then nail particleboard to them and the floor. Preassemble the back wall—including insulation and particleboard—and nail it into place.

12 Notch and nail rafters (see pages 238–239). Sheath the roof with ½-inch exterior-grade plywood. Short 2x4s provide nailers for the plywood and fascia boards.

9 *Fasten the front and one sidewall section to the slab using masonry nails. Shoot the nails with a rented gun or pneumatic nailer. Wear goggles to protect your eyes. Note that the corner has an extra 2x4 to provide a nailer for the interior walls.*

10 *Frame and insulate the floor. Because the walls will hold the floor in place, you needn't nail it to the concrete. Next, put up the other sidewall. But leave the back open so you'll have access to finish the interior walls. Wear gloves when working with fiberglass.*

13 *Finish the exterior walls with clapboard or plywood siding. A spacer like the one shown here helps you keep the laps uniform without a lot of measuring.*

14 *Nail shingles to the roof, then trim them. Hang a pet flap at the entry. Furnish the kennel with food and water dishes and an old blanket. Your dog will provide his or her own housewarming.*

Container plants and flowers in beds need more constant but less strenuous care than other landscape plants. Check pots daily for moistness. Beds need an inch of rain a week. Cut or pick dead flowers every day or so.

Wood structures will last longer if treated with stain and swept frequently. Occasional repairs are a given, as is eventual rebuilding, usually after a number of years of enjoyment.

Shrubs and trees, properly chosen for size and place, need only a bit of pruning. Vines need trimming more often. All drop leaves to renew your mulch and compost. Water trees deeply, especially young ones.

Because lawn maintenance takes more time than any other landscape chore (in times of rain, lawns sometimes need twice-weekly mowing), this yard makes generous use of paving, decks, ground covers, and mulch.

CHAPTER TWELVE

MAINTAINING YOUR LANDSCAPE

Y ou've designed your landscape; you've built and planted it. Now it's time to take care of your creation. Fortunately, with careful planning, you can shape a landscape that matches your ability and desire to maintain it. For the most part, you can schedule and pace the work to fit your life-style. And, if nothing else, this outdoor work gives you a great excuse for skipping other work that isn't nearly as pleasant.

OUTDOOR TASKS MONTH BY MONTH

COLD-WINTER CLIMATES

Month	Tasks	
January–February	Enjoy indoor gardening and rest. Read nursery catalogs. Order seeds and plants. Start slow growers like geranium, delphinium, and pansy indoors. Check tubers of stored dahlias; if too dry, sprinkle with	water. Inspect all stored bulbs, corms, and tubers, and cut off any decayed parts. Sweep snow off evergreens before it has a chance to break branches. Use deicing salt sparingly.
March	Begin pruning roses and fruit; feed all. Prune early-flowering shrubs only after bloom. Plant bare-root woody plants. Spray fruit trees with dormant oil when temperature exceeds 40 degrees and before	they leaf out. Remove rose cones when forsythia blooms; remove mounded soil gradually. Take leaves from beds in stages on dark days. Plant grass and hardy annuals outdoors. Check structures for damage.
April	Clean up. Spread compost around trees and shrubs. Pull mulch back from the crowns of perennials. Begin transplanting indoor seedlings outside; harden them off first with several short days outdoors.	Watch seedlings carefully for wilting; protect from wind. Start mowing when grass reaches 2½ inches. Spread preemergence herbicide to control crabgrass. Divide late-blooming perennials.
May	Plant tender bulbs. Water new trees and shrubs deeply. Sprinkle seedbeds to keep surface soil moist. Check the date of your area's last expected frost;	begin planting tender plants, seeds, and bulbs accordingly. Remove deadheads from spring bulbs; let foliage die down naturally. Stake plants early.
June	Water as needed. Feed roses. Remove spent roses by cutting back to a five-leaflet leaf. Spread and deepen mulch. Sweep decks and patios often. Check container plants daily for moistness. Pinch back	mum, petunia, and most annuals for low bushy growth. Break pine candles in half; prune other evergreens back to desired size. Trim clipped deciduous hedges before growth hardens.
July	Divide iris if overcrowded. Dig with fork. Trim decayed or corky ends; trim foliage to fan shape. Replant with rhizome near or on the surface and roots well buried. Bury sections of branches of low-	growing shrubs and vines so they can form roots for new plants. Harvest bush fruits daily. Check pool every few days and after every rain for chemical balance. Set mower blade higher in dry weather.
August	Move chrysanthemum plants to center stage as they begin to flower. Shear deadheads and feed annuals. Feed roses before mid-month so you won't	encourage late, winter-tender growth. Potted trees and shrubs can be planted anytime, but the longer they settle before winter, the better.
September	This is the best time for seeding or repairing lawns. Combine post- and preemergence herbicide. Plant trees and shrubs in mild climates. Divide early-blooming perennials. Take cuttings for winter	houseplants. Gather and compost all fallen fruits and nuts. Plant daffodils. Check structures again. Bring in houseplants before frost. Have covers ready to protect tender blooms from early frost.
October	Dig and store tender bulbs. Rake leaves; compost or use as mulch. Bag some leaves for insulation around foundations. Plant spring bulbs. Add a pinch of	bonemeal to every hole. Prepare pools and ponds for winter by lowering water level, adding floating logs, and covering. Mulch perennials.
November–December	Water plants well before freeze. Mulch to prevent freezing and thawing. Mound up soil around base of roses even under cones. Clean and oil tools. Feed	birds and provide water. Spray evergreens, Christmas trees, and treasured plants with antitranspirant spray. Save wood ashes to add to soil next spring.

WARM-WINTER CLIMATES

Month	Tasks
January–February	Place catalog orders. Prune roses and fruit trees; move woody plants while dormant. Seed cool-weather annuals like alyssum, stock, sweet pea, and larkspur outdoors; set out seedlings of pansy, petunia, snapdragon, and calendula. Spray full-strength dormant oil on fruit and deciduous trees; use half-strength spray on broad-leaved evergreens. Get lawn furniture and tools ready.
March	Plant tender bulbs and annuals outdoors when trees leaf out. Pick old blooms; feed blooming plants. Divide fall-blooming perennials. Plant seeds of astilbe, delphinium, hollyhock, and other biennials or perennials indoors. Feed lawn; mow grass when it's above 2½ inches. Check structures for damage.
April	Plant rest of tender plants after danger of frost passes. Feed lawn; aerate it anytime. Pinch mums until midsummer to keep bushy. Also pinch most annuals. Finish feeding or give booster to all plants. Spread mulch. Prune spring-flowering shrubs after bloom. Shorten pine candles; prune other evergreens just before growth starts. Remove diseased plants. Thin crowded fruit.
May	Sow seed, lay sod, or plant plugs of warm-season grasses now through summer. Keep watered until settled. Plant heat-resistant annuals like vinca, portulaca, celosia, and cosmos; use impatiens and coleus for shady spots. Start oleander from cuttings of mature wood. Stake large plants.
June	Prune and thin spring-blooming shrubs. Transplant when rainy season starts. Watch for insects; wash or pick them off plants before they can multiply. Use fungicide where diseases usually are a problem, especially on roses. Expose graft junctions of roses. Mow lawn as needed; dethatch now for fast recovery; treat chinch bugs. Continue to water plants as needed, especially newly set trees and shrubs.
July	Water and work outdoors in early morning or evening. Check pool chemicals every few days and after every rain. Sweep deck and patio often. Check evergreens for red spider and bagworm. For spiders, spray with miticide twice at two-week intervals. Plant evergreens toward end of summer.
August	Layer or take cuttings from plants during rainy season. Feed roses again. Renew mulches. Start pansies and other cool-weather annuals indoors for transplanting outside after summer heat. Move mums into empty spots for fall bloom. Now through late fall, cut back selectively the new buds along the branch sides of firs and spruces. Give last trim to deciduous hedges; trim evergreen hedges.
September	Plant sweet pea in deeply worked soil in sunny spot. Sow in trench 4 inches deep. Cover with 2 inches of soil. As plants grow, mound soil around roots and train tops up a fence. Sow winter-blooming plants in Sunbelt. Plant new trees and shrubs and spring bulbs. Make major lawn repairs; feed and lime old lawns.
October	Plant anemone and ranunculus tubers with the claws down. Plant biennials and spring-flowering bulbs. Gather and compost or bag leaves. Wrap young trees. Protect trunks from rabbits with loose wire wraps. Pull mulch back about 4 inches from trunks to discourage mice. Continue to mow so grass won't go into winter too long. Prepare pools and ponds for winter.
November–December	Mulch perennials for winter. Use herbicide for winter weeds when lawn is dormant. Update your landscape plan for any needed changes. Check structures again. Clean and oil tools. Dig and store tender bulbs before frost. Keep camellias moist to prevent bud drop. Be ready with frost protection to save plants of borderline hardiness. Water plants well and mulch before freeze.

MAINTAINING LAWNS

The secret to a successful lawn is constant and consistent care. If you make the work a pleasant habit instead of a dreaded chore, the right work will get done easily at the right time.

■ Water

Water deeply and thoroughly, 1 inch a week, or not at all. Dig down to be sure you are soaking 6 to 12 inches of soil. Sandy soils need less water more often. The more humus you have in your soil, the more it will soak up and retain water. A bluish tint, loss of resiliency so footprints show, and slower growth all indicate thirst. But even when grasses are allowed to go dormant for a whole summer, they usually green up quickly once rains return.

■ Feeding

Proper applications of fertilizer make grass plants strong and healthy so they can withstand drought and traffic and crowd out weeds. In the spring, use a fertilizer with a 2:1:1 ratio of nitrogen to phosphorus and potash. In fall, use a fertilizer with a 1:2:2 ratio for healthy root growth during winter. Apply about 4 pounds per 1,000 square feet. Slow-release fertilizer is the best form.

■ Weed and pest control

Thriving grass is the best control for weeds and pests. If problems do appear, begin treatment immediately. Check with your extension office for advice on effective and safe solutions.

MOWING YOUR GRASS

▶ *Mow the grass diagonally, alternating directions each time. This prevents a striped look and assures that grass blades are cut more sharply and evenly. Cut higher in a dry summer to conserve water and crowd out crabgrass. In the shade, cut grass higher or less often.*

▶ *Because grass naturally grows green on top and turns brown near its base, try to mow it often enough so that you cut only the top third of the blades. This encourages low, thick green growth and also discourages weeds.*

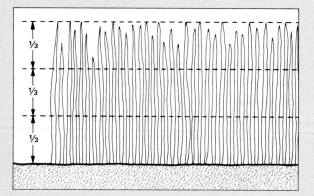

Mowing is a critical part of lawn care and yard neatness. Match your schedule to the growth rate of your grass: perhaps every five days in a wet season, every 10 to 14 days during dry times.

Cut grass to the ideal height specified for the kind. For bluegrasses, ryegrasses, and fescues, that's usually about 2 inches during active growth, 3 inches otherwise. Bent, Bermuda, and zoysia grasses can go as low as ¾ to 1¼ inches. Mow tall fescues, St. Augustine grasses, and bahia grass higher, from 3 to 3½ inches.

Get a mower you can push, turn, and change blade heights on easily. Sharpen blades monthly, more often if you hit stones or sticks. Dull blades wound and tear grass.

As long as you mow often enough, clippings can stay on the lawn. Short pieces will settle among new growth, decompose quickly, and add nutrients and humus to the soil.

Edging and trimming are easy with mowing strips and power equipment. Be careful not to damage tree bark.

■ Leveling

Level your lawn wherever freezing and thawing, worm activity, or planting changes like tree removal leave you with humps or dips that interfere with mowing.

Raise low spots by spreading a weedless mix of soil or sand and peat right on top of the grass, but no more than ¼ inch at a time. Smooth the soil, then repeat twice a year until level. For deeper hollows, slice and roll back the existing sod. Fill the depression with clean, rich soil. Smooth and tamp it firmly, then spread the sod back in place. Top-dress with ¼ inch of soil or peat; water deeply.

Remove humps by taking out wedges of turf 6 inches deep. Repeat at 10-inch intervals over the entire mound. Soak, roll, and repeat spring and fall until the hump disappears.

■ Bare spots

Reseed bare spots in early fall or spring. At other times, use sod or plugs.

To seed, prepare the soil by raking away debris and getting rid of weeds. If you use a herbicide, wait as directed before proceeding. Loosen the soil, then add humus and a light application of balanced fertilizer. Rake soil smooth, spread good seed, tamp down, and keep soil moist until seed germinates. See pages 296–297 for details on starting a new lawn.

▲ *To seed a bare spot, loosen soil 4 to 6 inches deep, then add humus and fertilizer. Rake smooth. Spread seed, tamp it down, and keep the soil moist with frequent sprinklings several times a day.*

▶ *Spread lawn fertilizer at least once in spring and again in fall. A hand-held spreader like this is fine for small areas. For larger yards, rent or buy a push spreader. Spread half while walking one direction, the other half in a second pass at right angles. Or use soluble food and a hose sprayer.*

▲ *If the thatch in your lawn gets too thick to let water and new growth through, use a heavy rake or rent a power rake. Or use thatch-removing sprays.*

For basic information on plants and planting, see pages 292–299.

MINIMIZING LAWN MAINTENANCE

Narrow side yards and strips near house or walk are hard to mow. These areas often are in shadow so grass does not grow well. Paving or mulch here is neater and easier to maintain.

This nonlawn focal point of flowers and small trees reduces mowing and adds interest and shade to the backyard. Plan a smaller area if you need open space for games.

Surfaces and structures like patios, walkways, and decks give high return in outdoor living space while reducing the time you have to spend mowing, watering, and fertilizing the lawn.

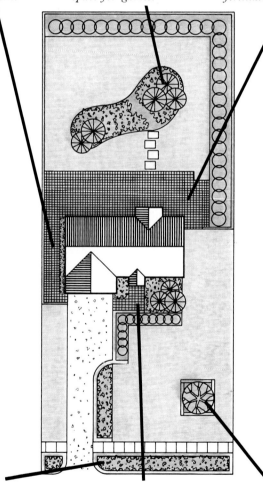

Strips of grass between curbing and sidewalk are difficult to mow and to keep looking good. Ground covers give them color, texture, and bloom. Put paving stones where needed for foot traffic.

Pave and plant the entryway so you don't have to mow bare-looking grass right up to the door. Paving keeps feet dry; plants along the walk give visitors a warmer welcome.

Place mulch and edging around trees so you don't have to duck under branches to mow. Trimming too close to trees and damaging their bark often leads to delayed growth or death.

A lawn, the most prevalent part of many yards, also is the part that takes the most work. Lighten your lawn-maintenance load by taking steps to make mowing easier and reduce the amount of grass you need to mow.

■ Making mowing easier
Your mower will move more effortlessly about your yard if you try some of the following.

■ Plant trees in groups, in swaths of mulch or ground cover, or in gardens. A lawn dotted with trees is a challenge to mow. Trees are safer anyway if lawn mowers never go near them.

■ As trees grow taller, prune their lower limbs. Continue to do this until the canopy of leaves is high enough for you to walk and mow under it comfortably. Such pruning also lets more light to your lawn and allows gentle breezes to reach your patio.

■ Install mowing strips: bands of concrete, brick, or other material on which the mower wheel can travel. These edges speed mowing and reduce trimming chores. They also can serve as attractive outlines in your landscape. Crucial to an effective mowing strip is that it be placed low to the ground. Locate sprinkler heads in the center of these bands to put them out of harm's and the mower's way.

■ Design your areas of lawn so that you can easily get the mower from one to another. In reducing the size of the lawn with other plantings, don't leave islands of grass.

■ Do lawn chores as needed: cut the grass before it needs raking, feed it before it needs reseeding, and treat pests and diseases before they do extensive damage. A lovely lawn is easily maintained if you take the work in stride. Fall behind and the problems can overwhelm you.

■ Lawn alternatives
Lawns began as status symbols for pastoral people who could finally afford to have a bit of pasture without any animals on it. The whole concept has since gotten so out of hand that

Americans now use more fuel and fertilizer on their lawns than some countries spend for their entire agricultural economies.

You can cut your lawn to a sensible size in several ways. Concentrate first on the areas where the grass is unsightly or does not grow well anyway.

■ Mulches

Removing unwanted sod and spreading a mulch—shredded bark or leaves, straw, or grass clippings, for example—in its place cuts your maintenance chores right away. It also conditions the soil for future plantings. Keep the mulch neat and safe with edging. Be careful of mower-thrown stones and sticks.

Put mulch where you're thinking of later adding a walk or patio so you can test the location. If you change your mind, it costs very little to restore the lawn and move the mulch.

To eliminate unwanted lawn without tilling, spread overlapping newspapers over the area, then top these with grass clippings, leaves, or any other organic mulch. Water well to hold all in place and speed decomposition.

Plant through these layers right away by digging the holes needed for trees or shrubs as usual. Plant smaller plants right on top of the newspapers; just place enough potting soil around the roots or over the seeds to cover. The roots will grow right through the papers (roots can split a rock), but weeds will not have the light they need to push up from underneath.

Consider using plastic under more expensive mulches like stone or bark to keep weeds from pushing through the shallow layer you're likely to use. Don't lay plastic, though, if you plan to put a lot of plants in the area; you'll tire of cutting through the plastic.

Many mulches are available free. Ask your neighbors to save leaves and grass clippings. As new laws banish these products from landfills, people will be glad to get someone to take them for free. Many utilities will dump truckloads of wood chips. Other by-products may be available in your area, too.

■ Ground covers

While mulches are not unattractive, ground covers make absolutely lovely carpets of various colors and textures with seasonal changes of bloom, fruit, or foliage color.

For best results, use plants that do well in your climate. Set cuttings or divisions in mulch. The closer you set the plants, the sooner they will cover the area. With plants 6 inches apart, 100 will cover 25 square feet. Do a section at a time and divide the plants as they multiply.

Pull weeds by hand until the ground cover fills the area. After that, the bed is self-sustaining. For an extra season of bloom, plant spring bulbs among ivy or pachysandra. See the next two pages, pages 66–67, and pages 317–319 for more details on ground covers.

■ Trees and shrubs

Plant trees and shrubs, too, to take up lawn space. Set them among the mulch and they will grow faster.

Include ground covers or shade-loving hostas or flowers under large trees; plant sun lovers under smaller trees until they cast more shade.

▲ *Some yards or sections of yards are greatly improved when they never need a mower. Here, slight berms (mounds of soil) give privacy, interest, and distinction. The brick path, curved deck, and low-growing plants stay attractive year-round with minimal attention.*

CHOOSING LOW-MAINTENANCE LAWN ALTERNATIVES

CHAMOMILE
Chamaemelum nobile

Height: 3–10 inches
Zones: 3–10
Soil: Average to below average
Light: Prefers full sun; will
take partial shade

Comments: The fragrant, ferny foliage of chamomile is delightful near walks, where footsteps send up clouds of scent. You also can mow it as a lawn substitute, forcing plants to form a tight carpet. Chamomile spreads fast, but sections may die without reason. Fill from surrounding area. Start from seed, or from cuttings or divisions set 6 to 12 inches apart. Chamomile has small daisylike flowers in summer. Survives drought well. Can be used for teas.

IVY: ENGLISH, BOSTON
Hedera helix and
Parthenocissus triscuspidata
Height: Will climb, but stays
5 to 10 inches above ground
Zones: 4–9
Soil: Rich, moist
Light: Prefers shade

Comments: Ivies come in many varieties. English is evergreen. Full sun can scorch it. Deep roots hold soil. Boston has larger, shiny, deciduous leaves that turn a brilliant red in fall. It takes full sun but does well in light shade. Mature ivies have small, inconspicuous flowers followed by dark blue berries that birds like. Ivies do well under trees. Prune for desired habit and compact growth.

LAMIUM
Lamium species

Height: 9–12 inches
Zones: 4–9
Soil: Any moist garden soil
Light: Tolerates shade

Comments: This easy, fast-growing, vigorous plant—also called spotted dead nettle and yellow archangel—can be set a little farther apart than most ground covers. Its crinkled leaves are variously colored and marked with silver and green. Flowers come in white, pink, lavender, and purple-red. Lamium can get weedy or take over; contain it with edgings. The word *dead* in the common name means this plant does not sting like a true nettle.

MOSS: IRISH, SCOTCH
Sagina subulata and
Arenaria species
Height: 2–4 inches
Zones: 4–10
Soil: Prefers moist, rich
Light: Full sun in cool areas,
afternoon shade elsewhere

Comments: The many species covered by these common names include pearlwort and sandwort, as well as many kinds of moss. Irish is usually dark green; Scotch, golden green. Both form low tufts of dense, linear foliage with white flowers in spring. Good between stepping-stones, among rocks, or under ferns. Mosses need a very acid soil. Leaves from deciduous trees should be removed; rake only after a hard freeze.

SPEEDWELL
Veronica species

Height: 6 inches–3 feet
Zones: 4–9
Soil: Tolerates many
Light: Full sun in North, some shade in South

Comments: Speedwells—often referred to as creeping, rock, or woolly—have dark green foliage with mostly blue, some pink or white, flowers. Bloom time ranges from late spring to September. Short varieties are good between paving stones or among bulbs. Speedwell makes a good, easy edging plant. Leaves are a rich, shiny green and plants spread to 2 feet wide. Similar to moss in effect. Takes considerable foot traffic.

THYME
Thymus species

Height: 2–15 inches
Zones: 3–10
Soil: Poor
Light: Sun; light summer shade in South

Comments: Creeping thyme has tiny, dark green leaves and a wonderful fragrance. It has clusters of red, pink, white, or purple flowers in summer. Woolly thyme has gray foliage and fewer flowers, but creates a more undulating and lower mat; it's perhaps the best thyme for use as a ground cover. Because crushing releases fragrance, both are good between stepping-stones or on a garden seat. Can be planted in or instead of a lawn.

VERBENA
Verbena peruviana

Height: 3–4 inches
Zones: 8–10
Soil: Tolerates dry
Light: Full sun to light shade

Comments: Verbenas include many species of annual or perennial herbs with leaves lobed or toothed and fuzzy. Flowers are small and sometimes stalked in roundish clusters. They come in pink, purple, white, or red. Verbenas are useful on dry banks, over walls, as ground covers, or in borders or hanging baskets. The prostrate stems root at the nodes and form dense mats. Does well in the Southwest. Prune in fall for denser growth.

WILDFLOWER AND NATURAL GRASS MIX

Height: To 5 or 6 feet by fall
Zones: 3–10
Soil: Mixes available for any
Light: Mixes available for sun or shade

Comments: An ever-changing tapestry of meadow or woodland blooms delights in the right place. But there's been much controversy about these natural lawn replacements; they are not neat enough for most front yards, and neighbors sometimes complain. Meadows, however, work well at the outer edges of larger lawns and on steep slopes. Use mixtures of native seed. Let annuals reseed to continue. Mow once in the fall.

In the South, try fragrant Confederate or star jasmine, lantana, or liriope. West Coast favorites are ice plant, gazania, African daisy, and Carmel creeper or ceanothus. For most of the country, anemone, artemisia, astilbe, lily-of-the-valley, bishop's weed, perennial geranium, hosta, primula, and vinca are good under trees. Keep mints and moneywort confined or they can take over.

Good ground covers for sun include bellflower, candytuft, ajuga, crown vetch, ivy geranium, mahonia, creeping phlox, dianthus, sedum, snow-in-summer, thrift or armeria, and woolly yarrow. For winter interest, plant bearberry, Japanese holly, wintergreen, box huckleberry, Oregon boxwood, or mountain cranberry. See pages 67 and 317–319 for more ground covers.

INSTALLING IRRIGATION SYSTEMS

The first step in planning an irrigation system is to check your home's water pressure, as explained at right. This determines how many sprinkler heads can operate at the same time.

Next, determine where you want heads. We decided on separate circuits for the right side and rear. The total flow rate of each circuit must not exceed 75 percent of a home's water pressure.

Make runs as straight as possible, avoiding layouts where piping doubles back. For 100 percent coverage, space heads so spray from one will nearly touch each neighboring head.

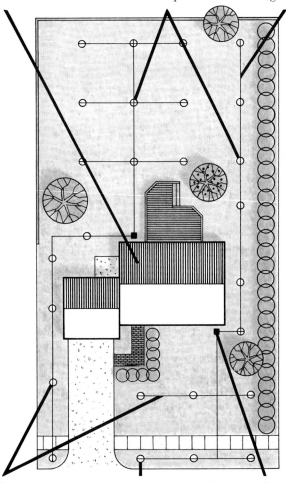

Our plan also provides separate circuits for the front and left side, a total of four in all. Plan your layout so that you don't have to tunnel under a driveway or other large paved area.

At borders, choose heads that won't waste water by throwing it onto a street, walk, drive, or neighbor's property. Some heads rotate, some spray a gentle mist, others bubble water.

Each circuit has a control valve. Two valves will go here, one for the front yard, one for the side. The plan calls for two more valves at the rear. Each valve can be wired to its own timer.

Tired of dragging hoses around your yard, returning from vacation to a parched lawn, or waking up to a marsh because you forgot to turn off the sprinkler last night? Go underground with a subterranean irrigation system that gives your landscaping exactly the amount of water it needs, when it needs it.

In-ground irrigation networks fall into two categories: drip systems and sprinklers. Drip irrigation carries water directly to trees, shrubs, and ground covers, bringing them a slow, steady trickle that sinks deep into the soil. Sprinklers toss water into the air, treating vegetation to a gentle shower. Drip systems are best for deep-rooted plants. Lawns require sprinklers. Your landscaping might benefit from a combination of the two.

■ Planning

In-ground irrigation systems are more affordable than ever, thanks to easily assembled components that let you do most or all of the installation work yourself. Planning the job can be tricky, however, so consult with a sprinkler parts dealer to determine the layout and equipment that will work best for you.

The dealer will need a detailed site plan that identifies all plant materials, soil conditions, and the like, along with the water pressure at your house in gallons per hour. This can be measured with a simple gauge that screws onto an outside hose cock. Most dealers will lend you a pressure gauge for a few days.

Pressure is important because the flow rate from all the heads in a system must not total more than 75 percent of available pressure; 60 percent is better. Need more heads than that? Break your system into separate circuits, as does the plan at left, then turn on each circuit at a different time of day.

Manual sprinkler controls are inexpensive, but require that you do the turning on and turning off. More costly controls consist of servomotors activated by programmable timers. These provide automatic, worry-free sprinkling.

1 *After you and a dealer have worked out a plan and you've bought the parts you need, familiarize yourself with those parts. The system begins with a loop of PVC pipe, shown at upper right, and an antisiphon valve, shown at upper left and on page 264. This prevents water in the sprinkler system, which could be contaminated with lawn chemicals, from being sucked back into your home's water supply.*

2 *Dig 6- to 10-inch-deep trenches with a spade or trenching machine. Plan to bury all but the top of sprinkler heads. Flexible plastic tubing is impervious to freezing and needn't be sunk below the frost line. Pressure causes heads like the one shown here to pop up when the water is turned on.*

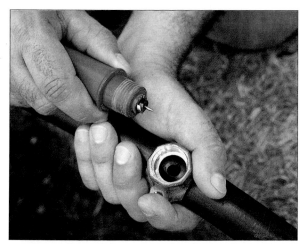

3 *Brass fittings clamp onto the plastic pipe wherever you need an outlet, then you punch a hole in the pipe by screwing this special tool into the fitting.*

4 *Start your system by clamping a hose bibb to a short piece of tubing. The bibb—located between the antisiphon and control valves— provides a connection for flushing out the system.*

(continued on page 264)

INSTALLING IRRIGATION SYSTEMS *(continued)*

5 Now install a control valve for each sprinkler circuit. This one is activated by a low-voltage solenoid that will be wired to a timer inside the garage. You also can buy manual control valves. Situate control valves so their cover boxes will be flush with the ground.

6 Lay tubing in trenches and piece together. T, elbow, and four-way fittings enable a circuit to branch out in one or several directions. Simply force each fitting into the plastic tubing, then tighten hose clamps with a screwdriver. For gentle curves, bend the tubing.

9 Drill a hole through the foundation or siding and connect PVC pipe to your home's water supply. You'll probably want to hire a plumber for this step. Caulk around the hole into the house. Connect antisiphon valve to water supply, then to irrigation system.

10 Use crimp connectors to wire each control valve to the antisiphon valve. Run wires from the antisiphon valve to the spot you've chosen for the timer that will operate the circuit. Low-voltage wires can be buried along with the tubing or in shallow trenches of their own.

7 *Attach clamps, puncture the tubing, and screw in sprinkler heads. Cut green risers to the right height with the pliers-like tool shown on the left. Lawn heads should be above ground level, yet low enough so that a mower can pass over them without nicking. Shrub heads should rise above foliage.*

8 *After all heads are in place, but before connecting to the house, attach a hose to the hose bibb and flush out the system. This also is a good time, before trenches are filled in, to check that each head provides good coverage.*

11 *Sprinkler timers resemble automatic-setback thermostats and the timers on videocassette recorders. You program the times you want the system to turn on and off. Watering in the early morning gives plantings a good start on the day.*

12 *Drop cover boxes over each control valve, fill the trenches with earth, tamp, and replace sod. Some sprinkler heads are adjustable so that you can fine-tune the system.*

MAINTAINING PLANTS

The amount of yard work you have to do depends largely on the kind of plants you have, the climate you live in, and how well the two suit each other. On these two pages, you'll find a few tips for maintaining common plants. See pages 256–257 for details on keeping a lawn in shape.

■ Watering
Water plants deeply whenever you get less than one inch of rain a week during active growth. Do this in the early morning or in the late afternoon; allow foliage to dry by nightfall. Drip and soaking systems are most efficient.

Water any newly set plants more often because of the damage to root systems caused by even the most careful transplanting. Each new tree can take five gallons of water weekly. Trees may take up to three years to reestablish good root systems.

■ Young trees
Stake young trees if necessary to keep them straight, but, because trees need to get used to some wind, use a minimum amount of support for only a few seasons. Wrap trunks of young trees with tree wrap or heavy paper during their first winter.

Prune ornamental trees very little, mostly to begin a proper shape. Generally, prune trees to a central leader; do not top trees unless you want shrubby growth. Remove any branches that form too low or at too narrow angles with the trunk. Because lower branches are usually removed as a tree grows, shorten any lower side branches that might take over too much of the tree and leave an unsightly canopy when later cut away.

Shrubs need only enough pruning to make them the shape you want. Remove unwanted, broken, crowding, or diseased branches whenever necessary. Vines may need some pruning all season long to keep them in place.

Weed ground covers until they spread. Separate perennials every several years. Replant annuals every spring. Remove dead flowers.

■ Feeding
Feed all plants at least once in early spring, annuals and woody plants again in the summer or after any pruning, perennials whenever buds form, and bulbs at planting time. Feed again as needed, depending upon the soil, the amount of rainfall that washes the nutrients away, and the type of plant. Let a soil test and advice from your county extension office be your guide.

■ Mulches
Mulching is the surest step anyone can take to promote faster, easier, and more vigorous growth. A layer of mulch lets the soil soak up and retain moisture longer. Soil temperatures stay more even, earthworm and bacterial action increase, and weeds are less of a problem.

To prevent pests and diseases, do all you can to keep your plants vigorous in the first place. Watch carefully for the first signs of damage and treat before any problems intensify.

▼*Fertilize as needed, depending on your soil and your plant. Do not feed too late in the summer or when soil is too dry. Brush granules from foliage with a broom or wash off with a hose. When possible, cultivate fertilizer into dirt so soil moisture can begin the benefits.*

For basic information on plants and planting, see pages 292–299.

◄ *Prune branches that cross, crowd, are damaged, or form too narrow an angle with the trunk. New research proves cuts will heal more quickly and surely if you cut just beyond the branch collar, usually a series of ridges, instead of absolutely flush.*

▲ *Water deeply. This root feeder, with the bubble on the right for fertilizer cartridges, gets the solution deep into the soil. Many feeder roots, however, even on trees, are near the surface, so deep feeding, though helpful, is not always essential.*

▶ *Nothing cuts work and promotes growth like mulch, for it conserves moisture and controls weeds. Organic mulches decompose from the bottom and become humus in the soil; replenish as needed.*

MAINTAINING CONCRETE, MASONRY STRUCTURES

Concrete and masonry promise permanence, but even the best-built walls, patios, driveways, and other structures require attention from time to time. Fortunately, most repairs can be accomplished in an hour or two, with no special skills and just a few hand tools.

Before you set out to make concrete and masonry repairs, try to diagnose what caused the damage. Water, especially ice, usually is the culprit. Frost in the ground causes heaving and settlement; water coursing down a wall or standing in low spots on a patio can leach away mortar and concrete, seep into joints, and wreck masonry units. The tactics shown at right and opposite cure minor concrete and masonry ailments. If the deterioration is chronic or extensive, you may need to solve an underlying drainage problem first. (To learn about improving drainage, see pages 52–55.)

■ Patching concrete
Repairing concrete is a lot like dentistry: You clean the cavity, then fill it. To fill shallow cracks and chips, use a commercial latex, vinyl, or epoxy patching compound mixed according to the manufacturer's instructions. These patching compounds hold better than conventional cement-sand mixtures and they require you to do far less preparatory work to the old surface.

For deeper cavities, apply the patching compound in several thin layers. Or use a conventional cement-sand mixture, making sure to apply a bonding agent (available at building centers) first. If you use concrete to fill a deep cavity, undercut the edges around the perimeter of the damaged area so that the crack or hole is somewhat wider at the bottom than at the surface. After you pack in the new concrete, the existing concrete helps hold it in place.

■ Tools
For most concrete and masonry repairs, you'll need a two-pound sledge, brick chisel, trowel, wire brush, and a bucket. When you chip away old material, protect your eyes with safety glasses. For removing stains, wear rubber gloves.

▲ *To replace a crumbling brick or stone, break away the mortar around it with a sledge and chisel, then smash the brick or stone and remove the pieces. Butter a new unit with mortar and slide it into place.*

◄ *To remove stains from concrete, sprinkle on a mixture of pumice and rottenstone or an industrial abrasive. Dip a wire brush in water and scrub vigorously. To learn about sealing concrete, see page 163.*

For basic information on working with concrete and masonry, see pages 282–287.

▲ *To patch a crumbling step, first chip away all loose concrete, then secure a retaining board with stakes. Moisten the concrete and trowel in patching compound. After the patch dries, remove the board.*

▶ *Break up disintegrating grout with a sledge and chisel. Use a vacuum or brush to remove all loose pieces from between stones. For new grout, mix mortar to a soupy consistency and pour it into place.*

◀ *To repair spalled concrete, first chip away all loose concrete with a chisel. Moisten the area well (don't let water stand, though), then apply a commercial patching compound. Let patch dry.*

▶ *Level sunken paver blocks, bricks, or stones by lifting them, then propping with a piece of 2x4. Fill underneath with equal parts sand, sifted earth, and cement. Tamp, if possible, or overfill to compensate for settling.*

269

MAINTAINING WOOD STRUCTURES

Rot is wood's worst enemy, so closely scrutinize decks, sheds, fences, and other wooden structures every spring and fall, paying special attention to members at or near ground level or anywhere else moisture might collect. If you detect any signs of rot (poke with a screwdriver if you're not sure), take immediate steps to remedy the problem before it gets worse.

Catch rot early and you may be able to arrest it by saturating the area with wood preservative. For more severe damage, you'll need to cut away the affected element and replace it. Use only redwood, cedar, or pressure-treated lumber for repairs.

During your semiannual inspection, also keep an eye out for decking boards, railings, or other items that might be pulling loose. These pose a safety hazard and should be hammered back in place right away.

■ Termites
Termites fall into two groups: *subterranean* ones eat wood but live underground, usually commuting back and forth via mud shelter tubes; *nonsubterranean* types live in the wood itself.

Nonsubterranean wood-boring insects—which include powder-post beetles and carpenter ants as well as several termite species—dig across the grain of the wood and sometimes break through the surface, leaving telltale piles of sawdust pellets. Subterranean termites bore along the grain of the wood and often leave nothing but a shell behind.

If you suspect termites, call a licensed exterminator. To eliminate subterranean termites, exterminators inject chemicals into the soil. For nonsubterranean termites, extermination consists of boring holes into the wood and injecting a liquid or powdered chemical.

▼ *Cut rotted boards back to sound wood. Plan cuts so they will expose framing to which you can nail a new piece of lumber. In this situation, caulking where the wood abuts concrete could prevent rotting in the future. Secure the new piece with galvanized nails or screws.*

▶ *Heavy sap deposits can bleed right through most stains. The cure: Sand the area, seal it with a nonbleed finish such as shellac or marine varnish, then restain. To remove mildew, scrub the area with a solution of water and household bleach, or use a commercial mildewcide.*

▶ *Pull popped nails, then drill pilot holes and drive galvanized screws adjacent to the old nail holes. Seal the holes with caulk. Reinforce a weakening structural member with galvanized L, angle, or T brackets. Again, use only galvanized screws.*

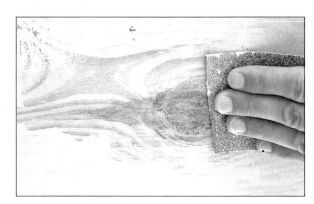

◄ *Posts are especially vulnerable to rot. Caulking here prevents water from seeping down alongside the post. Also cut back vegetation from around posts, fence rails, and other lower members of stuctures.*

▼ *To repair a splintered edge, remove the splinter and feather back the area around the wound. Drill holes and insert pegs along its length. Clamp a board to the edge and fill with wood putty. Let dry.*

◄ *End cuts can soak up moisture like a sponge. Saturate them with sealer-preservative every year or so. Reseal the entire structure, from top to bottom, every two or three years. An inexpensive pressure sprayer speeds the job.*

For basic information on working with wood, see pages 276–281.

CHAPTER THIRTEEN

CONSTRUCTION AND PLANTING BASICS

How long a nail do you need? What are the correct proportions for mixing concrete or mortar? When's the best time to start a lawn? Tackle any of the projects covered earlier in this book and you may puzzle over questions like these. For answers, turn to the pages that follow. Here you'll find a concise compendium of information about hardware and fasteners, wood, concrete, masonry, wiring, and plants.

HARDWARE AND FASTENERS

The hardware and fasteners you choose for a building project are just as important as the lumber and other materials they join. On this page, we look at nails, the fasteners you'll use most often. Then, on pages 274–275, we turn to screws, bolts, plates, and other hardware.

■ The right nail

The chart at right depicts a dozen nail types, each engineered for a specific purpose. Starting from the top:

■ *Doubleheaded* nails, also known as *scaffold* nails, are good choices for temporary nailing jobs, such as building forms or attaching braces to a post. The second head makes the nail easy to pull when you no longer need it.

■ *Masonry* nails are specially hardened so that they can penetrate into concrete or mortar.

■ *Spiral* and *ring-shanked* nails provide more holding power in wood. Spiral nails are threaded, somewhat like screws, and twist into materials; ring-shanked nails have barbs.

■ *Corrugated fasteners,* or *wiggly nails,* are used mainly to strengthen already-fastened joints. You also can use them alone for light-duty jobs such as building frames for screens.

■ *Brads* are miniature finishing nails, good for molding and finishing jobs.

■ *Finishing* and *casing* nails have small heads that are easily countersunk (set below the surface).

■ *Roofing* nails have wide, thin heads to hold down shingles and roofing paper.

■ *Box* and *common* nails are similar, but common nails have a thicker shank; this increases holding power but can cause splits in some boards.

■ Nail sizes

The scale at the bottom of the illustration compares nail sizes in pennies, a system still used by a few manufacturers, and inches. The higher the penny number (d), the longer the nail.

To determine the size nail you should use, multiply the thickness of the material you will be nailing *through* by three. A ¾-inch-thick board, for example, calls for a 2¼-inch nail. (See page 280 for more details.)

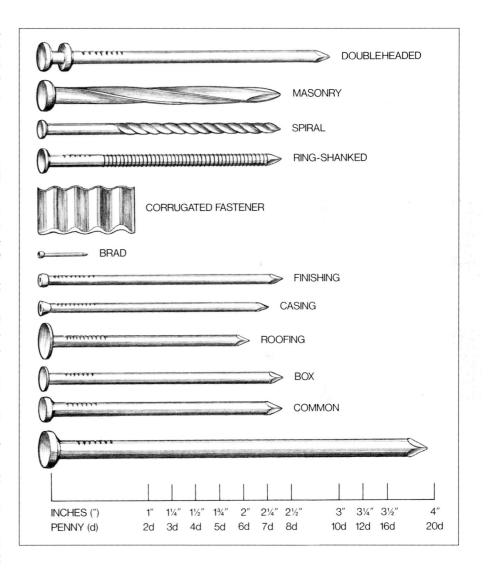

INCHES (")		1"	1¼"	1½"	1¾"	2"	2¼"	2½"		3"	3¼"	3½"		4"
PENNY (d)		2d	3d	4d	5d	6d	7d	8d		10d	12d	16d		20d

■ Nail coatings

All nails used for outdoor construction should be rust-resistant so they won't discolor the wood. Stainless steel and aluminum nails assure resistance to rust, but both are expensive, and aluminum nails bend easily. For economical rust protection, choose galvanized steel nails.

One other coating deserves mention. *Cement-coated* nails have an adhesive film that bonds to wood fibers under the heat and friction of driving. Use these for superior holding power.

(continued on page 274)

▲ *Here are profiles of the nails most commonly used in outdoor construction projects. To learn what each nail does best, check the text at left. Nails longer than 4 inches (20d) are called spikes.*

273

HARDWARE AND FASTENERS *(continued)*

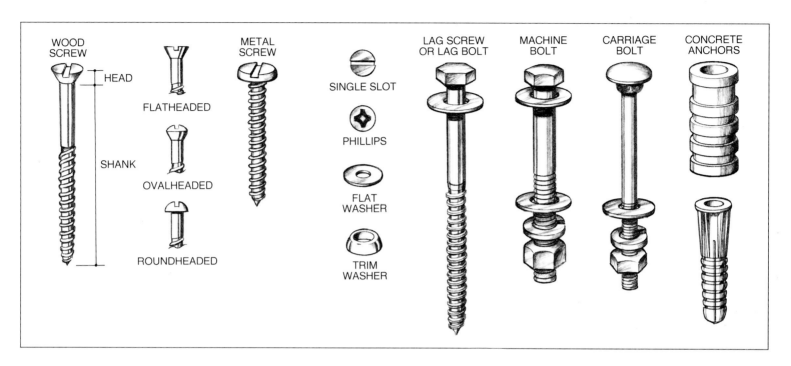

WOOD SCREW — HEAD — SHANK — FLATHEADED — OVALHEADED — ROUNDHEADED

METAL SCREW

SINGLE SLOT — PHILLIPS — FLAT WASHER — TRIM WASHER

LAG SCREW OR LAG BOLT — MACHINE BOLT — CARRIAGE BOLT — CONCRETE ANCHORS

▲ *Screws thread into wood or other materials. Bolts go all the way through and are secured by nuts. Tighten screws with a straight or Phillips screwdriver, or, in the case of lag screws, a wrench. Washers prevent the screwhead from marring the surface of the material. Use anchors when screwing into concrete or masonry.*

For the few seconds it takes to drive them, nails do a remarkable holding job. But at critical junctures, you'll want the strength and neatness of screws and bolts.

The illustration above shows, among other things, the two broad types of screws available: *wood* screws and *metal* screws. Metal screws have a flat, broad head and a shank that's threaded from head to tip, making them ideal for securing thin materials such as sheet metal and plastic. For wood-to-wood joints, use *flatheaded, ovalheaded,* or *roundheaded* wood screws. You can drive flatheaded screws flush with the surface. Ovalheaded screws add a decorative accent. Roundheaded ones do more utilitarian tasks. Use a *flat washer* with a roundheaded screw, *trim washers* with flat- and ovalheaded screws.

■ **Sizing up screws**

As with nails, the right size screw for the job goes about two-thirds of its length into the member you're fastening to. When ordering wood screws, specify the *length* (from ¼ to 5 inches), *gauge* or shank diameter (No. 0, which

is about 1/16 inch, to No. 24, about ⅜ inch), head type, and material (brass or galvanized steel for outdoor projects). The larger a screw's gauge, the greater its holding power.

Turn to *lag screws,* often called lag bolts, for heavy framing jobs. To order these, specify *diameter* (from ¼ to 1 inch) and *length* (from 1 to 16 inches).

Machine and *carriage bolts* handle all kinds of heavy fastening jobs. You need two wrenches to tighten a machine bolt, one for a carriage bolt.

When ordering bolts, specify the *diameter, length,* and the *type* (machine or carriage). To determine the correct length, add about ¾ inch to the combined thicknesses of the materials to be joined. Carriage bolts have diameters ranging from ¼ to ¾ inch and lengths from ¾ to 20 inches; machine bolts have diameters of ¼ to 1 inch and lengths of ½ to 30 inches.

Concrete anchors enable you to drive a screw into masonry or mortar joints. You drill a hole, insert the anchor, then turn a screw into it. As the screw cuts its threads, it expands the soft lead anchor snugly against the sides of the hole.

■ Plates and hangers

Want to beef up an otherwise weak wood joint? Reach for one of the devices shown at upper right. *Mending plates* reinforce end-to-end butt joints. *Corner braces* strengthen right-angle joints by attaching to edge surfaces. *Flat corner irons* do the same thing, but attach to the faces of the materials. *T plates* handle end-to-edge joints.

Framing fasteners, such as the *joist hanger* shown in our illustration, solve tricky framing problems. Other fasteners include *saddle brackets* for beam-on-beam or joist-on-beam applications, *post caps* for securing beams to the tops of posts, *rafter brackets,* and *stair cleats.* As with nails, screws, and bolts, all plates and hangers intended for outdoor use should be made of galvanized steel or other rustproof material.

■ Gate hardware

If your construction project will include a gate, you have some more choices to make. The illustration at lower right shows just a few of the hinges, latches, handles, and springs available at home centers.

Brick hinges install in the mortar between bricks. You chip out the old mortar, fit the hinge support into the recess, then force a light concrete or mortar mix around it.

Screw hinges thread into holes in a post. *Decorative hinges* typically attach to the post and gate with lag screws. *T hinges* reinforce the gate by covering its corner joints, always the weak spots in any gate. Use these for large garden gates, garage and barn doors, and any other application that calls for a sturdy, functional hinge.

Besides hinges, a gate requires a latch and some sort of handle. A *self-closing latch* automatically engages hardware on the post when the gate swings shut, protecting the gate and hinges from damage caused by strong gusts of wind.

You can make a *wood handle* like the one shown with scraps left over from building the gate. Or fit the gate with a store-bought *metal handle.* Regardless of whether your gate has a latch, a *spring* can keep it closed. Simply mount it as shown and adjust for fast or slow closure.

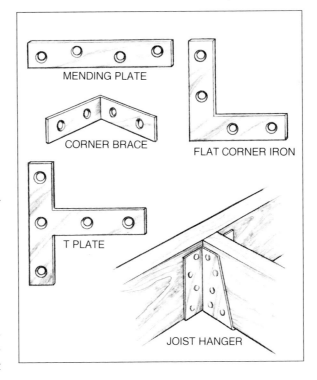

MENDING PLATE

CORNER BRACE

FLAT CORNER IRON

T PLATE

JOIST HANGER

◄ *These are only a few of the specialized items you can find in the hardware sections of home centers. Browse awhile and you'll find products designed for every conceivable carpentry situation.*

▼ *If your plans call for a gate, door, or other moving element, you have an equally wide selection of hinges, latches, handles, and other hardware to choose from. Let appearance and function guide you.*

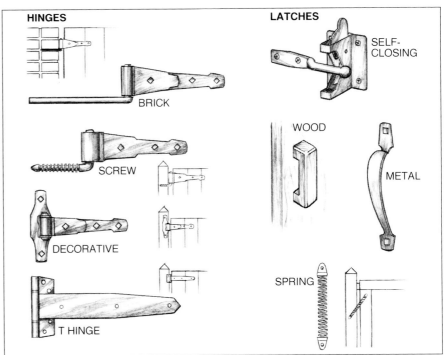

HINGES

LATCHES

SELF-CLOSING

BRICK

WOOD

METAL

SCREW

DECORATIVE

SPRING

T HINGE

WOOD

Because all successful outdoor woodworking projects start with the right tools and materials, we look first at these prerequisites. Then, on pages 279–281, we show you some basic techniques for working with wood.

■ Choosing tools

Though not exhaustive, the illustrations on the opposite page do depict many of the tools required for landscape construction with wood.

When selecting tools, keep in mind that good craftsmanship begins with quality tools. If, like most homeowners, you already have a few tools lying around, take a critical look at them before beginning a project. Toss out any that are bent or broken—and stay away from the bargain bins when you shop for replacements.

Instead, if at all possible, spend more money and invest in top-of-the-line professional-quality tools. Sturdily built to exacting standards, these tools will endure years of hard use. Some companies even offer lifetime guarantees.

■ Choosing lumber

Any lumber you select for outdoor projects must be naturally or chemically rot-resistant. Page 184 presents the pros, cons, and relative costs of your four choices: redwood, cedar, cypress, and pressured-treated lumber.

Once you've decided what species you want for your project, consider which *grade* of wood will work best for the project's various components. Softwood grading is tricky to learn, in part because there are several grading systems. But in general, you'll be on safe footing if you think in terms of two overall classifications: *select* and *common.* Use select lumber (*B* and *Better, C,* and *D*) for elements such as decking and fencing where good looks are important. For other elements, common lumber (*nos. 1, 2, 3,* and *4*) will do nicely. Not surprisingly, the better the grade, the more you will pay.

Also bear in mind that all pieces of lumber have a set of *nominal* dimensions (what you order) and a set of *actual* dimensions (what you get

after the lumber is milled and dried). To learn about nominal and actual dimensions of various-size members, consult the chart on page 278.

■ Ordering lumber

Before you set out for the home center or lumberyard, draw up a list detailing exactly what wood you will need. To order, state the quantity, thickness, width, length, grade, and species—in that order. Example: 40 pieces 2"x6"x10' construction-heart redwood.

Do everything you can to get a firsthand look at what you're buying. Some dealers will let you go out in the yard and hand-select your choices. Reject any boards that have serious defects. Realize, though, that few boards are absolutely perfect and that minor problems can be trimmed off when you cut the lumber or straightened out when you nail it in place.

■ Choosing plywood

Use only exterior-grade or marine-grade plywood for outdoor projects; moisture quickly wrecks the glues in interior plywood. If both sides of a panel will show, select grade A-A, which has two good faces. For applications in which only one side will show, you can save money with A-B or A-C plywood. Grade B-B is a thrifty choice for concrete forms, rough screening, and temporary walks.

One other exterior plywood worth knowing about is *medium density overlay* (MDO), which has a smooth, resin-impregnated fiber face designed especially for flawless painted finishes.

■ Storing lumber

Before your order is delivered, give thought to where you want to put the lumber. You may choose to stack it in the garage or near the project site. Use blocks to keep the stack up off the floor or ground, and cover it to protect against moisture. If you won't be using the wood for a while, separate layers with crosspieces so that air can circulate. Store sheet goods flat, if possible. Lumber isn't dimensionally stable until it's nailed or bolted together.

(continued on page 279)

▶ *You probably already own many or all of the carpentry tools you'll need for outdoor projects. If you don't have an electric drill or jigsaw, consider buying cordless ones. Besides freeing you from lengthy extension cords, they also present less of a shock hazard.*

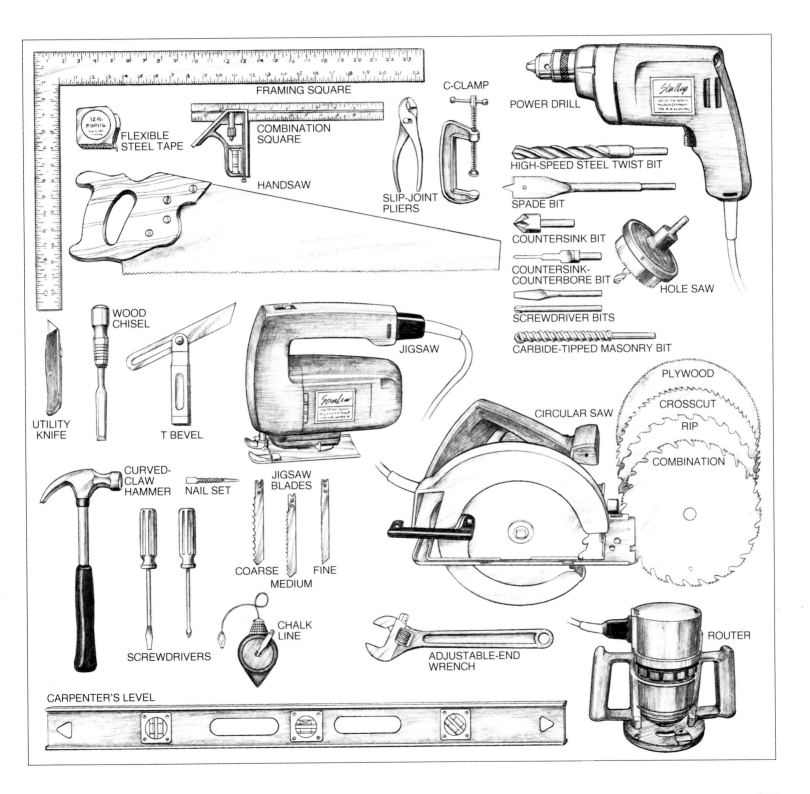

FRAMING SQUARE

FLEXIBLE STEEL TAPE

COMBINATION SQUARE

HANDSAW

C-CLAMP

SLIP-JOINT PLIERS

POWER DRILL

HIGH-SPEED STEEL TWIST BIT

SPADE BIT

COUNTERSINK BIT

COUNTERSINK-COUNTERBORE BIT

HOLE SAW

SCREWDRIVER BITS

CARBIDE-TIPPED MASONRY BIT

WOOD CHISEL

UTILITY KNIFE

T BEVEL

JIGSAW

PLYWOOD

CROSSCUT

RIP

COMBINATION

CIRCULAR SAW

CURVED-CLAW HAMMER

NAIL SET

JIGSAW BLADES

COARSE

MEDIUM

FINE

SCREWDRIVERS

CHALK LINE

ADJUSTABLE-END WRENCH

ROUTER

CARPENTER'S LEVEL

277

WOOD *(continued)*

LUMBER SELECTOR

Type		Nominal Size	Actual Size	Common Uses
Strips	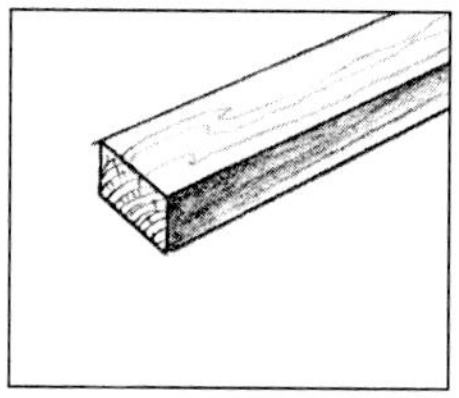	1 x 2 1 x 3	¾ x 1½ ¾ x 2½	Trim, spacers, shims, bridging, stakes, shallow forms, battens, screen frames, edging, lattice-work, and trellises. Strips are inexpensive and versatile building materials.
Finish Lumber (Boards)		1 x 4 1 x 6 1 x 8 1 x 10 1 x 12	¾ x 3½ ¾ x 5½ ¾ x 7½ ¾ x 9¼ ¾ x 11¼	Sheathing; siding and soffits; subflooring and flooring; decking; fencing; edging; walks; trim; planters; benches; storage sheds; and forms. Besides the ordinary board shown here, finish lumber also includes lumber with tongue-and-groove or shiplap edges.
Dimension Lumber	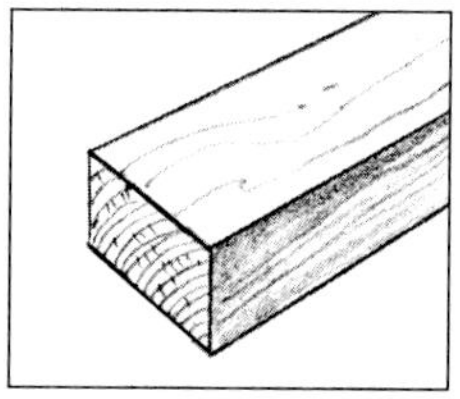	2 x 2 2 x 3 2 x 4 2 x 6 2 x 8 2 x 10 2 x 12	1½ x 1½ 1½ x 2½ 1½ x 3½ 1½ x 5½ 1½ x 7¼ 1½ x 9¼ 1½ x 11¼	Structural framing, stakes, decking, structural finishing, forming, fencing, walks, benches, screeds, and stair components. Dimension lumber pieces, often called "two-bys," bring strength and a sturdy appearance to outdoor woodworking projects.
Posts	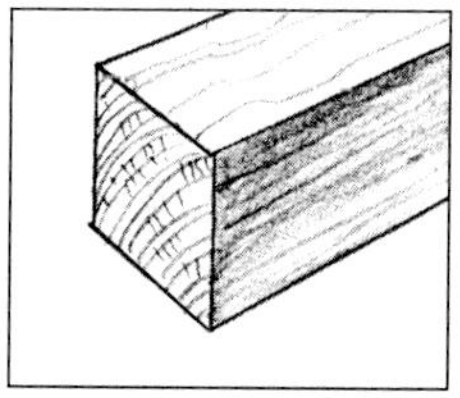	4 x 4 6 x 6	3½ x 3½ 5½ x 5½	Heavy-duty structural framing, support columns, fencing, retaining walls, and edging for patios and walks. You also can buy round posts in several diameters.
Timbers	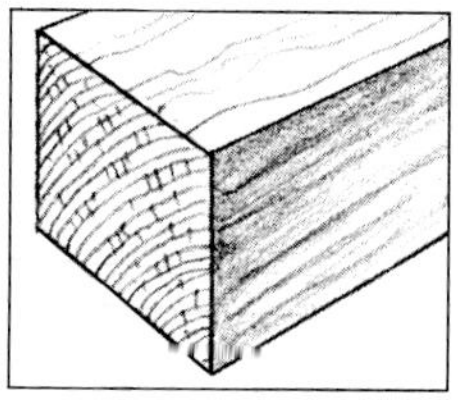	Rough-sawn; sizes vary	Actual sizes vary slightly up or down from nominal sizes	Heavy-duty structural framing, support columns, retaining walls, and steps. Timbers are a good building material for architectural and decorative interest. Maneuvering hefty landscape timbers is a two-person job.

All carpentry projects follow essentially the same steps. You begin with good measurements. After that, you cut pieces to size, then nail, screw, or bolt them together. Finally, when working outdoors, you often protect everything with a preservative. Here, and on pages 280–281, we take you through these processes.

■ Measuring basics

Whether you're building a 50-room mansion or a doghouse, there's no such measurement as *about*. Measurements must be exact.

Equally important to making correct measurements is to start square. Many boards aren't entirely square, especially at their ends. Fortunately, most building materials have a *factory edge* milled along at least one dimension. Refer to this edge when squaring the rest of the material.

Be sure, too, that your measurements take into account the narrow opening the saw will leave in its wake—called the *kerf*. If you're making just one cut, allow for the kerf by identifying the scrap side of the cutoff line with an X. This tells you which side to cut from. For multiple cuts along a board or on sheet goods, allow for the kerf between the cutoff lines.

■ Cutting basics

The vast majority of the cuts you'll be making fall into two categories: *crosscuts* across the grain and *rip cuts* parallel with the grain.

Crosscut boards with either a hand- or power saw. Start cuts by carefully positioning the blade so its kerf will be on the scrap side. With a handsaw, place the blade at a 45-degree angle to the work and, using the knuckle of your thumb as a guide, pull the saw back toward you; with a power saw, squeeze the trigger and let the blade get up to speed before easing it into the wood. As the cut progresses, let the weight of the saw—hand- or power—do the work.

For rip cuts, a power saw works best. To assure that you'll get a straight edge along the entire length of the cut, clamp a straight board or straightedge parallel to the cut line and guide the saw along it.

(continued on page 280)

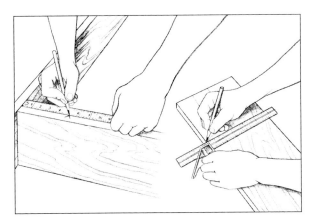

◀ *Mark cutoffs with a V; then place the point of your pencil at the V's tip, slide a square up to it, and strike your line. A combination square is ideal for marking most board widths. For longer lines, use a framing square or straightedge.*

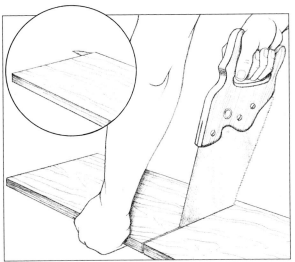

◀ *When you near the end of a cut, support the scrap side with slight upward pressure from your free hand. This keeps the piece from snapping off and splintering. Position your fingers well away from the saw blade.*

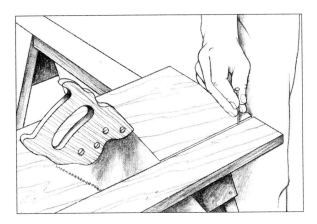

◀ *Saw blades tend to bind in longer rip cuts, especially near the end. If this happens, widen the kerf by wedging a nail or screwdriver into it. Be sure, too, that you adequately support the scrap side of the cut.*

WOOD *(continued)*

Fell a tree and its wood stops growing. But this organic building material has an afterlife of sorts, because humidity changes cause the grain to expand and shrink with the seasons—a process that can play havoc with weak joints in outdoor projects. To minimize twisting, racking, warping, and splitting, use nails, screws, or bolts at all critical structural points.

■ Nailing basics
Bend a few nails or split a perfectly good piece of wood and you'll soon discover that no one is born with an innate knack for pounding nails. Actually, you don't *pound* a nail at all; you *drive* it with a few well-directed blows. As with golf or tennis, learning to direct those blows means you must perfect your swing.

Grasp the hammer at the end of its handle, not up around the neck. Start the nail with a gentle tap, then lift the hammer in a gentle arc. Now, keeping your wrist stiff, drop the hammer squarely onto the nail. With practice, you'll find yourself driving nails smoothly, without straining (or maiming) your arm, wrist, or hand.

Your last blow should push the head of a common nail flush with the surface of the wood; drive the heads of finishing or casing nails below the surface with a nail set.

For maximum holding power in rough projects, use nails about an inch longer than the combined thicknesses of the pieces you're fastening. Drive the nails, then turn the members over and *clinch* (bend) the exposed portions of the nails in the direction of the grain so they're nearly flush with the surface. For showier projects, or when you can't get at the back of the materials, drive pairs of nails at opposing angles. For help selecting nails, see page 273.

■ Drilling basics
The electric drill has made all hand-powered boring tools obsolete. With the complement of bits shown on page 277, you can make holes in just about anything, and use the drill to drive screws as well. Here are some tips for using this jack-of-all-trades machine.

■ To prevent the drill bit from skating away from the point where you want a hole, make a shallow pilot hole first with an awl or the tip of a nail. Grip the drill with both hands and center the bit in the hole, then apply firm pressure and begin drilling. If you have a variable-speed drill, bring it up to full power gradually.

■ To assure that a hole will be perpendicular, hold a combination square against the wood and align the drill with the square's blade.

■ When you want to drill one or more holes to a certain depth, wrap masking or electrical tape around the drill bit so that the tape will touch the surface of the wood at the depth you want. Drill with gentle pressure, then carefully back the bit out as soon as the tape hits the surface.

■ To keep wood chips from clogging the bit and causing it to bind when you're drilling deep holes, feed the bit into the wood slowly, and back the bit out of the hole frequently with the drill's motor still running.

■ Screw basics
The threads along the shank of a screw grip the fibers of the wood being joined and pull them together with tremendous pressure. Here's how to get good results with these super fasteners.

■ First, drill pilot holes. Screws driven in directly can split all but the softest of woods. Make the holes slightly smaller than the screw's diameter.

■ Select the correct screwdriver for the screw you're driving. It should fill the slot completely for maximum torque.

■ Turning lots of screws—or even just a few—by hand can tire you. To reduce fatigue and speed up the operation, drive the screws with your drill and a screwdriver bit. Make sure the bit is firmly seated in the screw slot before beginning, and don't drive the screw too quickly or you'll strip the head. If you do damage a screwhead, you may be able to salvage it by deepening its slot with a hacksaw.

■ Faced with a hole that's a little too big for the screw you're driving? Insert a toothpick or sliver of wood into the hole. Tightening the screw forces the filler material against the wall of the hole, holding the screw tight.

■ Bolting basics

Nails and screws depend on friction between the fastener and the wood to do their jobs. Not so with bolts. When you tighten a nut on a bolt, you're mechanically clamping adjoining members together, creating the strongest joint of all. Here are ways to get the best out of bolts.

■ Tighten an adjustable-end wrench snugly onto the work. Otherwise, it could slip and strip a nut or bolt head.

■ Adjustable-end wrenches can handle most bolting jobs, but a set of automotive socket wrenches speeds the work and helps you out in tight corners. Socket-wrench sets typically include a crank-style handle for speedy tightening, and a reversible ratchet that lets you move the handle back and forth without removing the socket from the work.

■ With any wrench, pull it toward you; if the wrench slips, you run less risk of skinning your knuckles.

■ Never force a wrench by tapping its handle with a hammer. And don't slip a pipe over a wrench handle to gain leverage; you could snap the wrench or the material it's tightening.

■ Finishing basics

Redwood, cedar, cypress, and pressure-treated lumber can last for years outdoors with no finish at all, but periodic applications of preservative prolong the lives of all of these woods.

Apply clear preservative immediately to maintain the original appearance of redwood, cedar, and cypress. Or, wait a few months and let the wood weather before sealing it. Staining preservatives can give pressure-treated lumber the color of redwood or cedar.

Apply preservatives with a brush, roller, or an inexpensive pressure sprayer. If you spray, wear a mask, gloves, and eye protection.

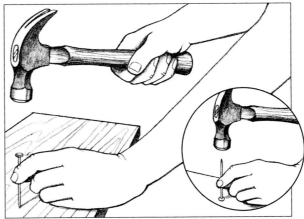

◄ *To make sure the hammer strikes the nail, not your fingers, keep your eye on the nail and let the weight of the hammer's head do the driving. Blunt the point of a nail that will be driven near the end of a board to reduce the chance of splitting.*

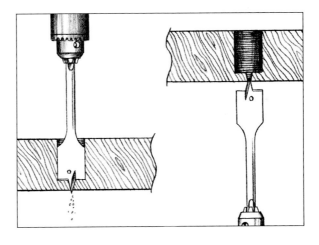

◄ *Spade bits can splinter wood when they exit through the back. To prevent this, drill until just the tip of the bit penetrates. Then carefully back out the bit and finish drilling from the other side.*

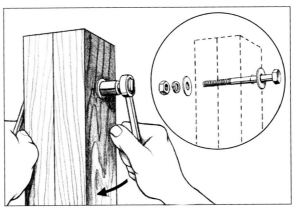

◄ *To bolt two pieces of wood together, slip a flat washer onto the bolt, then slide the bolt through the hole. Put another flat washer, then a lock washer, over the opposite end of the bolt; follow the washers with a nut. Tighten with two wrenches.*

CONCRETE AND MASONRY

▼*Mixed in the right proportions, concrete turns aggregate (gravel or crushed rock), sand, cement, and water into a pliable material that soon hardens into a stonelike mass. Mortar—made from sand, cement, lime, and water—bonds bricks, blocks, and stones.*

Everybody calls it *cement,* but you can't build much of anything with plain portland cement. Mix it with other materials, though, and cement becomes the key ingredient in the magic muds known as *concrete* and *mortar.*

On these two pages, we review some of the tools you'll need when you do concrete and masonry work. For details on the steps involved in working with concrete, see pages 284–285. Following that, on pages 286–287, is a discussion of mortar and masonry materials.

■ Concrete tools
As you decide which of the tools shown on the opposite page you will need for your project, bear in mind that you can either buy or rent most of them. If you buy, purchase only good-quality tools.

To aid in mixing and transporting masonry materials and concrete, lay your hands on a sturdy *contractor-quality wheelbarrow*—the kind with a 3-cubic-foot or larger tray and a pneumatic rubber tire. Also handy, but not essential, are a *mortar box* and *mortar hoe* for mixing ingredients.

To prepare sites and move concrete and mortar ingredients, you must have either a round-bladed shovel or a couple of specialists: a *spade* for squaring up excavation edges and a *square-bladed shovel* for moving sand and wet concrete.

For placing concrete, you'll need a *tamper,* a *wooden float,* a *screed* (not shown), and a *darby* or *bull float.* Screeds, used to level just-poured concrete, often are nothing more than straight lengths of 2x4. Use the darby, bull float, or a small hand float to smooth screeded concrete and push larger stones below the surface. You can make these from scrap lumber, if you like.

To finish, use a magnesium or steel *trowel* to further smooth and compact the concrete, an inexpensive *edger* to round off and strengthen the edges of concrete slabs, and a *jointer* to put grooves in slabs to control cracking. If you plan to cut control joints after the concrete hardens, fit a circular saw with a *masonry blade* for the jointing work.

■ Masonry tools
If you're working with mortar, you can dispense with the tools needed for finishing concrete, but you'll need several others. To cut bricks, blocks, and stones, buy or rent a *brick hammer,* a *brick set* or *masonry chisel,* and a 2-pound *sledgehammer* (often called a baby sledge or mash hammer).

And, when building concrete or masonry walls, lay your hands on *line blocks,* a *modular spacing rule,* and a *plumb bob.*

For placing mortar, use a well-balanced, pointed *brick trowel.* Use a *pointing trowel* or a *caulking trowel* to force mortar into joints being repaired. A *joint strike* or a *joint raker* (not shown) helps you finish mortar joints.

Because dried concrete and mortar are almost impossible to remove, wash and dry tools thoroughly after use. Follow the drying with a light coat of oil on all metal parts.

(continued on page 284)

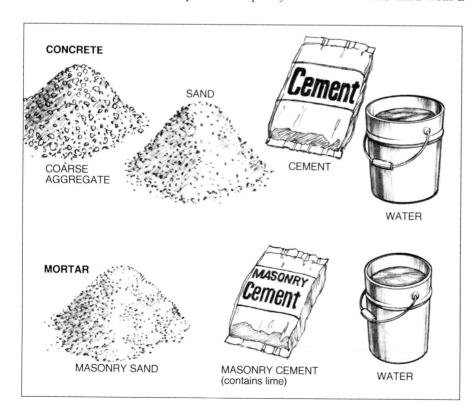

CONCRETE

COARSE AGGREGATE

SAND

Cement

CEMENT

WATER

MORTAR

MASONRY SAND

MASONRY Cement

MASONRY CEMENT
(contains lime)

WATER

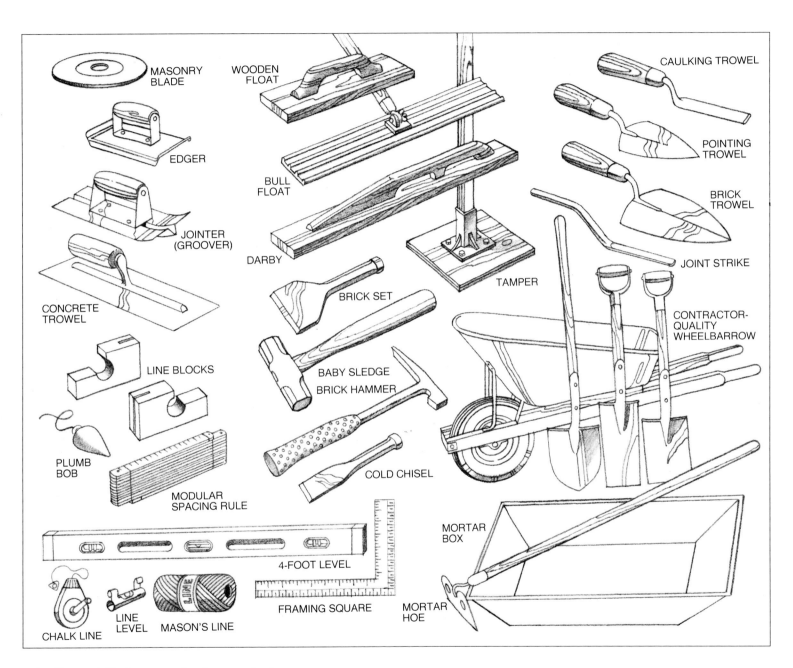

MASONRY BLADE

WOODEN FLOAT

CAULKING TROWEL

EDGER

BULL FLOAT

POINTING TROWEL

JOINTER (GROOVER)

BRICK TROWEL

DARBY

CONCRETE TROWEL

TAMPER

JOINT STRIKE

BRICK SET

LINE BLOCKS

BABY SLEDGE

BRICK HAMMER

CONTRACTOR-QUALITY WHEELBARROW

PLUMB BOB

COLD CHISEL

MODULAR SPACING RULE

4-FOOT LEVEL

MORTAR BOX

CHALK LINE

LINE LEVEL

MASON'S LINE

FRAMING SQUARE

MORTAR HOE

▲ *Besides specialized concrete and masonry tools, you'll need carpentry tools—such as a claw hammer, handsaw or portable circular saw, levels, chalk box, mason's line, and framing square— for building forms and batter boards.*

CONCRETE AND MASONRY *(continued)*

Working with concrete is a six-step process: You prepare the site, build forms, pour the mix, level it, trowel the surface, then help it cure. Here's what each of these steps entails.

■ Preparing the site

If at all possible, place your slab on undisturbed soil. If you must pour on top of recently filled soil, as would be the case around a new foundation, pack the soil by watering it for several days and allowing it time to settle.

Lay out the site with strings and stakes or batter boards, as explained on pages 58–59.

▶ *With form boards that butt end to end, drive stakes that lap the joint. At corners, stake near the end of each board. Strengthen curved forms with stakes every 1 to 2 feet.*

▼*Dividing a large project such as a drive-way or big patio into smaller slabs lets you pour a manageable amount of concrete at a time. The dividers can be temporary or permanent.*

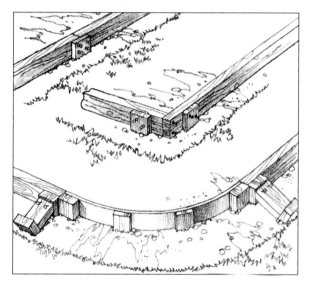

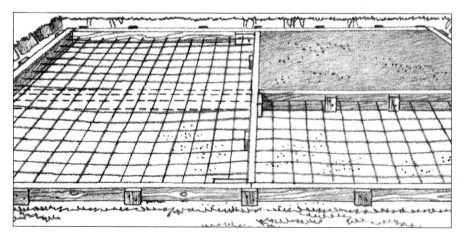

Then excavate to a depth equal to the thickness of the slab you've decided on, plus 2 to 3 inches for a sand or gravel drainage bed, minus 1 inch so the slab's surface will be above ground level. Make the excavation about 3 inches larger all around to provide room for forms.

■ Building forms

Because slabs generally run about 4 inches thick, 2x4s that are smooth and straight make ideal forming material. Securely anchor the form boards with foot-long stakes (1x4 lumber works well) every 3 to 4 feet. Attach the stakes to the form boards with doubleheaded nails, which are easy to pull later. Or nail through the form boards and into the stakes using regular-headed nails. Hammer the stakes' tops level with the top of the form, or cut them at that level, so you can drag a screed across the form.

For proper drainage, forms should slope at least ¼ inch per foot. To establish the proper slope, measure down from both ends of a level string stretched from the top end of the slab (perhaps at the house or garage) to the point where the slab will end. For a 20-foot slab, for example, the downhill edge should be 5 inches lower than the uphill edge.

Shape curves with 3½-inch-wide strips of ¼-inch-thick hardboard or plywood. With plywood, cut the strips perpendicular to the grain so they will be easier to bend. For a snug fit, tack one end in place, driving two 4-penny nails through the thin form member into a stake. Then spring the board into the desired shape, cut it to length, and nail it to a second stake.

To control cracking, prop up ½-inch-thick expansion strips wherever the new concrete will abut old concrete. (See opposite for details on tooling control joints into the poured concrete.)

■ Mixing or ordering concrete

Compute how much concrete you'll need by multiplying the form's width and length; for circles or cylindrical forms, multiply the square of the radius by 3.14. After you know how many square feet you'll have, consult the Concrete Estimator at right. To assure you won't run short, increase your estimate by 10 percent.

When buying concrete, you have three options. For small jobs, such as setting a few fence posts, buy premixed concrete. Premix bags include cement, sand, and aggregate. You simply add water. Each sack yields from ⅓ to ⅔ cubic foot of concrete, depending on its size.

For jobs that require a half cubic yard of concrete or more, buy the cement, sand, and aggregate separately and mix them yourself, or order ready-mix concrete. Mixing it yourself—using 10 shovelfuls of portland cement, 22 shovelfuls of sand, and 30 shovelfuls of aggregate for each cubic foot—lets you make a small batch at a time. This allows you to place and finish one section before repeating the process.

If time and energy mean more to you than cost, order ready-mix concrete. You'll get a more reliable mix and also avoid hauling and mixing messes.

■ Pouring and finishing concrete

Spread sand or gravel in the form, then lay reinforcing mesh of a gauge appropriate to the job. Next, pour wet concrete into the form, spreading it with a garden rake. Use the rake's tines to pull the mesh midway into the slab's thickness.

Level the surface by screeding it with a 2x4 laid across the slab, from one side of the form to the other. Move the screed back and forth in a sawing motion and draw it horizontally across the unleveled concrete, as shown on page 161.

Smooth the concrete with a darby or bull float (see page 161). Then, when water no longer rises to the surface, run an edger between the slab and the form. After that, use a jointer and a straight board to hand-tool shallow control joints (every 8 feet or so in a patio; every 4 feet or so in a walk). Finish with a wood or steel trowel, or give the surface a special texture (see pages 162–163).

Keep concrete wet during the first week after you pour. One way to do this is with a hose or lawn sprinkler. You also can retard evaporation by covering the slab with plastic sheets.

(continued on page 286)

CONCRETE ESTIMATOR
In Cubic Feet and (Cubic Yards)

Thickness	Surface Area of Job in Square Feet				
	20	50	100	200	500
4 inches	6.7 (.2)	16.7 (.6)	33.3 (1.2)	66.7 (2.5)	166.7 (6.2)
6 inches	10 (.4)	25 (.9)	50 (1.9)	100 (3.7)	250 (9.3)
8 inches	13.3 (.5)	33.3 (1.3)	66.6 (2.5)	133.3 (5.9)	333.3 (12.5)

CONCRETE MIXING PROPORTIONS

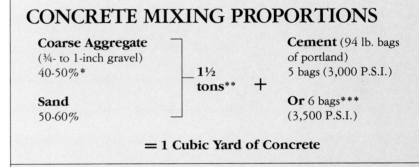

Coarse Aggregate
(¾- to 1-inch gravel)
40-50%*

Sand
50-60%

1½ tons**

+

Cement (94 lb. bags of portland)
5 bags (3,000 P.S.I.)

Or 6 bags***
(3,500 P.S.I.)

= 1 Cubic Yard of Concrete

*   The more aggregate, the stronger the mix.
** These ingredients can be purchased separately in the proportions described here or together in a mixture commonly known as *con-mix*.
*** For projects requiring extra lateral strength such as a driveway.

◄ *To control the wetness of concrete, watch it as you mix in water. The leftmost example is too dry; the middle mix is too soupy. The rightmost example shows a proper mix: it holds most of its shape when sliced but is still soft enough to pour and form.*

CONCRETE AND MASONRY *(continued)*

STONES

RUBBLE

FLAGSTONE

ASHLAR

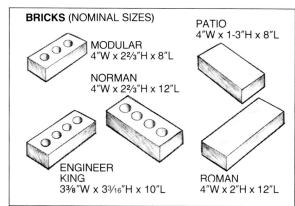

BRICKS (NOMINAL SIZES)

PATIO
4"W x 1-3"H x 8"L

MODULAR
4"W x 2⅔"H x 8"L

NORMAN
4"W x 2⅔"H x 12"L

ENGINEER
KING
3⅜"W x 3³⁄₁₆"H x 10"L

ROMAN
4"W x 2"H x 12"L

◄ *Stone is classified according to how it's cut. Rubble is uncut and highly irregular. Flagstones—typically sandstone, limestone, or quartzite—are big, flat rocks. Ashlar consists of squared but still irregular shapes.*

▲ *Bricks and stones come in myriad sizes. To estimate how many you will need, figure the area of your project in square feet. A masonry dealer can tell you how many bricks or stones of a given size will cover 1 square foot.*

▶ *To determine if your mortar mix has the right adhesiveness, pick up a small amount of it with your trowel, stick it to the trowel with an upward jerk, then turn the trowel upside down. If the mortar sticks to the trowel, it's ready for use.*

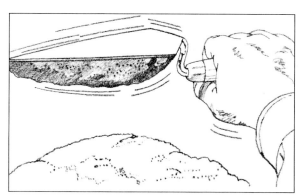

Easy to work with and nearly indestructible, stones, bricks, and blocks make sense for a wide range of outdoor building projects. First, we look at your choices in masonry units; then we tell you how to put them together.

■ Options
Masonry work can be accomplished with any number of different building materials.
■ *Stones* fall into the three broad categories illustrated at far left. *Rubble* stones interlock like three-dimensional jigsaw puzzles. Because they're irregular, rubble stones work well for walls but not horizontal surfaces such as patios and walks.

With *flagstones,* it's the other way around. These come in irregular shapes or precut squares and rectangles that are more or less uniform in thickness. Use flagstones for walks, steps, and patios, and anywhere else you want a durable, dressy surface.

Ashlar or dimensioned stone is cut on all sides, making it easy to stack. You still have to do some final cutting and fitting, though.
■ *Bricks* vary widely in color, texture, and dimensions. *Modular* bricks are sized to conform to modules of 4 inches, which makes it easy to estimate how many you will need. *Non-modular* bricks do not conform to the 4-inch module in one or more dimensions.

When a dealer tells you the dimensions of a brick, he is talking about its *nominal size,* which is the brick's actual size, plus a normal mortar joint of ⅜ to ½ inch on the bottom and at one end.

For outdoor projects that must withstand moisture and freeze-thaw cycles, ask for SW (severe weathering) bricks. If temperatures in your area are moderate year-round, you can get by with MW (moderate weathering) bricks. Use NW (no weathering) bricks only for interior projects such as fireplaces.
■ *Concrete blocks* are cast from a stiff concrete mix into hundreds of different sizes and shapes. A typical block has a nominal size of 8x8x16 inches and weighs 40 to 50 pounds.

Concrete blocks come in two grades—*N*, designed for outdoor freezing, and *S*, for use above grade and where the blocks won't be directly exposed to weather.

■ Masonry *veneers* of brick, terra-cotta, slate, and stone offer a way to put an attractive face on otherwise plain materials, such as concrete. Terra-cotta quarry tiles are made in many colors and shapes. They measure ⅜ inch or ½ inch thick. Slate tiles also come in several colors, in uniform thicknesses ranging from ¼ inch to 1 inch. Flagstones aren't uniformly thick, which means you must lay them on sand or in a thick mortar bed. See pages 164–165 for details.

■ Dry vs. wet setting

Once you've settled on the sort of masonry units you'd like for your project, you need to decide what to put between them. Here your choices are two: *dry-set* the units without mortar or *wet-set* the units using mortar to bond them.

To dry-set a patio or other surface, you simply excavate, lay down a bed of sand, set the masonry on this bed, then sweep more sand into the joints. More about this on pages 154–157. You also can lay up a stone retaining wall without mortar, as shown on page 72.

Dry setting is far and away the easier way to go, but mortaring isn't as difficult as you might imagine, once you get the hang of it.

■ Mixing mortar

How you go about preparing the mortar for a job depends on the project's size. For small jobs and repairs, buy premixed mortar that already contains sand. For larger ventures, you'll save money by purchasing the sand and masonry cement separately and mixing them yourself.

To mix mortar, carefully measure three parts sand and one part cement into a wheelbarrow or mortar box. Spread half of the sand first, then the cement, then the rest of the sand. Use a hoe to thoroughly mix the dry materials.

After you've completely blended the sand and cement, make a depression in the center of the dry mix, pour a small amount of water into

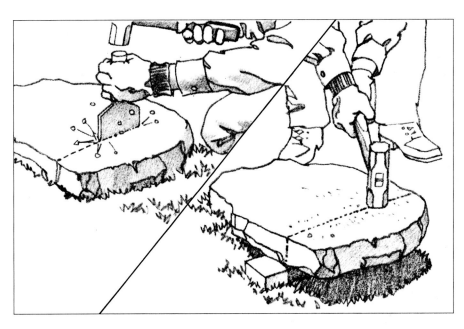

it, then fold the mix into the water with a hoe or trowel. Add more water until your mix behaves as shown opposite, bottom. Be sure to take your time. Generally, you'll need about 2½ gallons of water for each bag of cement, but this can vary, depending on the moisture content of the sand. Don't run water from a hose into the mix; you might drown the mortar.

■ Working with mortar

Lay mortared masonry paving units only on top of sound, clean concrete. If you have to pour a concrete slab first, follow the steps explained on pages 284–285, skipping any steps after the concrete is screeded.

Wet the surface just before troweling on an even ¼- to 1-inch layer of mortar. Use a thinner layer for even-surface paving units such as brick, a thicker one for irregular stones. Screed this to a uniform depth with a piece of 2x4, then place the paving units on the mortar, leveling each one as you position it. Let the mortar holding the masonry set and cure for a day or two before you fill the joints between them with more mortar. For more about working with mortar, see pages 124–125 and 164–165.

▲ *To cut a stone, score all around the desired break line. Lay the stone across a support; tap the unsupported part. Wear goggles when doing this.*

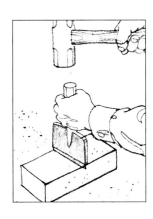

▲ *To cut a brick, score around it. Set the brick on sand, hold a brick set with its bevel away from the side of the finished cut, and rap sharply.*

WIRING

If you've successfully pulled off a few indoor wiring projects, the principles you learned there can help you do the same outside. Exterior electrical equipment differs slightly, however, and you must take a few more precautions to protect wiring against moisture.

Read these two pages for details on the tools and components you'll need. Pages 290–291 discuss the techniques you'll need to master.

(*Caution:* If you've never worked with electricity before, outdoors is not the place to start. For this reason, we've omitted any discussion of basic procedures such as making connections and hooking up receptacles and switches.)

■ Cable

In planning an underground installation, first find out whether local codes permit plastic-clad UF cable, or whether they require that you run standard TW wire through rigid conduit. If you're permitted to use cable, you'll still have to protect it with conduit in aboveground situations. Keep in mind, too, that cable should be buried at least 12 inches below the surface. Rigid conduit need go only six inches underground; thinner EMT conduit (the kind used indoors) requires 12 inches of earth protection.

When you buy fittings, make sure they're the weathertight type designed for outdoor use. Exterior components look much like the ones used inside, but they're heftier and have gaskets, waterproof covers, and rubber-sealed connections.

Also, because the potential for serious shock is much greater outdoors, you must protect all exterior receptacles with *ground fault circuit interrupters* (GFCIs). These devices, which can be installed in your home's service panel or in lieu of a standard receptacle, instantly shut off power should a malfunction occur.

■ Tools

You may not need all the items pictured on the opposite page, and you may already have quite a few of them, but let's explain what each does.

Long-nose and *linemen's pliers* are musts. The first help you curl wires into the loops needed for many electrical connections. Linemen's pliers handle heavier cutting and twisting jobs. *Side-cutting pliers* are handy when you have to snip wires in tight places.

A *utility knife* slices through anything that calls for a cutting edge. A *combination tool* does a variety of tasks—cuts and strips wires, sizes and cuts off screws, crimps connectors, and more. If your wiring is protected by cartridge-type fuses, a plastic *fuse puller* lets you remove them without danger of electrical shock.

Several types of testers are available. The *continuity* type has a small battery and bulb for testing switches, sockets, and fuses with the power off. A *neon tester,* on the other hand, lights up only when current is flowing. It tells you whether an outlet is live and hooked up properly.

You'll need one of each of these, or you can invest in an inexpensive *voltmeter* instead. If you'll be installing a number of new receptacles, you also might want a *receptacle analyzer.*

With an *electric drill,* a *spade bit,* and a *bit extension,* you can bore holes for wiring in just about anything, even through the side of your house.

If codes permit UF cable in your area, use a *cable ripper* to cut open the plastic sheathing. The one shown also strips insulation from conductors. For conduit, you'll need a *tubing cutter,* a *bender,* and a *fish tape* to pull wires through.

Low-voltage jobs are often soldered. Use a *soldering gun* and a spool of rosin-core *solder.*

Most of the gear shown here packs easily into a *tool pouch.* Electrical work keeps you on the move, and you'll appreciate the convenience of having everything you might need at your hip.

■ Low-voltage wiring

If you don't relish the arduous job of burying 120-volt wiring underground, consider choosing a low-voltage lighting system instead. These step down house current to a six- or 12-volt tickle, which means you can safely string fixtures like so many Christmas tree lights. Simply plug a transformer into a standard 120-volt receptacle and run lightweight cable to the fixtures. See pages 214–215 for more details.

(continued on page 290)

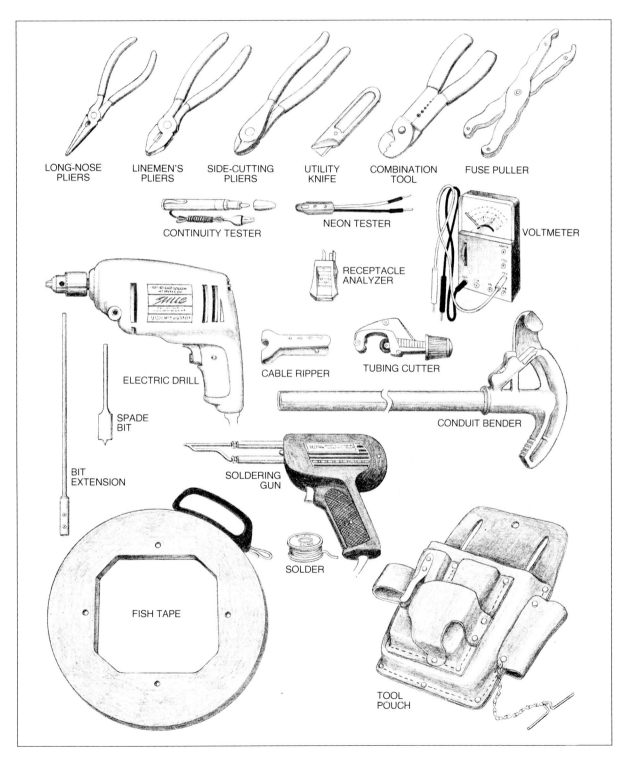

LONG-NOSE
PLIERS

LINEMEN'S
PLIERS

SIDE-CUTTING
PLIERS

UTILITY
KNIFE

COMBINATION
TOOL

FUSE PULLER

◀ *Armed with these tools, you can do just about any electrical job, indoors or out. If you'll have a lot of digging to do, you might also want to rent a gasoline-engine trenching machine. Even for short runs, you can count on a hard day of excavating by hand.*

CONTINUITY TESTER

NEON TESTER

VOLTMETER

RECEPTACLE
ANALYZER

ELECTRIC DRILL

CABLE RIPPER

TUBING CUTTER

SPADE
BIT

CONDUIT BENDER

BIT
EXTENSION

SOLDERING
GUN

SOLDER

FISH TAPE

TOOL
POUCH

WIRING *(continued)*

To complete an outdoor electrical installation, you first have to decide where the power is going to come from. Next, you dig a trench from that point to the site or sites where you would like lights or receptacles. Then you lay conduit, cable, or a combination of the two and make the final connections.

■ Tapping power

If there's an exterior receptacle nearby, you're in luck. Simply dig a trench to the receptacle and hook up to it as shown at upper right.

If there's no convenient source of power outside, look around your basement for a junction box, or run a new circuit from the service panel. This requires boring a hole through the wall, as shown at lower right.

In some localities, you can run sheathed cable through the wall to a new box outside; in others, you're required to use conduit or armored cable. Find out what codes permit. In most cases, it's best to install a junction box back to back with the exterior box, then connect the two with conduit or cable.

A third option is to take power from an exterior light fixture, as shown on the opposite page. This is probably the least desirable way to go, because you have to run conduit up to the eaves, and your new outlet will be live only when the light switch is turned on.

■ In the trenches

Once you know where power is going to come from, it's time to plan an itinerary for the trench or trenches you will need. Route these well away from water, gas, electric, telephone, sewer, and sprinkler lines. For conduit, keep the trenches as straight as possible; sheathed cable can easily snake around obstructions.

After you've laid out a trench, strip away sod and set it aside on plastic sheeting. Keep the sod slightly damp. For EMT tubing and UF cable, you'll need a trench that is about 8 inches wide by 1 foot deep; rigid conduit requires one that is 4 inches wide by 6 inches deep.

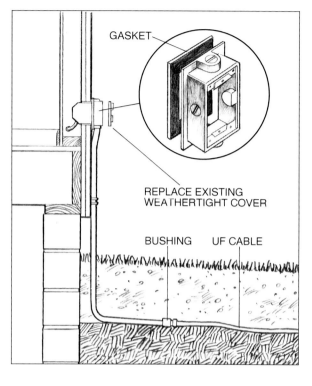

GASKET

REPLACE EXISTING WEATHERTIGHT COVER

BUSHING   UF CABLE

◄ *To tap into an exterior receptacle, add a weathertight box extension and run conduit from it. Be sure to caulk all around the extension. If you use UF cable, it should exit from conduit about 12 inches below grade through a special insulating bushing.*

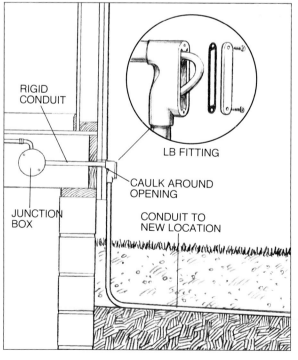

RIGID CONDUIT

LB FITTING

JUNCTION BOX

CAULK AROUND OPENING

CONDUIT TO NEW LOCATION

◄ *Here, threaded rigid conduit connects a basement junction box to an LB fitting. This fitting has a removable plate that makes it easy to pull wires through, but there's not enough space inside to make connections. Caulk where conduit enters the wall.*

► *If you want a post lamp or other light to go on at the same time as an under-eave light, tap into it. To do this, you'll need the round box extension shown in the inset drawing.*

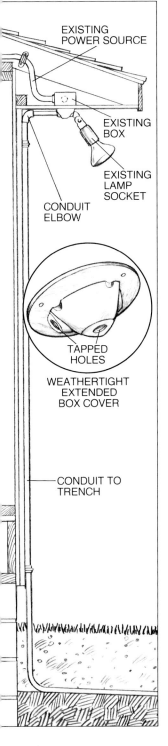

EXISTING POWER SOURCE

EXISTING BOX

EXISTING LAMP SOCKET

CONDUIT ELBOW

TAPPED HOLES

WEATHERTIGHT EXTENDED BOX COVER

CONDUIT TO TRENCH

To avoid tearing up a sidewalk, dig to one side of it, then resume on the other. After you've finished digging, flatten one end of a piece of conduit, lay it in the trench, and drive it through the ground under the walk. After it emerges on the other side, cut off the flat end. You also can rent an auger.

■ **Bending conduit**

Conduit comes in 10-foot sections: ½, ¾, or 1 inch in diameter. To work with conduit, first shape it with a bender like the one shown on page 289, then cut it to length. Always bend the conduit before cutting it because each bend shortens the total run by a few inches.

If you've never worked with conduit before, buy an extra length or two and experiment until you get the knack of bending the tubing in gentle arcs, with no crimps that might impede the pulling of wires.

To bend conduit, slip the conduit into a bender, with its handle pointing up and away from you. Then, with one foot on the conduit, pull the handle slowly and steadily toward you. Make a bend gradually, with a series of tugs along its radius. Pull too sharply at any point and you'll crimp the tubing. When the handle reaches a 45-degree angle with the ground, you've completed a 90-degree bend.

EMT conduit bends easily. Bending rigid tubing requires more muscle; for simple runs, consider substituting elbow connectors for bends. Codes forbid a total of more than 360 degrees in bends along any run. This limits you to four 90-degree quarter bends, three if you'll have offsets at the ends (which you'll need for a box that's mounted on a wall).

■ **Cutting and connecting**

Cut conduit with a hacksaw or, better yet, an inexpensive turning cutter like the one shown on page 289. Clamp the cutter onto the conduit, rotate a few times, tighten the handle, then rotate some more. A wheellike blade slices through the metal.

A second pointed blade on the cutter lets you remove sharp burrs that could chew up wiring insulation. Stick the point into the cut tubing end and rotate the cutter.

Join conduit sections end to end with waterproof couplings. At boxes, use special connectors. Some of these connectors include offsets, which can save a lot of bending.

Connect conduit carefully. Pulling wires through conduit can subject components to stress, and good grounding depends on secure metal-to-metal connections.

■ **Pulling wires**

Now comes the time when you learn why codes are so specific about bends, crimps, and burrs in tubing. As you pull wires through your conduit, you'll quickly notice that any hang-ups can lacerate insulation or even make the task impossible.

For a relatively straight run, you can probably push the wires from one box to another. If you can't push the wires, you'll need a fish tape and a helper. Snake the tape through the conduit, then hook the tape and wires together.

Next, begin pulling with gentle pressure. As the wires work past bends, expect to exert more muscle. Have your helper gently feed wires into the conduit. With lots of wires or a long pull, lubricate the wires with talcum powder or pulling grease, available from electrical suppliers.

Leave 6 to 8 inches of extra wire at each box. And never splice wires inside conduit. They must run continuously from box to box.

■ **Aboveground receptacle**

When installing a freestanding exterior receptacle that rises out of the ground on a conduit stalk, be sure to firmly root the stalk in concrete below. First, cut the bottom out of a large coffee can and slip it over the conduit. Then plumb the stalk and brace it with guy wires. Next, fill the can with concrete. Bevel the top so water will run off. Extend the stalk 20 to 24 inches above ground so no one will trip over it.

PLANTS

Essential to all landscapes, of course, are plants. On these two pages, we outline some of the tools you'll need when working with plants, and offer a brief discussion about improving your soil. On pages 294–295, you'll find details on choosing and starting plants. Pages 296–297 discuss starting a lawn, and pages 298–299 give information on the climate zones that should guide you in selecting plants. For information on maintaining plants and lawns, see pages 254–267. And for plant recommendations, see pages 300–323, plus the charts sprinkled throughout the book.

■ Tools

Having the right yard tool at hand can make all the difference in how, when, or if a job gets done, and in how much you enjoy or resent it.

Your tool choices depend largely on the size and makeup of your yard, as well as your temperament and the time you have for yard work.

Most garden work can be done with a hoe and a trowel. But a power shredder, edger, composter, and bicycle-tired cart add greatly to the ease and satisfaction for some people.

Examine tools before you buy. If a handle is too long, short, or heavy for you, try another. Check connections. The best spades, forks, and long-handled shovels have a metal shank extending part way up the handle for additional strength. Trowels are more durable when they have wooden handles driven into a metal shank.

Wheelbarrows and carts come in many materials and sizes: small enough to go down the cellar steps or big enough for six bags of leaves.

Choose hoses for weight, length, durability, and ease of repair. Consider soaker hoses, mist nozzles, and sprinklers according to your yard's needs. Hose attachments for fertilizers and sprays have finally reached the no-plug stage and work well.

■ Tool care

With care, well-made tools will last for years. Here are some maintenance hints.

■ Clean tools after each use with a paint stick or steel brush to keep soil from encrusting.
■ Wipe wooden handles with linseed oil. Paint them a bright color if you tend to lose tools.
■ Sharpen tools for efficiency and safety. Follow manual instructions. Use a file on the inside edge of your hoe.
■ Check and tighten bolts and screws regularly.
■ Wind up hoses between use. Excessive sun shortens their life. Drain well before winter.
■ Remove grass clippings, dirt, and grease from your mower and sharpen as needed. Before winter, run until gasoline is used. Drain the crankcase. Clean the oil filter. Add clean oil.
■ Sharpen the blades of shears, mowers, spades, and hoes before storing for winter. Apply oil, floor wax, petroleum jelly, or lard.
■ Wash and dry sprayers thoroughly after each use. Oil plunger rod and leather plunger often.
■ Have a storage area handy to the garden.
■ Store all sprays, dusts, and poisons out of the reach of children and pets.

■ Soil improvements

There are three main types of soil, one of which is best for growing plants. Loam—the ideal soil—molds into a loose mound when squeezed lightly. Squeezed harder, however, it crumbles. Soil high in clay forms a tight, sticky mass if squeezed when wet. Sandy soil feels grainy and crumbles when wet.

If your yard's soil is clayey or sandy, turn it to a depth of at least 1 foot wherever you want to garden and add humus in the form of compost, peat, grass clippings, shredded leaves, or any other organic matter. If you religiously use all organic material produced in the garden and house as mulch or compost, you'll soon have a wonderfully friable, workable soil that smells of life. For more about composting, see page 235.

Also important are a soil's acidity and its levels of certain nutrients. To judge your soil, buy and use a soil test kit or have your soil tested. The test will tell you exactly what your soil needs. Check with your county extension office for more details.

(continued on page 294)

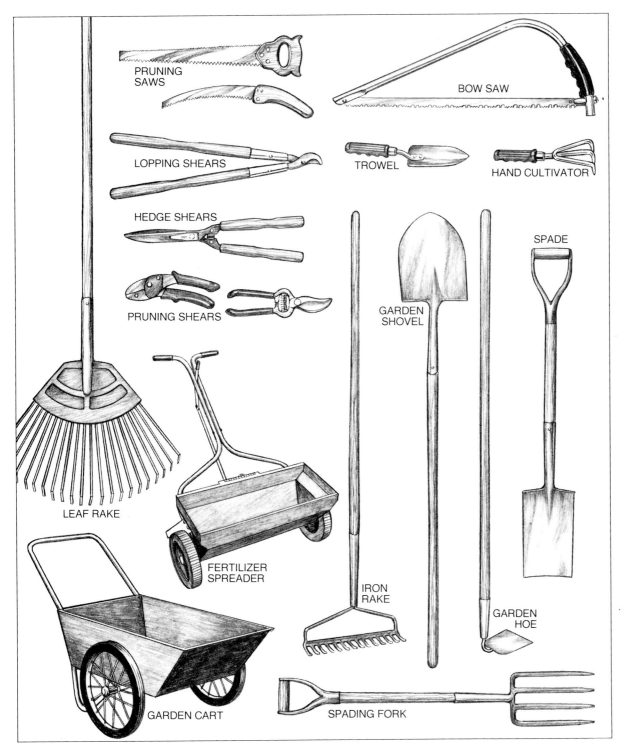

PRUNING SAWS

BOW SAW

LOPPING SHEARS

TROWEL

HAND CULTIVATOR

HEDGE SHEARS

SPADE

PRUNING SHEARS

GARDEN SHOVEL

LEAF RAKE

FERTILIZER SPREADER

IRON RAKE

GARDEN HOE

GARDEN CART

SPADING FORK

◀ Here are most of the basic garden tools you'll need. You may prefer to rent rather than store a spreader. You also will need a lawn mower, perhaps an edger, and hoses. The final choice depends largely on the jobs you'll be doing most often, and the tools that you prefer.

PLANTS *(continued)*

To begin creating the green part of your landscape, buy plants from a reputable local or mail-order nursery or start them yourself. The decision depends mainly on the size of plants you want to start with.

■ Nursery plants

Bare-root stock, the most economical nursery plants, must be purchased and planted while dormant, usually late winter or early spring. Some nurseries can extend that dormancy for several weeks into the spring with cold storage. Bare-root plants come as rather dead-looking twigs, so the reputation of the nursery and its guarantee are important. Swelling of buds and suppleness of branches indicate life. Place roots and as much of the rest of the plant as possible in water for several hours to overnight, then plant.

Mail-order stock may arrive at the beginning of a week of rain. If you can't plant soon, heel in the plants by placing them slantwise in a shallow trench and covering the roots with soil (see page 61). As soon as possible, move the plants to their permanent homes.

When selecting container plants, pick ones with good foliage color. If the choice is between present blooms and basic shape, make yourself choose the best branch structure and you'll get more blooms in the long run.

Balled-and-burlapped or potted trees and shrubs can be planted any time of the year, but spring and early fall are the best times. Worst is late fall before a hard winter or in a hot summer without proper aftercare.

■ Planting

For years, the rule was that it was better to dig a $5 hole for a $1 plant than vice versa. It still is necessary to dig a generous hole so the roots will not be crowded, but it is no longer advisable to fill it with such good soil amendments that the roots will never push outward.

Dig your hole 2 feet wider than the root ball. It need be no deeper. If roots have become tangled within a pot, pull some of them apart. Fill the hole with good soil; replace subsoil or clay with topsoil.

Remove any labels, instruction tags, or strings that encircle branches so they won't restrain or become imbedded in the growth.

Whenever you plant anything, water well, as much to settle as to moisten the soil. Then mulch the soil surface and leave a surrounding doughnutlike ridge—a foot or so from a tree trunk, several inches from the crown of a perennial flower—to hold in waterings or rain.

Most trees are already pruned at the nursery. Remove any broken or crowding branches, then prune only as needed to start the shape you want. See pages 266–267 for more about care after planting.

Very large trees should be planted by an expert who has the special equipment needed. This equipment also will require a certain amount of space, so plant your big trees before you put in surrounding plantings.

▲ *For a bare-root tree, dig a hole large enough to spread the roots without crowding. Place the tree at the same depth it was before, as indicated by the darker area of the trunk. Stake on the windward side.*

▲ *Dig a large hole for balled-and-burlapped trees as well. You can leave the burlap to rot away, but remove any plastic, wire, or cords. Adjust height; planting too deep could kill the tree. Stake as needed.*

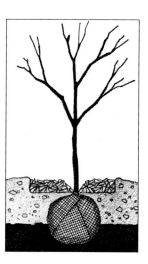

▲ *Elevate the grade if your soil drains poorly or if your yard has a high water table. (Test for these conditions by filling a hole with water. The water should drain overnight.) Slope softly back to existing grade.*

■ Starting plants

For starts of shrubs, perennials, or ground covers, consider seeking divisions from friends' plants. Or, try planting one section of your yard this year—say with a ground cover—then letting the plants multiply there until you have enough to start another section.

Shrubs are best divided in early spring, when they're still dormant. For late-blooming perennials like phlox and mum, divide just as shoots are coming up. Divide after flowers fade for early bloomers like iris or peonies.

For some plants—like Japanese iris, rhubarb, and the offshoots of a lilac bush—simply cut a chunk of branch and root from the edge of the clump with a spade. You won't disturb the rest of the plant at all.

Many clumps, such as those of ajuga, can be carefully dug with a spading fork and divided by pulling the crowns apart. Others, like ferns, may have such entangled roots that you'll have to pry the clumps into sections with two spading forks or cut them apart with a sharp knife. Replant each section in good soil with ample room for the plant's natural spread.

■ Seeds

Seeds are the most inexpensive way to start many plants, but they take longest and may not always be true to color. Annuals and herbs are often started from seed planted indoors in late winter or outdoors as soon as cold weather is past. Most packets give the best time to plant and instructions as to depth and distance apart.

Indoors, plant in a sterile medium like purchased potting soil or perlite in any container that has bottom holes for drainage. Pack and moisten the medium. Scatter the seeds and press them. Tiny seeds need no covering; larger ones can be planted as deep as their greatest width.

Cover the container with a loose piece of plastic. Bread wrappers work fine and usually keep the medium moist enough for several days. Heat from the bottom speeds sprouting, so put containers on the refrigerator, dryer, or TV. Most seeds do not need light at this point.

◄*After planting, remove any branches that have too narrow an angle (top cut) or are crossing or crowding (middle and lower cuts). Such pruning leaves a strong scaffold of branches. For best healing, cut just beyond the branch collar (inset), almost but not quite flush.*

Packets or catalogs also may tell you when to expect germination, which can vary from two days to a few weeks, depending on the kind of seed. (Some tree seeds take several seasons.)

As soon as the first sprouts begin to emerge, move the container to a bright, cool place and take off the plastic. Keep the medium moist but don't overwater. Feed and transplant when the second set of leaves appears.

Harden-off the seedlings before transplanting them outdoors. To do this, carry them slightly on the dry side, but don't let them wilt. Place the containers outdoors for a few more hours each day until they are used to the sun and wind. If the weather is harsh the first few days after transplanting, put milk jugs or other protection around the seedlings.

If you plant your seeds outdoors, you'll have less control over seedling growth, but more space. Prepare the soil. Water it well. Plant seeds, cover a tad more deeply than indoors, and keep the soil moist until seedlings appear.

The main drawback to seeding outdoors is that you must be familiar enough with the seedling to know if it is that or a weed coming up. Seed packets, rows, and time will help you tell for sure.

Thin and transplant seedlings as needed, and pinch most annuals to encourage bushiness.

(continued on page 296)

PLANTS *(continued)*

Since a good lawn will last for generations, it is vital to plant it carefully. (For details on maintaining established lawns, see Chapter 12, pages 254–265.)

■ Grading
Before starting, make sure the lawn area is as level as possible and drains properly. For good drainage, slope the lawn gently away from your house. Consider ground covers or a retaining wall for severe grades (see Chapter 3). Mowing steep slopes is difficult and can be dangerous.

Whenever building or drastically changing grades, remove the topsoil first, then respread it over the leveled surface. You can do small jobs yourself with a spade and rake or an old tire pulled by a rope. Hire a tractor for big jobs.

For more information on grading and drainage, see pages 52–57.

■ Improving the soil
Also before starting, test your soil with a simple test kit or contact your county extension agent and follow instructions. Most grasses thrive at a neutral or slightly acid pH of 6 to 7. Add lime as needed to improve the structure and provide the best environment (less acid, better chemical balance) for beneficial bacteria and earthworms.

Adding organic matter, such as moist peat or weed-free compost, and additional topsoil, if needed, will increase growth and decrease maintenance. Also broadcast a complete fertilizer (10-10-10, for example) using 10 to 20 pounds per 1,000 square feet, depending on the fertility of the soil. Till or spade 6 inches deep, making the soil pebbly, but not powdery. Remove any rocks or debris and rake smooth, leaving shallow crevices to catch grass seeds.

■ Choosing the kind
Choose from new, improved grasses according to how much sun your lawn will get, and how you will use the yard. In the southern states, warm-season grasses grow most from March

◀ *After your soil is ready, use a mechanical spreader, a shoulder planter, or hand broadcasting to apply half of the seed while walking back and forth one way. Then spread the rest going in a perpendicular direction over the same area.*

◀ *When sodding, prepare the soil well as for seeding. Lay the sod within a few hours after delivery. Stagger the end seams. Roll and water. Mound soil around exposed edges. Keep the area well watered until new growth starts.*

◀ *Planting sprigs or stolons is another way to start a new lawn vegetatively. Again, prepare the soil well. Bury the sprigs with only the top nodes above ground. Space most 12 inches apart, zoysia 6 inches. Mulch will help. Keep area watered.*

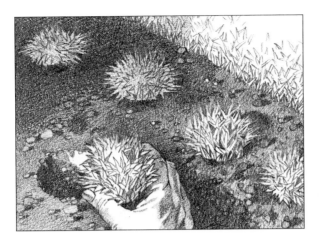

► *Plugging is a convenient and economical method to repair or establish a lawn with warm-season grasses. Most southern lawns are started this way. The runners spread above ground to fill in quickly and crowd out weeds.*

through August. They turn brown after frost. Over-seed with a winter grass in the fall to keep weeds out and extend and intensify the lawn's green color.

Bahia is the only southern grass often started from seed and thus is less expensive. It also is less elegant but takes less care. St. Augustine makes a thick turf and is beautiful as long as it is protected from its several and serious enemies.

Bermuda is used on southern golf courses and athletic fields. 'Meyer' zoysia will thrive farther north than any other southern grass. 'Cashmere' zoysia has finer texture, grows faster, and tolerates shade better.

In the northern two-thirds of the country, use mixtures of cool-season grasses. These grasses flourish in spring and fall, and turn brown in the dead of winter and during summer drought.

Most sunny cool-season lawns use largely bluegrasses. New varieties like 'Bonnieblue', 'Eclipse', and 'Sydsport' have superior color, density, and heat and drought tolerance.

Fescues are the best for shade and for play areas that get rough treatment. New ryegrasses are especially good for getting a lawn established fast.

When buying grass seed, always check the label for percentage of germination, varieties included, and percent of inert ingredients. Better seed is worth the price; cheap is no bargain if you have to redo all the work or settle for an inferior lawn.

■ **When to start**

The ideal time for planting seed is early September, with very early spring second best. Sow the amount listed in the package directions (too much seed can cause the tiny grass plants to choke each other out). Then walk backward and rake lightly so that the seed is covered with no more than ⅛ inch of soil.

Sod, sprigs, and plugs can go in almost anytime, though spring or fall is preferred. When you choose sod, look for well-rooted, moist rolls that are uniformly green and not yellowing.

Roll the area after planting seed or sod, then, if seeding, cover with mulch to conserve moisture. If you rent a drum roller with a surface of mesh fabric, you can roll the ground and apply a thin mulch of peat moss at the same time. Or spread straw about ⅛ inch thick—so you can see soil through it—after you've rolled the area. If you use burlap to retain moisture, remove it as soon as germination begins. A mesh material that the grass can grow through is available, though more expensive. Use it only on steep slopes or difficult spots (see pages 66–67).

■ **Watering and mowing**

The main cause of lawn failures is lack of moisture. Water new lawns with a fine mist from two to several times a day for the first week; the next week, water at least once a day. Water less frequently but more deeply as grass grows.

Weeds also may germinate, but your new grass soon will crowd them out. Keep traffic off until the lawn is well established.

Mow the grass with sharp blades set at about 1½ inches when the new growth is 2 inches tall. Fertilize it lightly after mowing, then monthly for three or four months, giving thinner spots a bit more food to equalize growth.

(continued on page 298)

PLANTS *(continued)*

O ne key to successful landscaping is planting the right plant in the right place. The hardiness zone map on these two pages was prepared by the U.S. Department of Agriculture, and is based on a study of the average annual minimum temperatures recorded by 14,500 weather stations throughout North America.

Find and keep in mind your zone number when choosing any plant for your landscape. In this and other garden books and catalogs, zones of hardiness are given for many plants.

As the environment is increasingly threatened, it becomes more and more important to use our bit of land wisely and carefully. The right plants will need less coddling, less water, and fewer pesticides, and reward us with more success and enjoyment.

■ Microclimates

This zone map and others, though, are only general guides. Most yards have several microclimates determined by exposure, wind, elevation, and surroundings. In the warmer microclimates of your yard, you may be able to grow a few plants from the next zone to your south. Or you may find that most of your yard requires extra hardiness, and you'd be wiser to choose from the zone to your north.

In yards near the water or in cities surrounded by much concrete, tender plants may escape damage while the same plants a few miles away suffer mild to severe winterkill.

Here are some other factors to consider when choosing plants and deciding where they might grow best.

■ Southern and western sides of houses and other structures are sunnier and warmer than northern or eastern exposures.

■ Southern and eastern exposures usually are protected from chilling winter winds.

■ Strong winds can damage plants, by either drying the soil or knocking over fragile growth.

■ Cold air sweeps down hills and rests in low areas of neighborhoods.

■ Your microclimates will change as your trees grow larger or when you add a fence or deck.

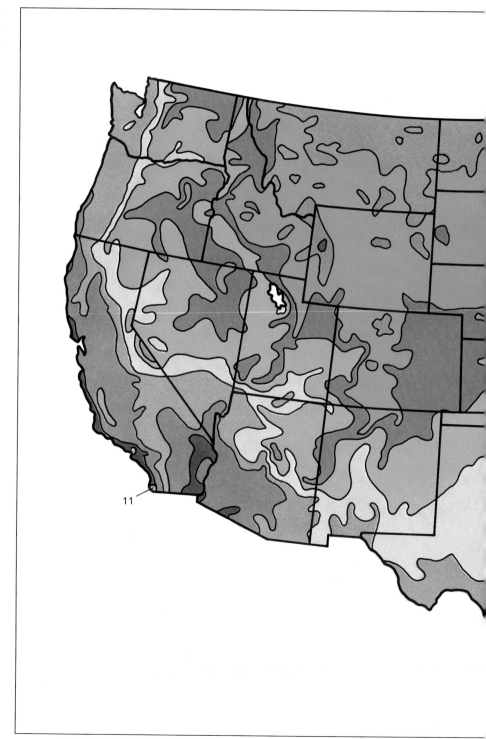

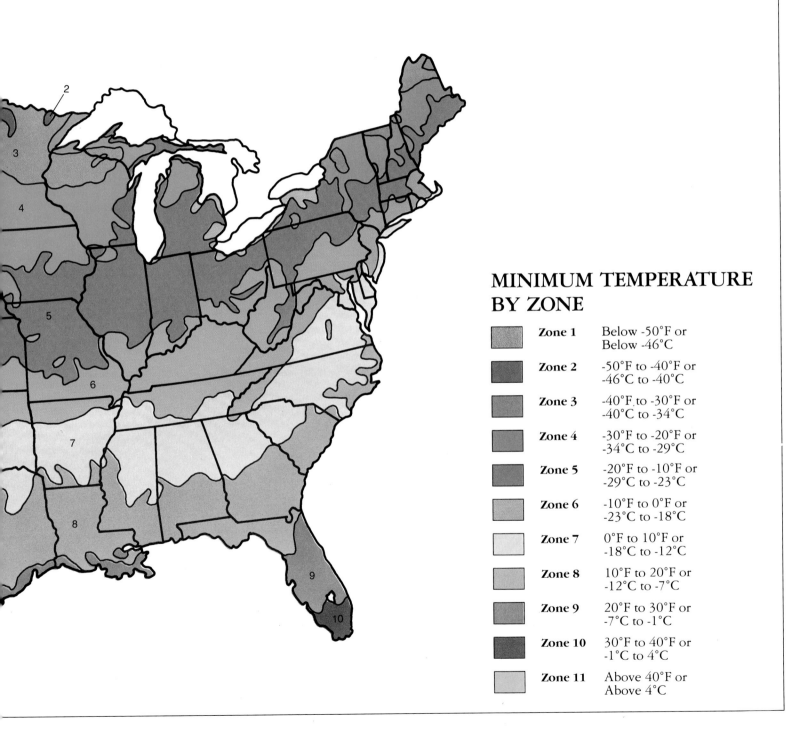

MINIMUM TEMPERATURE BY ZONE

	Zone 1	Below -50°F or Below -46°C
	Zone 2	-50°F to -40°F or -46°C to -40°C
	Zone 3	-40°F to -30°F or -40°C to -34°C
	Zone 4	-30°F to -20°F or -34°C to -29°C
	Zone 5	-20°F to -10°F or -29°C to -23°C
	Zone 6	-10°F to 0°F or -23°C to -18°C
	Zone 7	0°F to 10°F or -18°C to -12°C
	Zone 8	10°F to 20°F or -12°C to -7°C
	Zone 9	20°F to 30°F or -7°C to -1°C
	Zone 10	30°F to 40°F or -1°C to 4°C
	Zone 11	Above 40°F or Above 4°C

CHAPTER FOURTEEN

RECOMMENDED PLANTS

After completing your general plans, you are ready for the fun of picking particular plants. To help you begin, this chapter describes many popular trees, shrubs, vines, ground covers, and flowers. While making your decisions, keep in mind that your selections will satisfy you more if they serve several purposes and offer interest for several seasons. Remember, too, that the botanical world is vast, and that there are many fine plants beyond those listed in this review.

DECIDUOUS TREES

SMALL (up to 30 feet tall)

Crab Apple (*Malus* species and hybrids)
Many flowering crab apple varieties and cultivars make excellent small to medium landscaping trees that provide year-round interest. Crab apples prefer acid soil, but plant where dropping fruit won't create cleanup chores. Select disease-resistant varieties. (See also page 108.) 15–25 feet/Zones 3–8.

Dogwood: Flowering, Japanese
(*Cornus florida, C. kousa*)
Dogwoods are among the choicest trees for interest all year. They like light shade and acid soil. A new disease is causing some trouble. (See also page 108.) 15–30 feet/Zones 4–9.

Franklinia (*Franklinia alatamaha*)
Rare and lovely, franklinia is a slow grower that prefers sheltered valleys and partial shade. Camellialike flowers, 3 inches across, open singly over many weeks. Leaves turn crimson in autumn. Franklinia likes rich, acid soil. It's sometimes hard to grow, and can die suddenly. 20–30 feet/Zones 6–8.

Fringe Tree (*Chionanthus virginicus*)
This slow-growing native tree has fleecy white flowers in early June and bright yellow fall color. Foliage is bold and similar to magnolia. The vase-shaped crown is wider than it is tall. Leaves and flowers come late; blooms are aromatic and long lasting. Good near patios, fringe tree can be trained as a shrub or tree. 20–30 feet/Zones 5–8.

Fruit Trees (stone) (*Prunus* species)
Peach, cherry, plum, apricot, and others in this group offer fine edible landscaping; highly ornamental fruitless varieties also are available. All are covered with bloom before leaves show in spring. Some have interesting shapes or bark and good fall color. (See also page 110.) 20–25 feet/Zones 4–10.

Hawthorn (*Crataegus* species)
Tough, thorny hawthorn has delicate clusters of white or pink flowers in spring, glossy green foliage, orange to red fall color, and scarlet or yellow fruits. Hawthorn tolerates clipping, salt, pollution, and other adverse conditions, but can get fire blight. 15–30 feet/Zones 5–9.

Hazelnut (*Corylus avellana*)
Perhaps the easiest nut tree for the homeowner to grow, the small hazelnut—also called filbert—works well near a patio or entry, or as a screen or accent. Hazlenut adapts well to many soils but needs full sun. Two or more are required to bear nuts, but you can plant them in clumps or as a hedge. Catkins bloom on winter branches, dark green leaves are woolly underneath, and nuts come in frilly green clusters. 6–25 feet/Zones 4–8.

Lilac, Japanese Tree (*Syringa reticulata*)
A true tree, this lilac has a spreading umbrella form, cherrylike bark, a fragrance similar to privet, and large trusses of white flowers in mid-June. It is attractive, disease free, and drought resistant. 20–30 feet/Zones 5–8.

Magnolia: Merrill, Saucer, Star
(*Magnolia kobus x loebneri* 'Merrill,'
M. x soulangiana, M. stellata)
All three trees have large, striking flowers of pink and white, and bloom when young. Velvety buds, cucumberlike pods with red seeds, and multitrunked habit all add interest. Magnolias like full sun or light shade, and rich, acid soil with plenty of root room. Late frosts can damage flowers. 15–30 feet/Zones 5–10.

Maple, Amur (*Acer ginnala*)
Usually multitrunked, this maple has fragrant, nonshowy flowers, bright red winged seeds in summer, and brilliant fall foliage. Its leaves are oval or globe shape. This tree withstands cold and wind better than Japanese maple. (See also page 108.) 15–20 feet/Zones 5–10.

(continued on page 302)

DECIDUOUS TREES *(continued)*

Maple, Japanese (*Acer palmatum*)
Japanese maple is a fine accent tree with dense green to red star-shaped leaves, scarlet autumn color, and gray horizontal branches. Japanese maple likes slightly acid soil and some protection from wind. It produces its best color when grown in sun to part shade. (See also page 108.) 15–20 feet/Zones 6–9.

Redbud (*Cercis canadensis*)
Redbud is prized for its purple spring bloom, heart-shaped leaves, yellow autumn color, multiple trunks, and rounded habit. Good in woodlands or shrub borders or as an accent plant, redbud tolerates shade and many soils. Unfortunately, it is susceptible to wilt and borer. 25–35 feet/Zones 4–8.

Serviceberry (*Amelanchier canadensis*)
Also called shadblow, serviceberry has white flowers that briefly cover its branches early in spring; its fall color ranges from beautiful yellow to red. Edible maroon and purple berries attract birds. This tree gives light to medium shade, and does best in acid soil and natural settings. Serviceberry doesn't tolerate pollution well. 6–20 feet/Zones 4–5.

Silver-Bell, Carolina (*Halesia carolina*)
This small tree, also called snowdrop tree, has bell shaped white flowers in May. An open grower—sometimes multitrunked—it is fine for light shade and screening; it also combines well with evergreen backgrounds or underplantings of azaleas or rhododendrons. Its leaves turn yellow in fall. Carolina silver-bell likes moist, acid soil, and has no pest problems. 25–30 feet/Zones 5–10.

Smoke Tree (*Cotinus coggygria*)
Smoke tree makes a fine tree or shrub because it is fast growing and easy to move. Flowers followed by fruit panicles are lovely all summer; autumn colors are brilliant. Variety 'Purpurea' has purple foliage. For best effect, plant smoke tree where the sun will shine through it. 15–20 feet/Zones 5–9.

Sorrel (*Oxydendrum aboreum*)
Also known as sourwood or lily-of-the-valley tree, sorrel is superior for landscaping and not used enough. Its laurellike leaves are lustrous, dense, and leathery. They turn deep red in late August and remain so until mid-October. Blooms in mid-July are pendulous clusters of white. Sorrel does best in full sun and moist, acid soil. 25–30 feet/Zones 5–9.

MEDIUM *(30 to 50 feet tall)*

Amur Cork Tree (*Phellodendron amurense*)
This fast grower gives light, open shade beneath low, spreading branches. Do not crowd. Compound leaves turn yellow in autumn and drop quickly. Male plants have clusters of black berries. Corklike ridged bark gives winter interest. Tolerates drought and pollution. 30–40 feet/Zones 4–9.

Birch: River, Weeping
   (*Betula nigra, B. pendula*)
River birch has peeling bark with layers of gray and reddish brown. The trunk often divides near ground and looks like two or more trees growing together. Likes wet soil but resists borers. Weeping birch is not as hardy. It has delicate foliage and paper white bark for a dramatic effect. It's often used in clumps, but is short-lived and prone to borer attack. (See also page 110.) 40–50 feet/Zones 2–9.

Cherry, Sargent (*Prunus sargenti*)
This, the largest and hardiest of the Oriental cherries, bears masses of pearly pink flowers. Dark green shiny leaves turn red-bronze in fall. The tree's bark is attractive, dark, and lustrous. Good dense shade and specimen tree. Columnar varieties available. 50–75 feet/Zones 5–9.

Hornbeam (*Carpinus* species)
The adaptable European hornbeam is good as a street tree or in paved areas. American blue beech and Japanese hornbeam are smaller. All are slow growers with fluted gray bark and elm-like foliage that turns yellow to orange-red in fall. They bear interesting clusters of nutlike fruit and are pest free. 30–60 feet/Zones 4–8.

Horse Chestnut, Red (*Aesculus x carnea*)
This buckeye relative has upright conical clusters of red to pink flowers in May, five-fingered leaves, and a dense, mushroom form. It can become slightly untidy and grows slowly. Prone to leaf scorch in hot winds, so does best where summers are cool and moist. No notable fall color. 30–40 feet/Zones 4–8.

Linden (*Tilia cordata, T. x euchlora*)
Linden, with its dense pyramid of dark green, heart-shaped leaves, makes a good street, lawn, or shade tree. Bees will buzz around the tiny clusters of fragrant, early-summer white flowers. Linden withstands adverse city conditions, heat, and drought, and yields fast, hardy growth. 'Greenspire' and 'Redmond' are choice cultivars. 35–70 feet/Zones 4–9.

Mountain Ash (*Sorbus alnifolia*)
This fine, upright tree is prized for its white clusters of spring flowers, striking red-orange berries that attract birds, and smooth, gray bark. Lustrous foliage turns orange and scarlet in the fall. Mostly problem free, this tree doesn't tolerate city pollution well. 25–50 feet/Zones 5–9.

Pear, Bradford Callery
  (*Pyrus calleryana* 'Bradford')
This formal-looking, upright, pyramidal tree is covered with white flowers in spring, bears no fruit, and produces brilliant crimson-red fall foliage. Thornless and fire-blight resistant, it is a good, undemanding street or specimen tree. Prune this tree only when damaged by ice. 25–35 feet/Zones 5–9.

(continued on page 304)

TREES FOR SPECIAL INTEREST[1]

Fast Growing, Temporary
Acacia
Alder
Black locust
Catalpa
Elm, Siberian
Empress tree
Eucalyptus
Poplar
Silk tree
Tallow, Chinese
Willow

Spring Flowering
Butternut
Cherry, sargent
Crab apple
Dogwood
Fruit trees
Hawthorn
Magnolia
Mountain ash
Pear, Bradford
Redbud
Serviceberry

Summer Flowering
Catalpa
Chestnut, Chinese
Crape myrtle
Dogwood, Japanese
Franklinia
Fringe tree

Golden-chain tree
Golden-rain tree
Jacaranda
Linden
Silk tree
Sorrel
Tulip tree
Yellowwood

Fruiting
Chinese jujube
Crab apple
Loquat
Pecan
Persimmon
Prunus species
Serviceberry

Fragrant
Acacia
Arborvitae[2]
Bayberry[2]
Black locust
Cedar[2]
Crab apple[3]
Eucalyptus[2]
Fringe tree[3]
Fruit trees
Hemlock[2]
Katsura tree[2]
Linden, littleleaf[3]
Magnolia
Maple, amur
Pine[2]
Russian olive
Silk tree

Silver-bell
Sorrel
Viburnum
Yellowwood

For Winter Interest
Alder
Birch
Crab apple
Crape myrtle
Dogwood
Ginkgo
Holly
Katsura tree
Magnolia
Poplar
Oak
Oak, amur
Tulip tree
Tupelo, black
Willow

Avoid Near Street, Drive, Pipes
Ash
Black locust
Box elder
Catalpa
Hawthorn
Honey locust
Horse chestnut
Maple, red or silver
Mulberry
Poplar
Walnut, black
Willow

[1]*For more information about many of the trees listed, see pages 34, 108–111, and 301–306.*
[2]*Fragrant foliage.*   [3]*Fragrant after dark.*

DECIDUOUS TREES *(continued)*

Sassafras (*Sassafras albidum*)

Sassafras has short, stout, contorted branches that produce an open shape and dappled shade. Its bark is corky and dark red. Lustrous leaves—irregularly shaped like mittens with one, two, or no thumbs—turn orange to scarlet in fall. Sassafras will grow in poor soil, but its long taproot can cause transplant problems. 30–60 feet/Zones 5–9.

Yellowwood (*Cladrastis lutea*)

A broad tree with rounded crown, slow growing yellowwood is good in a grouping or as a specimen. Smooth, gray, beechlike bark provides winter interest. White, fragrant, pea-shaped flowers in hanging panicles are abundant in early June, though plants initially take time to bloom and bloom may be heavy only every three years. Crotches can be brittle; to keep the tree from bleeding, prune only in summer. 30–35 feet/Zones 4–9.

LARGE *(50 to 120 feet tall)*

Ash (*Fraxinus* species)

Fast growing and adaptable, ash likes full sun and has good yellow to purple fall color. Grass grows well under this tree. Some ash can get too large for small yards. Insects can be a problem for this tree. New cultivars like 'Marshall's Seedless' and 'Autumn Purple' are worth trying. 30–90 feet/Zones 2–9.

Beech (*Fagus* species)

Magnificent trees for forest or park. If you have one, treasure it for its smooth, silvery gray bark and golden bronze autumn color. Some have bronze leaves all year. Beech is too slow growing to figure in landscaping plans for decades to come, and only moss will grow beneath it. 50–100 feet/Zones 5–10.

Birch, Paper (*Betula papyrifera*)

Also called canoe birch, this native of Canada and Alaska has bright yellow autumn color. Bark is reddish brown on younger branches; later it turns chalky white and peels. Usually planted in clumps, birch does best in ample sun and well-drained, sandy, moist, acid soil. Borers can be a problem. (See also page 110.) 40–70 feet/Zones 2–8.

Chestnut (*Castanea mollissima*)

The Chinese chestnut and the newer disease-resistant forms of the American chestnut make majestic, spreading trees. Plant two or more in the same hole in smaller yards—for pollination. Chestnut does best on a north-facing slope in fertile, slightly acid soil. Train to central leader. 30–60 feet/Zones 5–9.

Gingko (*Ginkgo biloba*)

Also called maidenhair tree, ginkgo has unique fan-shaped leaves that turn golden yellow in fall. Its open habit and stiffly diagonal, uplifted branches provide filtered shade. Easy to care for, ginkgo is one of the best street trees. Ginkgo needs sun for best results. (See also page 110.) 50–80 feet/Zones 5–10.

Hickory (*Carya* species)

Bitternut, shagbark hickory, pecan, and pignut are prized for their lovely yellow autumn color, general sturdiness and stateliness, and shaggy bark. They make fine shade or specimen trees. Large, slow growing, and late to leaf out in the spring, they have long taproots that make transplanting difficult; buy hickory from a nursery. 60–120 feet/Zones 4–9.

Honey Locust (*Gleditsia triacanthos inermis*)

Honey locust's delicate leaflets give light shade and need little raking. Honey locust adapts to seashore or difficult conditions, but has some pest problems, especially in warmer climates. To avoid thorns and seedpods, choose the improved cultivars. 30–70 feet/Zones 5–9.

Katsura Tree (*Cercidiphyllum japonicum*)
This tree gives medium to dense shade with open foliage that allows good air circulation. Fine-textured, heart-shaped leaves turn yellow to scarlet. It resists diseases and insects, and can have multiple trunks. Kept to one trunk, it will be a slim oval while young, then spread at maturity. 40–60 feet/Zones 5–9.

Larch, Golden
(*Pseudolarix amabilis* or *P. kaempferi*)
This unique tree has cones and feathery, needle-like foliage that turns golden yellow in autumn, then falls. It is a large, broadly pyramidal tree that grows easily but needs plenty of room. Slow growing, it likes acid soil and needs some wind protection. 50–120 feet/Zones 6–8.

Maple, Norway (*Acer platanoides*)
This tough, versatile tree has improved cultivars like 'Emerald Green,' 'Summer Shade,' and the red-leaved 'Crimson King.' It gives dense shade, has bright yellow autumn color, and grows quickly. Spreading roots make growing grass underneath it difficult. (See also page 108.) 40–70 feet/Zones 4–9.

Maple: Red, Sugar
(*Acer rubrum, A. saccharum*)
Fast-growing red or swamp maple has tiny, profuse red blooms in early spring and brilliant red leaves in early fall. Winged seeds also are bright red. The varieties 'Bowhall' and 'Scanlon' are narrow. 'Red Sunset' and 'October Glory' are most colorful. The slow-growing sugar, hard, or syrup maple of New England does poorly in crowded or city conditions. (See also page 108.) 50–100 feet/Zones 3–7.

Oak (*Quercus* species)
Oaks are among the most useful native trees and are preferred for landscaping where room permits. Cherish any you have. Long-lived, they are fast growing where soil suits them. Plant them where acorns will be no trouble.

Pin oak and scarlet oak are fine pyramidal trees. Pin oak's drooping lower branches can create problems for traffic underneath. It is the easiest oak to transplant.

Quick-growing red oak, one of the best oaks, likes acid, sandy soil and full sun. It transplants easily and tolerates city conditions.

Cork, holly, live, and laurel oaks are evergreen in warm climates. They grow quickly and spread broadly, giving medium to dense shade.

English oak is susceptible to powdery mildew and has little autumn color.

For more about oaks, see page 108. 30–100 feet/Zones 4–9.

Sweet Gum (*Liquidambar styraciflua*)
Named for its fragrant, sticky sap, sweet gum has star-shaped, glossy leaves that turn yellow to scarlet to purple in fall. Given room, it develops unmatched Christmas-tree elegance. Ball-shaped fruit gives winter interest. Sweet gum needs full sun and likes acid soil. It takes time to settle in, then is trouble free and fast growing. 60–120 feet/Zones 5–10.

Tulip Tree (*Liriodendron tulipifera*)
Beloved for its pyramidal form, square leaves, tuliplike flowers, and yellow autumn color, tulip tree has green, yellow, and orange flowers that hide among the leaves, but are striking when viewed from above. Tulip tree can have weak wood and its roots can become invasive. (See also page 109.) 60–100 feet/Zones 5–9.

Walnut (*Juglans* species)
Black walnut, English or Persian walnut, butternut, and heartnut are stately trees, even in winter. Walnuts leaf out late and drop colorless leaves early. They can inhibit some plants beneath their spread. All are good for shade and screening. Walnuts need space and are self-pollinating (although having two trees spurs a better harvest). 20–80 feet/Zones 3–9.

EVERGREEN TREES

NEEDLED

Arborvitae (*Thuja* species)
This stately, reliable tree has flat sprays of scale-like foliage. Slow growing, it is excellent for natural or clipped hedges, screens, columnar accents, or windbreaks. It tolerates wet soils unless winds are high. Plant in sun to part shade; train to a central stem. Choose improved cultivars like 'Nigra' or 'Hetz Wintergreen.' (See also pages 82 and 313.) 40–60 feet/Zones 3–8.

Cedar: Deodar, Atlas
   (*Cedrus deodar, C. atlantica*)
True cedars are fairly rare, but they make excellent specimen or skyline trees where hardy and given enough room. Cedars grow at a slow to moderate rate. Upright cones on upper side of branches grow 4 inches long. The bluish needles are borne in starlike clusters in a picturesque, open pattern. 'Glauca' is the bluest. 40–70 feet/Zones 6–10.

Douglas Fir (*Pseudotsuga menziesi*)
More beautiful and dependable than spruce or true fir, quick-growing douglas fir has soft, spiraling, bluish green needles. New spring growth is an attractive apple green. Foliage is fragrant. Pendulous cones are 2 to 4 inches long. Dwarf varieties of douglas fir make good hedges. 80–100 feet/Zones 5–9.

Fir (*Abies* species)
Good specimen trees, firs may lose their lower branches as they age. Two-inch, bristly needles are dark bluish green on top, silvery gray beneath. Firs do best in cool climates, full sun, and rich soil. White fir withstands city conditions, heat, and drought. 55–80 feet/Zones 4–8.

Hemlock (*Tsuga canadensis*)
With nodding top and drooping branches, hemlock exhibits a special grace. Use it as a background plant, among pines in a grove, or as a clipped hedge. Hemlock likes deep moist loam and takes light shade. Do not plant it near the house. Usually problem free, it does need water in dry periods. Prune to make it dense. 50–80 feet/Zones 4–8.

Pine (*Pinus* species)
Pines vary widely and fill many landscaping needs, from windbreaks and tall hedges to shade and specimen trees. White pine is one of the hardiest and most graceful. Austrian pine is stiffer and more rugged. Scotch pine, with its horizontal spreading branches and red bark, often gets an interesting, contorted shape as it ages. Lace-bark has multiple trunks. (See also pages 110 and 313.) 30–100 feet/Zones 3–9.

Spruce (*Picea* species)
Spruces have short, squarish needles and hanging cones. Cultivars come in shades of white, red, and blue. Spruces are moderate to fast growing and often overgrow their location. For small yards, choose smaller cultivars. Spruces do best in cooler climates. (See also pages 109 and 313.) 50–100 feet/Zones 2–9.

BROAD-LEAVED

Holly (*Ilex* species)
Many hollies make handsome shrubs or even trees, especially in warmer climates. In colder areas, they may shed their leaves in winter, yet survive. Hollies like acid soil and nearly full sun; most need male and female trees to produce berries. (See also page 312.) Hollies have some insect problems. 20–70 feet/Zones 6–10.

Magnolia, Southern (*Magnolia grandiflora*)
Also called bull bay, southern magnolia has large, lustrous, dark green leaves with brownish undersides and huge, waxy white blooms from May to August. Most are dense and heavy looking; 'St. Mary's' is smaller, about 20 feet. 60–75 feet/Zones 7–9.

DECIDUOUS SHRUBS

SMALL (*up to 5 feet tall*)

Note: Dwarf cultivars of dogwood, rose, spirea, viburnum, and yellowroot are available.

Azalea

'Exbury' hybrids grow to 4 feet, with good fall color, as well as spring bloom. See pages 308 and 311 for more details on azaleas.

Barberry (*Berberis* species)

Barberry, with thick, thorny growth, makes a good hedge and barrier plant. Flowers are small; fruit and foliage vary in color according to variety. Easy to grow, barberry likes full sun and will attract birds. (See also page 82.) 3–5 feet/Zones 4–8.

Cinquefoil, Shrubby (*Potentilla fruticosa*)

Shrubby cinquefoil stays dainty and is choice for small gardens, borders, or mass plantings. It has soft, needlelike foliage and flowers like buttercups that begin in May and continue all summer. Easy to grow and to transplant, it needs full sun. 1–4 feet/Zones 2–9.

Cotoneaster, Cranberry
(*Cotoneaster apiculatus*)

Cranberry cotoneaster is ideal when used as a ground cover, at the front of a shrub border, or to hold banks. It has small shiny leaves, inconspicuous flowers, ornamental red berries, and spreading wishbone-patterned branches. Cotoneaster likes sun. It has red fall color in the North, and is evergreen in the South. (See also pages 67 and 317.) 2–4 feet/Zones 5–8.

Currant or Gooseberry (*Ribes* species)

These fruits are useful for edible landscaping in foundation plantings or under spreading trees. Some gooseberry bushes will cascade over walls or banks. Others are thorny and make effective barrier plants. Both kinds do well in large containers for patios. 3–5 feet/Zones 3–8.

Daphne, February (*Daphne mezereum*)

February daphne is an upright shrub that produces small, lilac or rosy purple, fragrant flowers. Hardiness varies with species; some types demand limestone soil. February daphne prefers sun or partial shade; its berries, which are toxic, turn red in summer. (See also page 311.) 3–5 feet/Zones 5–8.

Forsythia, Arnold Dwarf
(*Forsythia x intermedia* 'Arnold Dwarf')

This variety and the even lower 'Bronx Greenstem' grow with typical arching branches that root at the soil line. Small, greenish yellow flowers in early spring aren't quite as showy as on taller kinds. This forsythia has vigorous, dense foliage; it likes sun or part shade. (See also pages 111 and 308.) 2–4 feet/Zones 5–8.

Forsythia, Korean White
(*Abeliophyllum distichum*)

Not a true forsythia, this shrub has flowers of similar shape and bloom time, but they're white and very fragrant. It has arching stems, is easy to grow, and likes full sun. 3–5 feet/Zones 5–8.

Hydrangea, Hills-of-Snow
(*Hydrangea arborescens*)

Six-inch clusters of white bloom in midsummer on this plant. Hydrangea likes full sun or partial shade, and rich, moist soil. In dry times, water. Hydrangea usually dies back in hard winters. 3–5 feet/Zones 4–8.

Kerria (*Kerria japonica*)

Also known as globeflower, kerria is a good foundation or border shrub. Its green twigs are attractive in winter; golden yellow flowers appear in mid-spring. Double varieties bloom longer. Several cultivars include variegated leaves. Kerria likes shade and needs pruning to remove dead wood. 4–8 feet/Zones 5–8.

(continued on page 308)

DECIDUOUS SHRUBS *(continued)*

Quince, Flowering (*Chaenomeles speciosa*)
Flowering quince is widely planted for its bright, often orange, flowers in early spring. Available cultivars range from white to dark red. These shrubs are dense and thorny, and make good hedge, border, or barrier plants. Fruits are edible in jams. 2–6 feet/Zones 3–9.

MEDIUM *(5 to 10 feet tall)*

Azalea (*Rhododendron* species)
Among the most loved flowering shrubs, hardy azaleas vary in form and color. They are useful in beds, as foundation plants, as accents, or below spreading trees. Some are fragrant. All need good humidity, full sun or partial shade, and moist, acid soil. (See also pages 307 and 311.) 4–10 feet/Zones 4–10.

Blueberry (*Vaccinium* species)
Blueberry works well as an interest plant, ground cover, or screen, or in a hedge, border, or container. Foliage is bronze in spring and glossy green all summer. Delicious berries follow clusters of pinkish white flowers. Likes full sun but tolerates part shade in hot areas; needs acid soil. 1–18 feet/Zones 3–9.

Chokeberry (*Aronia arbutifolia*)
A dependable native shrub, chokeberry has dense flower clusters of white with pinkish tints in May, followed by bright red fruits, too sour even for birds, that are colorful all fall and winter. Leaves turn red in fall. Does best in full sun in borders. 6–10 feet/Zones 6–8.

Clethra (*Clethra alnifolia*)
Also called summer-sweet, clethra is a native that thrives along the seashore and in damp places. It makes a good border plant because of its fragrant white spikes in summer and its yellow to orange fall color. Clethra likes part shade or sun in moist, acid soil. 3–8 feet/Zones 4–9.

Dogwood: Red-Osier, Tartarian
(*Cornus sericea, C. alba*)
In winter, dogwoods are standouts, as their red wood contrasts with the snow below. Their flowers and fruits are not showy, but their foliage turns dark red in the fall. Dogwoods like moist soil and are good in borders, near foundations, and beside water. (See also page 108.) 7–10 feet/Zones 3–9.

Elderberry, American (*Sambucus canadensis*)
Also called sweet elderberry, this shrub has clusters of white, fragrant flowers and purple-black edible berries. Elderberry is fine for borders, screens, or hedges. It needs sun and moist, fertile soil. 6–10 feet/Zones 3–9.

Forsythia (*Forsythia* species)
Loved for its bright, early spring flowers of yellow, forsythia has good foliage and is an easy, adaptable shrub. It spreads by underground stems and may outgrow small spaces. Get improved cultivars like 'Meadowlark' or 'Ottawa' for sure bloom in North. Forsythia needs full sun. Prune right *after* flowering. (See also pages 111 and 307.) 8–10 feet/Zones 5–8.

Fruit, Dwarf (stone) (*Prunus* species)
Bush forms of plum and cherry are lovely in hedgerows, as flowering accents in foundation plantings, or near patios. Genetic dwarf plants of almond, apple, apricot, cherry, nectarine, peach, pear, and plum have many uses: as informal hedges, in foundation plantings, as interest plants in shrub borders, and especially in containers. 4–10 feet/Zones 3–9.

Hibiscus (*Hibiscus* species)
The hibiscus species includes mallows that die to the ground each winter, the southern shrub, and the popular rose-of-sharon. Hibiscus works well as a border or hedge. Two- to 6-inch blooms come in white, pink, and blue; some plants include all three. All like moist soil and sun to partial shade. 5–10 feet/Zones 5–10.

Honeysuckle (*Lonicera* species)
Tartarian and winter honeysuckles are best used for mass effect in borders and screens, and where their fragrance and berry-eating bird visitors can be enjoyed. Easy to grow, these vigorous bushes need sun and well-drained soil. (See also pages 82 and 315.) 6–12 feet/Zones 3–9.

Lilac (*Syringa* species)
Hundreds of lilac types enchant gardeners yearly with their plumes of fragrant springtime flowers. Choose several bloom times to stretch the season to weeks. Give full sun and well-drained, slightly acid soil. (See also page 111.) 3–20 feet/Zones 2–9.

Mock Orange (*Philadelphus* species)
Mock orange is prized in mass plantings because of its fragrant white flowers that come at spring's end, when few other shrubs are in bloom. This shrub is easy to grow in full sun or light shade. 'Minnesota Snowflake' is very hardy, with 2-inch double flowers. 'Belle Etoile' has pinkish-blush flowers. The variety 'Virginal' has semidouble blooms throughout the summer. 4–12 feet/Zones 4–8.

Privet (*Ligustrum* species)
Popular for clipped hedges, privet is vigorous and usually problem free, and withstands adverse conditions. It has glossy foliage, white flower clusters, and black berries. In the South, it is evergreen. It will grow in some shade. 9–15 feet/Zones 4–9.

Rose (*Rosa* species)
Now the official U.S. flower, many roses are true and hardy shrubs. Meadow rose has red twigs for winter interest. Rugosa roses have hips that can be used in drinks and jellies. Roses make good barrier, accent, and border plants. Landscape roses are easy to grow, are disease resistant, and usually bloom from early summer to fall. (See also pages 82, 107, and 316.) 3–15 feet/Zones 3–10.

(continued on page 310)

SHRUBS FOR SPECIAL INTEREST[1]

For Quick Screens

Beautybush
Elaeagnus
Euonymus
Forsythia
Honeysuckle
Mock orange
Privet
Viburnum:
  arrowwood,
  nannyberry,
  siebold

Spring Flowering

Andromeda
Azalea, Korean
Barberry
Bayberry
Cinquefoil
Forsythia
Fruit, dwarf
Honeysuckle
Kerria
Lilac
Pussy willow
Rhododendron
Spirea
Viburnum
Witch hazel

Summer Flowering

Arrowwood
Azalea, flame
Butterfly bush

Crape myrtle
Hydrangea, peegee
Leucothoe
Mock orange
Mountain laurel
Privet
Rose
Rose-of-sharon
Spirea,
  'Anthony Waterer'
Stewartia

Fruiting

Almond
Apple[2]
Apricot[2]
Blueberry
Cherry, bush[2]
Cherry, Surinam
Citrus, dwarf
Currant
Gooseberry
Guava, pineapple
Nectarine[2]
Peach[2]
Pear[2]
Plum, bush
Plum, natal
Pomegranate
Quince
Rose (hips)

Fragrant

Azalea hybrids
Bayberry[3]

Boxwood[3]
Butterfly bush
Clethra
Honeysuckle
Lilac
Privet[4]
Rhododendron
  hybrids
Rose
Viburnum, Korean
  spice
Witch hazel

With Toxic Parts[5]

Apple: seeds
Azalea: all parts
Black locust: seeds,
  sprouts, foliage
Cherry: seeds
Chokecherry: leaves,
  stems, bark, seeds
Daphne: berries,
  leaves
Elderberry: all parts
Golden-chain: seeds,
  pods
Holly: berries
Hydrangea: leaves,
  buds
Jasmine: berries
Magnolia: flower
Oleander: bark, leaves
Peach: leaves, seeds
Privet: leaves, seeds
Wisteria: pods, seeds
Yew: all parts

[1]*For more information about many of the shrubs listed, see pages 34, 67, 82–83, 90, 109, 111, 186, and 307–313.*
[2]*Genetic dwarf.*   [3]*Fragrant foliage.*   [4]*Fragrant after dark.*
[5]*No need to avoid, but warn children.*

DECIDUOUS SHRUBS *(continued)*

Spirea (*Spirea* species)
Also called bridal wreath, spirea once was over-planted because of its fountains of white spring flowers and ease of growth; now many improved varieties bloom in white to red from April to August. 'Goldflame' has pink flowers and golden foliage; 'Plena' has double flowers. Spirea likes sun, but will tolerate partial shade. 1–12 feet/Zones 5–9.

LARGE *(more than 10 feet tall)*

Buckeye, Bottlebrush (*Aesculus parviflora*)
Little used but an excellent shrub for accent, borders, or banks, bottlebrush buckeye has midsummer spikes of white florets and yellow to orange autumn color. Trouble free, with a spreading habit, this shrub likes sun or partial shade and soil that's moist and slightly acid. 8–15 feet/Zones 5–9.

Butterfly Bush (*Buddleia* species)
The fountain, 'Sun Gold,' and orange-eye versions of this plant have long spikes of fragrant flowers in white, pink, red, purple, blue, or pale yellow on arching branches. Some bloom in early summer; the orange-eye blooms summer to fall. Blooms attract butterflies in profusion. In the North, this plant may die to the ground, but it will grow back and bloom by summer. 6–15 feet/Zones 5–9.

Crape Myrtle (*Lagerstroemia indica*)
These useful, vase-shaped, quick-growing large shrubs (or small trees) bloom all summer long in the South. Crape myrtle makes a good accent shrub. New varieties are hardy as far north as Washington, D.C., and can withstand temperatures to minus 23 degrees. In bad winters, crape myrtle may die to the ground, but it will grow back from its roots. 10–30 feet/Zones 7–10.

Honeysuckle, Amur (*Lonicera maacki*)
This late-blooming bush has small, whitish yellow, fragrant flowers and scarlet, inedible berries. Leaves and berries often last to Thanksgiving. Use in hedge or border, or as screen or specimen. 15 feet/Zones 3–8.

Hydrangea, Peegee
(*Hydrangea paniculata 'grandiflora'*)
Peegee hydrangea is a big, rather coarse shrub with large clusters of summer flowers that turn pink or purplish as they dry, often keeping the bush attractive even after its leaves have fallen. Use in borders. 25–30 feet/Zones 4–8.

Pussy Willow (*Salix* species)
Pussy or goat willow grows quickly and roots easily in water from spring-blooming twigs, but is coarse and can be pest ridden. Use sparsely in screens or border. 10–25 feet/Zones 2–8.

Viburnum (*Viburnum* species)
Viburnum (or arrowwood or cranberry bush) includes medium shrubs to small trees that are among the finest landscaping plants. Pink buds open to varied, showy white flowers, many of them fragrant in spring. Lush summer foliage turns red in autumn, and clusters of black or red berries attract birds. Some are edible. All are hardy and easy to grow. Viburnums prefer sun and moist, slightly acid soil; they will tolerate salt spray. Select choice varieties: pink 'Dawn,' yellow-leaved 'Aureum,' small 'Compactum.' (See also page 83.) 5–30 feet/Zones 3–9.

Witch Hazel (*Hamamelis* species)
Witch hazel blooms in fall or late winter—even in snow—with small, inconspicuous to moderately showy, fragrant, ribbonlike flowers of yellow to copper. Witch hazel has good yellow autumn foliage. Mostly native, these shrubs like full or partial sun and rich, moist soil. 5–30 feet/Zones 5–8.

BROAD-LEAVED EVERGREEN SHRUBS

SMALL (can be kept under 5 feet tall)

Azalea (*Rhododendron* species)
Dense and often spreading, azaleas have trusses of flowers in many colors that stand proudly above the foliage in mid-spring to early summer. Some varieties lose their leaves in harsh winters. Azaleas tolerate partial shade and like well-drained, acid soil. (See also pages 307 and 308.) 3–6 feet/Zones 4–8.

Boxwood (*Buxus microphylla*)
A Japanese evergreen with small, glossy leaves and a spreading habit, littleleaf box is prized for clipped or natural hedges and foundation plantings. 'Green Beauty' and 'Wintergreen' retain green color all winter. Some turn yellowish, especially in cold winters. Box likes mulch over its shallow roots and full or part sun. Protect it from wind, and remove snow that collects on the bush. 3–4 feet/Zones 6–8.

Daphne (*Daphne* species)
Several evergreen or semievergreen daphnes make excellent foundation plantings. They have clusters of long-lasting, fragrant spring flowers. Some are low enough for rock gardens. Burkwood has whitish flowers and red berries. The upright *D. odora* is an evergreen in Zone 8 and warmer climates. Water daphnes sparingly. Some like alkaline soil. (See also page 307.) 3–5 feet/Zones 5–10.

Gardenia (*Gardenia jasminoides*)
Gardenia has thick, glossy evergreen leaves 2 to 3 inches long. Aromatic flowers bloom spring to summer. Gardenia needs moist, acid soil and likes sun to partial shade. For thrips, spray with liquid soap mixed with water. 'Veitchii' and 'August Beauty' have longer bloom; 'Radicans' is a 12-inch miniature. 2–6 feet/Zones 8–9.

Heather (*Calluna* species)
Small leaves and clusters of tiny midsummer flowers in white, pink, or purple are heather's trademarks. Use this plant in borders or rock gardens. Needs acid soil and full or part sun. 2 inches–2½ feet/Zones 4–7.

Leucothoe (*Leucothoe* species)
Coast and drooping leucothoe have sprays of fragrant white, bell-shaped blooms in spring and glossy leaves that are deep green in summer and bronze in winter. Branches arch gracefully for covering banks or the leggy feet of other shrubs. Good in borders or near foundations. Likes acid soil and shade. 3–6 feet/Zones 5–9.

Mahonia (*Mahonia aquifolium*)
Also called holly grape or Oregon grape, mahonia has hardy, attractive leaves that turn bronze in winter, clusters of bright yellow flowers in spring, and bluish black, grapelike berries in summer. Good as a barrier, foundation, or border plant, mahonia likes acid soil and partial shade, and needs protection from heat and drying. (See also page 318.) 3–6 feet/Zones 5–8.

Santolina (*Santolina chamaecyparissus*)
Santolina (or lavender cotton) is a low, silvery-leaved shrub often used for edging flower beds or walks. Easy to grow and aromatic, santolina likes poor soil and full sun. Prune before or after flowering. 1–2 feet/Zones 5–8.

MEDIUM TO LARGE
(taller than 5 feet)

Andromeda (*Pieris* species)
Beautiful and dependable, andromeda should be used more often in landscapes. Its flowers bloom with fragrant upright or pendulous spires of white to pinkish bells in early spring. It likes wind protection and part shade. (See also page 109.) 2–9 feet/Zones 4–8.

(continued on page 312)

BROAD-LEAVED EVERGREEN SHRUBS *(continued)*

SHRUBS AND TREES BY SHAPE[1]

Shrubs with Arching Branches

Beautybush
Butterfly bush
Daphne, lilac
Deutzia, slender
Forsythia
Spirea

Erect Shrubs

Cranberry, highbush
Dogwood, red-osier
Hibiscus
Lilac, common
Mock orange, lemoine

Rounded Shrubs

Hydrangea
Kerria
Lilac, Persian
Quince, flowering
Weigela
Witch hazel

Spreading Shrubs

Cotoneaster, spreading
Crab apple, sargent
Ninebark, dwarf
Quince, Japanese
Sumac, staghorn
Viburnum, fragrant

Weeping Trees

Apricot, weeping
Ash, weeping
  European
Beech, weeping
Birch:
  slender European,
  Young's
Boree, weeping
Cedar, deodar
Cherry, weeping
Crab apple,
  pink weeper
Hemlock, pendula
Hornbeam, weeping
  European
Linden, pendent silver
Pines (several
  varieties)
Spruce: brewer,
  Koster weeping
  blue
Willow (several
  varieties)

Columnar Trees

Arborvitae
Cedar, pyramidal red
Ginkgo, sentry
Hornbeam:
  'Columnaris,'
  'Fastigiata'
Juniper, blue columnar
Lombardy poplar
Maple, red: 'Bowhill,'
  'Scanlon'
Maple, sentry
Tulip tree, 'Fastigiata'

Pyramid-Shaped Trees

Beech
Birch
Black gum
Cedar
Hemlock
Holly
Larch
Linden
Magnolia
Pine
Pin oak
Sorrel
Spruce
Sweet gum

Trees with Horizontal Branches

Chestnut, Chinese
Dogwood
Fir
Hawthorn
Oak (notably white
  and live oak)
Redbud
Red pine
Scotch pine
Silk tree
Spruce

[1]*For more information about many of the plants listed, see pages 34, 67, 82–83, 90, 108–111, 186, and 301-313.*

Camellia (*Camellia* species)
Slow growing and dependable, camellias produce exquisite flowers and dark, lustrous foliage. They thrive in temperate, humid areas and as far north as Philadelphia in sheltered spots or containers. By choosing for a succession of bloom, you can have flowers from late fall into spring. Camellias need shade and acid soil. 6–25 feet/Zones 7–9.

Euonymus (*Euonymus* species)
Also called spindle tree, hardy evergreen euonymus is a cousin of the deciduous burning bush. The evergreen euonymus is good in hedges or borders, or as a barrier. It tolerates many soils and city conditions and likes sun or shade. Some types are semitrailing. 6–15 feet/Zones 5–9.

Fire Thorn (*Pyracantha* species)
Fire thorn produces clusters of white flowers in spring that give way to showy orange to scarlet berries. Plants grow quickly and are excellent for espaliers or hedges, or as specimen, barrier, or border plants. Fire thorn will tolerate dry soil, but needs sun for berry production. 6–15 feet/Zones 7–10.

Holly (*Ilex* species)
Evergreen holly is useful for accent, barrier, foundation, hedge, and border plantings. Some low, compact varieties are good for edging and hedges. Leaves are glossy and leathery, but flowers are inconspicuous. Berries on female plants are showy. Evergreen hollies are easy, but slow, to grow. Keep moist. (See also page 306.) 3–20 feet/Zones 5–9.

Mountain Laurel (*Kalmia latifolia*)
Mountain laurel—one of the most beautiful shrubs—is ideal for foundations, as an accent plant, or in woodland settings. Its great masses of delicate blooms range from deep pink to white. Lovely with dogwoods and rhododendrons, it needs acid soil and prefers partial shade. 3–10 feet/Zones 5–8.

NEEDLED EVERGREEN SHRUBS

Arborvitae, American (*Thuja occidentalis*)
A slow-growing, compact, columnar shrub or tree, American arborvitae has green or blue-green, scalelike, fan-shaped foliage. Use it as a foundation, hedge, or accent plant. It likes rich, moist, well-drained soil and a cool climate. Prune in early spring. (See also pages 82 and 306.) 7–20 feet/Zones 3–8.

Cephalotaxus (*Cephalotaxus harringtonia*)
Also called Japanese plum yew, cephalotaxus is similar to true yews, but less dense. It usually is multistemmed and wide spreading. ('Fastigiata' is columnar with dark green, 1½-inch needles and 1-inch, purple-green fruits.) Use cephalotaxus in a hedge or as a screen. It needs moist, acid soil. Shear it in spring before growth starts. 20–30 feet/Zones 6–8.

Cryptomeria (*Cryptomeria japonica 'nana'*)
Also called Japanese cedar, cryptomeria has reddish brown bark, bluish green needles that pick up a bronze tinge in winter, and a broad, pyramid shape. Use it along foundations or in patio tubs. Cryptomeria likes moist soil and is pest free, but it doesn't tolerate drought very well. 3 feet/Zones 5–9.

Cupresso-Cyparis (*Cupressocyparis leylandi*)
A cross between Alaska cedar and Monterey cypress, this narrow, columnar evergreen has scalelike, gray-green to pale green foliage. It grows fast—3 to 5 feet a year—but is easily sheared to any size for hedges and screens. Prune in early spring. It tolerates many soils and climates. 40–50 feet/Zones 5–10.

Cypress, False (*Chamaecyparis* species)
This evergreen has deep green, scalelike, fanned foliage and reddish brown shredding bark, making it a fine accent plant. Be sure to get dwarf cultivars: 'Gracilis,' 'Nana,' 'Golden Mop.' Basic species will grow too large in foundation plantings. False cypress likes sun, humidity, and moist, neutral to acid soil. It needs protection from wind. 4–100 feet/Zones 4–8.

Juniper (*Juniperus* species)
Creeping cedar and junipers that carry the names dwarf common, Hollywood, pfitzer, and shore all have dense, broad, spreading foliage in many hues (depending on variety), blue berries, and wood that smells like cedar. Well-chosen cultivars make fine ground covers or foundation plants. Shore juniper withstands salt spray. All like sun and dry, sandy soil. (See also page 318.) 1–20 feet/Zones 3–9.

Pine (*Pinus* species)
Bristol-cone hickory, dwarf white pine, and mugo or mountain pine are slow-growing, dense shrubs with bright or dark blue-green needles, 1 to 4 inches long. Use pines as specimen, border, or foundation plants, and in rock gardens or containers. Pines need full or part sun. They are subject to scale. For thicker bushes, prune. (See also pages 110 and 306.) 4–100 feet/Zones 3–9.

Spruce, Dwarf White (*Picea glauca 'conica'*)
A dense, pyramidal evergreen with a single trunk and tufted, ½-inch light green needles, dwarf white spruce grows slowly. Use it as an accent or dense hedge, with low-growing shrubs, or in rock or formal gardens. It likes sandy soil and a cold climate. (See also pages 109 and 306.) 6–8 feet/Zones 2–6.

Yew (*Taxus* species)
The darkest, richest green of all the evergreens, yew has soft, flat needles. Female plants have red berries. Many shapes and sizes fill a large range of garden uses: along foundations, in hedges, or as group plantings. Canada yew, the hardiest, is a good ground cover or low woodland plant. Japanese yew does well in sun, shade, and most soils, as long as drainage is good. It prefers moist, sandy loam. (See also page 83.) 3–20 feet/Zones 2–7.

VINES

PERENNIAL

Actinidia (*Actinidia* species)
This group includes kiwi, Chinese gooseberry, and some 40 species of twining, woody vines. Grown mostly for its handsome foliage, actinidia has small, fragrant white flowers in spring. It is trouble free and vigorous, and creates an attractive pattern on a wall, fence, or arbor. The right varieties in the right light and climate produce delicious fruits that keep well. (See also page 107.) 40 feet/Zones 5–10/Deciduous.

Bittersweet (*Celastrus* species)
Hardy and twining, thorny bittersweet is good for screening, on banks, or as a barrier. It has inconspicuous flowers, leaves that turn yellow in fall, and red fall berries in orange capsules. It grows in ordinary soil and will tolerate shade, but it fruits best in sun (male and female required). Do not plant on trees. 30 feet/Zones 4–8/Deciduous.

Bougainvillea (*Bougainvillea* hybrids)
This thorny twiner grows best in the deep South—in full sun in cooler areas and in afternoon shade in hottest climates. (In the North, grow it as a houseplant.) Bougainvillea has flower clusters with showy bracts in red, pink, orange, and purple. Limit its water—it can withstand drought—but feed well. Frost will damage it. 6–30 feet/Zones 9–10/Evergreen.

Carolina Jessamine (*Gelsemium sempervirens*)
A twining vine, carolina jessamine is good on a fence, trellis, mailbox, or lamppost, or used as a ground cover. It has fragrant yellow flowers, and long, glossy leaves. A double-flowered form is available. It needs fertile soil and sun or light shade. 10–20 feet/Zones 7–9/Evergreen.

Clematis (*Clematis* species and hybrids)
Among the most exquisite and showiest of all vines, clematis sports single or semidouble white, blue, pink, red, or purple flowers—as large as 9 inches across—that can cover the vine in early summer. A dainty plant, clematis works best when it's used as an accent or to frame an entrance rather than as a screen.

Curly clematis has long, purple, bell-shaped flowers all summer on current year's wood.

Golden clematis has gray-green leaves, long-lasting bright yellow flowers in late spring, and plumed seed heads in early fall.

Virgin's bower clematis has small, white flowers in late summer and seed heads in fall. It's good in a wildflower garden, grows rapidly, and tolerates wet soil.

All clematis climb by twisting leaf stalks. They do best with their flowers in sun and their roots in shade. Do not plant too shallow or allow to dry out for long. (See also page 111.) 5–30 feet/Zones 4–9/Deciduous.

Creeper, Virginia (*Parthenocissus quinquefolia*)
Virginia creeper climbs by clinging with disklike ends on aerial rootlets. Self-supporting, it can hang like a lacy curtain from a screened porch, covering but not damaging. Then, in winter, it will drop its foliage to let sunshine in. Five-finger, whorled leaves turn dark red in fall; flowers are inconspicuous. Birds love its blue autumn berries. It grows rapidly in sun or light shade. 50 feet/Zones 4–9/Deciduous.

Grape (*Vitis* species)
Hardy, dependable vines for fruit, screening, or shade, grapes climb by clinging tendrils. Vigorous, they need pruning yearly (or more often), and are excellent as covers on arbors or small structures, or espaliered against a wall. Some can be trained as small weeping trees. Flowers are fragrant but not showy. (See also page 107.) 50–100 feet/Zones 4–10/Deciduous.

Honeysuckle (*Lonicera* species)
A good climber, honeysuckle has trumpet-shaped, fragrant flowers in profusion, in many colors, and over much of the summer; red or black berries appear in the fall. Honeysuckle also is good as a ground cover on banks, and is ideal for quick screening. Vigorous, almost rampant in some climates, honeysuckle can die to the ground in severe cold, but is semievergreen in the South. Tolerates drought and sun to dense shade. (See also pages 82 and 309.) 12–50 feet/Zones 3–10/Deciduous.

Ivy, Boston (*Parthenocissus tricuspidata*)
Carefree Boston ivy will quickly cover a building facade with no support. Its large, waxy green leaves turn bright red in fall, and provide shelter for birds (dark blue berries provide food). In winter, it creates a dense pattern of gray on walls. It grows in full sun to partial shade. (See also page 260.) To 60 feet/Zones 5–9/Deciduous.

Ivy: English, Algerian
(*Hedera helix, H. canariensis*)
Both ivies are fast growers that cling by their rootlets to walls and stone. They also will quickly cover wire fences, and can be used as ground covers. Both produce black berries in the fall and have variegated varieties. These ivies do best in rich, moist soil on north or east walls. Both tolerate shade; Algerian can take more sun than English. (See also pages 260 and 318.) 50–90 feet/Zones 4–9/Evergreen.

Jasmine (*Jasmine* species)
Winter jasmine is the hardiest jasmine, growing as far north as Boston. Common white and Japanese jasmine thrive farther south. All grow as shrubs with some support. Flowers are dainty and fragrant. Jasmine likes sun and moist or wet soil. 10–30 feet/Zones 5–9/Semievergreen.

VINES FOR SPECIAL INTEREST[1]

Rapid Growing[2]

Actinidia, bower
Bittersweet
Cathedral bells
Chinese gooseberry
Clematis
Creeper, Virginia
Dutchman's-pipe
Five-leaf akebia
Grape
Honeysuckle
Hop vine
Ivy, Boston
Ivy, English
Trumpet vine
Wisteria

Flowering

Cathedral bells
Clematis
Honeysuckle
Hydrangea, climbing
Jasmine
Mandevilla
Passionflower

Plumbago
Silver-lace vine
Wisteria

For Interesting Fruits

Beans, white and
  scarlet runner[3]
Bitter melon[3]
Bittersweet
Clematis (most
  species)
Creeper, Virginia
Euonymus, running
Grape[3]
Hop vine[3]
Kiwi[3]
Magnolia vine
Rose[3]
Scarlet kadsura
Winter creeper

For City Conditions

Bean, scarlet runner
Cathedral bells
Cypress vine

Hop vine
Ivy, Boston
Ivy, English
Silver-lace vine
Wisteria

For Use as a Ground Cover

Akebia
Bittersweet
Euonymus, running
Hop vine
Honeysuckle
Ivy, Boston
Ivy, English

Fragrant

Clematis,
  sweet autumn
Honeysuckle
Jasmine
Kiwi
Madeira vine
Moonflower
Rose

[1]*For more information on many of the vines listed, see pages 35, 106-111, 166, and 314–316.*
[2]*Vines that grow 4 to 20 feet in one year.*   [3]*Edible.*

Passionflower (*Passiflora caerulea*)
The hardiest passionflower survives as far north as Iowa, dying back in winter but returning from roots. Others are more tropical. All have exquisite flowers of white, blue, or red. Use on sunny fences and arbors. To 20 feet/Zones 7–10/Evergreen until frost kills top growth.

(continued on page 316)

VINES *(continued)*

Rose (*Rosa* species and hybrids)
Climbing and rambler roses offer fragrant flowers in many colors. Good for borders or arbors, or lovely above gates. All need support, pruning, six hours of sun daily, shelter from north winds, and fertile, well-drained soil. (See also pages 82, 107, and 309.) 15–20 feet/Zones 4–10/Deciduous.

Wisteria (*Wisteria* species)
Vigorous wisteria has superb panicles of white, rose, or lavender blooms in spring. Its twisting trunks provide winter interest. Wisteria is slow to establish; grafted plants bloom sooner. It likes fertile soil and full sun to partial shade; prune to keep in bounds. Provide strong support. (See also page 107.) 30–40 feet/Zones 4–9/Deciduous.

ANNUAL

Balloon Vine (*Cardiospermum halicacabum*)
Balloon vine has inconspicuous flowers, feathery foliage, and balloon-shaped seedpods; it is a perennial in the South. 10 feet/Sun.

Balsam Pear (*Momordica charantia*)
Balsam pear's small yellow flowers bear gourdlike fruits that turn yellow and open to expose large, bright red seeds. Rapid growing, it covers a porch quickly but can become weedy. 8–30 feet/Sun.

Black-Eyed Susan (*Thunbergia alata*)
Yellow or orange daisylike flowers—some with dark throats—bloom all summer. This vine needs a long season. 6–10 feet/Sun or shade.

Canary-Bird Flower (*Tropaeolum peregrinum*)
Canary-bird flower has 1-inch, yellow, feathery flowers in summer. It thrives in poor soil, needs moisture and shade, and prefers cool nights. 6–10 feet/Shade.

Cardinal Climber (*Ipomoea x multifida*)
Cardinal climber has 2-inch, crimson, tubular flowers all summer; its foliage is deeply cut. It twines and likes sandy soil. Good with blue morning-glory. 10–20 feet/Sun or shade.

Cathedral Bells (*Cobaea scandens*)
Also called cup-and-saucer vine, cathedral bells has large, deep bluish purple or creamy white, campanula-shaped flowers for six months, from spring into summer. A southern favorite, cathedral bells grows rapidly and clings by tendrils. It's slow to germinate, so start it eight weeks early indoors. A native of Mexico, it likes heat. 10–20 feet/Sun.

Cypress Vine (*Ipomoea quamoclit*)
Cypress vine produces white, red, or pink flowers all summer; its foliage is ferny. Grows wild in the South, and starts easily from seed or cuttings. 10–20 feet/Sun or part shade.

Dutchman's-Pipe (*Aristolochia durior*)
The huge leaves of dutchman's-pipe are unequaled for cooling shade or dense screens. This vine needs space to avoid crowding other plants. Pipelike flowers blend a rare shade of mahogany and white, but are not showy. Soak seeds 48 hours in hot water before planting. 30 feet/Sun or shade.

Moonflower (*Ipomoea alba*)
This rapid grower is ideal for screening. It has large, heart-shaped leaves and deep-throated, large, fragrant white flowers that open at dusk. A native of Florida swamps, moonflower needs a long season and likes poor soil. 15 feet/Sun.

Morning-Glory (*Ipomoea purpurea*)
Morning-glory's flowers open at dawn, then close when the sun gets too hot. Good on fences, porches, and lampposts, it thrives in almost any soil in sun. (See also page 111.) 8–10 feet/Sun.

GROUND COVERS

African Daisy (*Osteospermum* species)
African daisy produces carpets of 3-inch pink or lilac-fading-to-white blooms from November to March, sporadic blooms the rest of the year. Excellent for covering slopes, it's used mostly on the West Coast. It will survive on one or two waterings a year. Mow or cut back every year or two in spring. 1–3 feet/Zones 9–10/Sun.

Ajuga (*Ajuga reptans*)
Also called bugleweed or carpet bugle, ajuga is one of the best ground covers. It has dark green foliage rosettes with bronze, purple, or rainbow overtones; variegated types have white edges and purple centers. Colors intensify in fall. Blue flower spikes bloom in spring. Good for edgings, ajuga spreads quickly but is not rampant. (See also page 129.) 3–6 inches/Zones 3–10/Sun or light shade.

Bearberry, Common (*Arctostaphylos uva-ursi*)
Common bearberry has tiny, evergreen, trailing leaves and red autumn berries. This ground cover is good on banks, in poor or acid soils, and on seashores. It's vigorous and trouble free. 6–8 inches/Zones 2–8/Part shade or sun.

Bellflower (*Campanula* species)
Also called campanula or harebell, bellflower is low and trailing. It has neat foliage and a profusion of blue to purple, upright bells or star-shaped cups, mainly in late spring or early summer. Bellflower is adaptable for small areas in moist soil. 6–10 inches/Zones 3–10/Sun or light shade.

Bishop's Weed
(*Aegopodium podagraria 'variegatum'*)
This ground cover has gray-green, compound leaves with white edges. White flowers resemble wild carrot; remove to control spreading and prevent plants from becoming rampant. Excellent for problem areas, and for edgings where it can be controlled. Tolerates any soil. 6–12 inches/Zones 3–10/Sun or shade.

Candytuft (*Iberis sempervirens*)
Candytuft's evergreen foliage is attractive all year. Masses of white, 2-inch-tall flower spikes cover the top in spring. Improved varieties bloom at intervals all season. Candytuft is excellent for edging or covering small spaces; tolerates salt and seashore conditions. 10–12 inches/Zones 3–8/Sun or light shade.

Carmel Creeper
(*Ceanothus griseus 'horizontalis'*)
This California coast native has dark green, glossy, round leaves and violet-blue spring flowers. It tolerates salt spray and strong winds; it can get root rot with too much water. 1½–4 feet/Zones 7–10/Sun.

Chamomile (*Chamaemelum nobile*)
English (or Roman) chamomile is a fragrant herb with fernlike foliage and small, daisylike flowers in summer. Place it where it will be brushed or crushed so it releases its fragrance. Can be a lawn substitute. (See also page 260.) 3–10 inches/Zones 3–10/Sun or light shade.

Corsican Mint (*Mentha requieni*)
Corsican (or creeping) mint makes a fragrant, green carpet. In spring, it produces small, pale lavender blooms. Its shallow roots need constant moisture. It will take some traffic and is good as a container or bonsai ground cover. 1–2 inches/Zones 6–10/Sun or light shade.

Cotoneaster (*Cotoneaster* species)
The shiny green leaves of rockspray, cranberry, and bearberry cotoneaster spread 4 to 15 feet in a fish-bone pattern. White or pinkish summer blooms yield to red berries and leaves in fall. Cotoneaster is ideal for larger spaces or steep slopes. *C. dammeri* is evergreen. (See also pages 67 and 307.) 6 inches–3 feet/Zones 5–10/Sun or light shade.

(continued on page 318)

GROUND COVERS *(continued)*

Ferns
The fern family includes many hardy and adaptable plants that offer a light, airy, and cooling look. Their textures contrast well with bolder foliage. Charming in woodlands or shady areas, most ferns die back in winter. (See also pages 37 and 203.) 6 inches–3 feet/Zones 2–10/Shade.

Forget-Me-Not (*Myosotis scorpioides* 'semperflorens' and *M. sylvatica*)
M. scorpioides is a perennial; *M. sylvatica* self-sows. Both have pale blue flowers with pink, yellow, or white centers in spring and summer. Persistent but not invasive. Forget-me-not needs moisture; good along stream banks or with tulips. (See also page 321.) 2–18 inches/Zones 4–10/Partial shade.

Germander (*Teucrium chamaedrys*)
This plant has dark green, ¾-inch leaves, with lavender flower spikes in spring. Evergreen in milder zones, germander is ideal for poor soils and hot locations; makes a good edging. Bees love its blooms. 8–18 inches/Zones 5–10/Sun.

Ginger, Wild (*Asarum* species)
Also called snakeroot, these woodland plants have large, heart-shaped leaves. Red-purple flowers hide at the base of the leaves in spring. Cool weather tints the leaves purple. 6–10 inches/Zones 4–10/Sun or shade.

Ivy: English, Algerian
(*Hedera helix, H. canariensis*)
See pages 260 and 315. 6–12 inches/Zones 4–9/Shade.

Juniper (*Juniperus* species)
This low-growing evergreen group includes plants with many textures and subtle hues; most are good on banks and slopes. Junipers are slow to grow, but will deter traffic when established. (See also page 313.) 4 inches–4 feet/Zones 2–10/Sun or light shade.

Lily-of-the-Valley (*Convallaria majalis*)
Familiar because of its light green basal leaves and nodding stalks of delicate, fragrant, bell-shaped flowers in spring, lily-of-the-valley tolerates wet or dry soil. (See also page 129.) 6–12 inches/Zones 3–9/Sun to dense shade.

Mahonia, Creeping (*Mahonia repens*)
Creeping mahonia has hollylike leaflets that are bluish green on top and powdery underneath; often, they turn deep red in fall and winter. It has fragrant yellow spring flowers and will deter traffic. Protect this ground cover from wind. Its roots stop erosion, and the plant resists drought. (See also page 311.) 24 inches/Zones 5–10/Sun or shade.

Moneywort (*Lysimachia nummularia*)
Also called creeping jennie, moneywort has bright yellow, buttercup flowers in spring—some continuing all summer—and penny-shaped leaves. A moisture lover, it grows anywhere, and is especially good around rocks and pools. It can be rampant and will bear some traffic. 2–6 inches/Zones 2–10/Sun or shade.

Moss, Irish (*Sagina subulata*)
Also called Corsican pearlwort, this tufted ground cover's needlelike leaves form an evergreen matting. White flowers appear in spring. Irish moss is good between stepping-stones, in rock gardens, and under ferns. 'Aurea' has golden leaves. Can become a weed. (See also page 260.) 3–4 inches/Zones 4–10/Sun or light shade.

Pachysandra (*Pachysandra* species)
Also called Japanese spurge, pachysandra has whorls of spoon-shaped leaves toothed on their outer edges; some have leaves that are mottled or edged in white. Evergreen in mild areas, pachysandra quickly forms a dense carpet, and is excellent under trees or shrubs, or as an edging along shady walks. (See also page 67.) 8–10 inches/Zones 4–8/Part sun or shade.

Sedum (*Sedum* species)
Also called stonecrop, these succulents have many forms, sizes, and colors. Their flowers are yellow, white, or pink to rose. Sedums prefer poor soil and some drought, and can spread to cover an acre, but won't stand traffic. 2–10 inches/Zones 3–10/Sun.

Silver Mound Artemisia
  (*Artemisia schmidtiana*)
This plant's silvery leaves have woolly texture, are aromatic when crushed, and form attractive mounds. Its yellow flowers aren't showy. An excellent accent plant, artemisia tolerates heat and drought but not dampness. 6 inches– 2 feet/Zones 3–9/Sun.

Snow-in-Summer (*Cerastium tomentosum*)
Snow-in-summer has tiny, silver leaves that form a low mat and send up an abundance of delicate white flowers in late spring. Good for rock gardens or edgings, or among bulbs. Does well in desert, coastal, or mountain areas. 3–6 inches/Zones 2–10/Sun.

Strawberry (*Fragaria* species)
Alpine strawberry and some ornamental varieties have attractive foliage, white flowers in spring, and fruits both edible and decorative. Tolerant and adaptable, strawberry will stand a little foot traffic and light shade. (See also page 67.) 6–12 inches/Zones 3–10/Sun.

Sweet Woodruff (*Galium odoratum*)
Sweet woodruff's dark green, sandpapery, edible leaflets are like spokes on square stems. Tiny white flowers in clusters bloom in early summer. Grow sweet woodruff beneath rhododendrons and high-branched conifer trees. 6–12 inches/Zones 4–10/Light shade.

Thyme (*Thymus* species)
Creeping, woolly, lemon, and many more thyme varieties vary from matlike growth to small shrubs, all with tiny, dark green leaves

---

GROUND COVERS FOR SPECIAL INTEREST[1]

Quick Spreading

African daisy
Ajuga
Bearberry
Bellflower
Carmel creeper
Crown vetch
Ivy, Algerian
Lamium
Mondo grass
Moneywort
Sedum
Snow-in-summer
Verbena
Yellowroot

For Showy Flowers

African daisy
Agapanthus
Ajuga
Astilbe
Bellflower
Bougainvillea
Candytuft
Carmel creeper
Cinquefoil
Crown vetch
Daylily
Deutzia
Forget-me-not
Gazania
Geranium
Heath
Heather
Hosta
Lantana, trailing
Lily-of-the-valley
Phlox, creeping
Pink, moss or maiden
Potentilla
St. John's wort
Snow-in-summer
Speedwell
Spirea
Verbena

Edible

Chamomile
Cranberry
Mint
Natal plum, dwarf
Rosemary, dwarf
Strawberry
Thyme
Violet

Potential Weeds

Bishop's weed
Buttercup, creeping
Crown vetch
Evening primrose
Honeysuckle, hall's
Ivy, ground
Knotweed
Matrimony vine
Mint
Moneywort
Ribbon grass
St. John's wort

[1]*For more information on many of the ground covers listed, see pages 35, 37, 67, 129, 166, 186, 203, 260–261, and 317–319.*

---

and aromatic red, pink, white, or purple summer flowers. Thyme makes a good lawn substitute for limited-traffic areas. (See also page 261.) 2–15 inches/Zones 3–10/Sun.

Vinca (*Vinca minor*)
Also called periwinkle or myrtle, vinca has dark, glossy, evergreen leaves and lovely lavender spring flowers. Grow under trees or shrubs, or among bulbs. (See also page 67.) 10–12 inches/Zones 4–9/Shade.

FLOWERS

PERENNIAL

Anchusa (*Anchusa azurea*)
Also called summer forget-me-not, anchusa is covered in summer with intense, true blue flowers. Anchusa grows easily from seed or divisions, and has lance-shaped basal leaves. 3–4 feet/Zones 4–8/Sun.

Aster, Hardy (*Aster* species)
Also called michaelmas daisy, hardy aster produces flowers of blue, purple, or pink in late summer and fall. It combines well with lily, kniphofia, and mum. Good as a cut flower, it has small, green leaves and needs support. 3–4 feet/Zones 4–9/Sun.

Astilbe (*Astilbe x arendsi*)
Also called false spirea, astilbe has feathery flower heads from June through August, seed heads that provide winter interest, fernlike mounds of foliage, and shallow roots. 15–30 inches/Zones 4–8/Shade.

Baby's-Breath (*Gypsophila paniculata*)
Baby's-breath produces a cloud of dainty white or light pink blooms from June through September. Excellent as a filler or for cut flowers, baby's-breath has silvery green, fine foliage. 6 inches–4 feet/Zones 3–8/Sun.

Bee Balm (*Monarda didyma*)
Bee balm has unusual round clusters of flowers in red, pink, white, or lavender that attract bees and butterflies. An aromatic herb, it spreads aggressively. Good for naturalizing in woodland settings or bog gardens. 2–3 feet/Zones 4–9/Sun or light shade.

Bleeding-Heart (*Dicentra spectabilis*)
Bleeding-heart is a favorite for its reliability and heart-shaped spring flowers. Its foliage turns yellow and disappears by midsummer. Dutch-man's-breeches, of the same genus, likes more shade and has ferny foliage. 1½–3 feet/Zones 4–9/Sun or shade.

Butterfly Weed (*Asclepias tuberosa*)
A form of milkweed, this handsome native plant is covered with bright orange flowers, which butterflies love, all summer long. Attractive ornamental pods follow the flowers. Butterfly weed stands drought well. Striking with daylily and red-hot-poker, it is slow to emerge in spring, so mark your planting spot. 1½–3 feet/Zones 4–9/Sun.

Chrysanthemum
(*Chrysanthemum x morifolium*)
Mums, the glory of the fall garden, come in many forms and rich autumn colors plus lavender. Gray-green foliage is attractive all year. Mums can be moved even when in full bloom. 1–4 feet/Zones 4–10/Sun.

Daylily (*Hemerocallis* hybrids)
Daylilies are the glory of the midsummer garden. Each lilylike bloom lasts only a day, but every plant can have dozens of blooms. Plants have attractive, grasslike foliage and combine well with speedwell, liatris, and butterfly weed. 1½–4 feet/Zones 3–9/Sun or shade.

Delphinium (*Delphinium* species)
Delphinium has few rivals for color and form. Spikes of white, pink, or marvelous blues bloom in early summer, then rebloom in fall. Palm-shaped gray-green leaves are nice all season. 2½–6 feet/Zones 2–7/Sun.

Flax (*Linum* species)
Flax has delicate flowers in golden yellow or sky blue for weeks in early summer. Excellent when planted alongside Iceland poppy and columbine, flax has attractive, feathery foliage all season. 1–2 feet/Zones 5–8/Sun.

Hosta (*Hosta* species)
Also called plantain lily or funkia, hosta is prized for its foliage, which varies in color, variegation, texture, and edging. Some also have lovely fragrant flower spikes in summer to early fall. Easy to grow, hosta is excellent as a ground cover or garden accent. (See also pages 37 and 203.) 1–3 feet/Zones 4–9/Shade.

Loosestrife (*Lythrum salicaria*)
Loosestrife, with its slender spires of pink-purple flowers from June to September, is excellent for the back of a border. 1½–4 feet/Zones 4–9/Sun.

Peony (*Paeonia* species)
Peony is a favorite for its large, fragrant spring flowers. It is long-lived and easy to grow. New cultivars have stronger stems. Place in front of shrubs, or use as a border or low hedge. 2–4 feet/Zones 3–9/Sun.

Phlox (*Phlox* species)
Different varieties of phlox can produce everything from creeping splashes of spring color to tall clusters that give mass and substance from June to early September. Phlox's ferny or lance-shaped foliage is good all season. 6 inches–4 feet/Zones 3–9/Sun.

Shasta Daisy (*Chrysanthemum x superbum* or *C. maximum*)
Shasta daisy is a classic of simple beauty either in the garden or as a cut flower. If you select several varieties, you can get single and double blooms all summer. Basal foliage is dark green. Plants may die out and need replacing every few years. 1–4 feet/Zones 5–10/Sun.

Speedwell (*Veronica* species)
Also called veronica, speedwell has lovely spikes of blue or white flowers—perfect for a rock garden or border—from June to September. Its foliage is dark green. (See also page 261.) 6 inches–3 feet/Zones 4–9/Sun.

BIENNIAL

Canterbury-Bells (*Campanula* species)
Biennial bellflowers have cuplike blooms in white, pink, blue, or purple. Sow seed in June. 1½–4 feet/Zones 4–9/Sun.

Forget-Me-Not, Alpine (*Myosotis* species)
Along with a few perennials, the myosotis group includes this blue-flowered biennial star of the spring garden. It's excellent mixed with spring bulbs or naturalized in a woodland. Sow seed in July or August. (See also page 318.) 8 inches–2 feet/Zones 3–8/Part shade.

Foxglove (*Digitalis purpurea*)
The first spiked flower of spring, foxglove produces thimble-shaped blossoms in a wide range of soft colors. It has bold basal foliage. Sow seed in June. 2½–5 feet/Zones 4–9/Sun.

Hollyhock (*Alcea rosea* or *Althaea rosea*)
Hollyhock produces towers of white, pink, yellow, red, or purple flowers; its foliage can be coarse. Once established, hollyhock self-sows. 3–8 feet/Zones 3–9/Sun.

Pansy (*Viola x wittrockiana* or *V. tricolor*)
Pansies are delightful in earliest spring when their painted faces defy the cold. They bloom until fall, come in many colors, and are perfect for edgings, for rock and wall gardens, in containers, and among spring bulbs. Keep flowers picked. Sow seed in August outdoors or in January inside. 6–8 inches/Zones 4–9/Shade.

Sweet William (*Dianthus barbatus*)
Sweet william's lovely, spicy-smelling floret clusters of rich reds, pinks, and white are excellent for the front to middle of flower borders, for cut flowers, in rock gardens, or naturalized at the edge of woodlands. Sow seed in June. Sweet william self-sows once started. 6 inches–2 feet/Zones 4–8/Sun.

(continued on page 322)

FLOWERS *(continued)*

ANNUAL

Ageratum (*Ageratum houstonianum*)
Ageratum's fluffy blue, pink, or white flowers make it good for edgings, border fronts, or containers. 4–10 inches/Sun.

Alyssum, Sweet (*Lobularia maritima*)
Sweet alyssum has low mats of fragrant, delicate flowers in white, rose, lavender, or purple. For continual bloom, shear. Will self-sow. (See also page 129.) 3–6 inches/Sun or part shade.

Bachelor's-Button (*Centaurea cyanus*)
Also called cornflower, this annual has gray-green foliage and round flowers in white, pink, blue (which is loveliest), or purple. Repeat sowing for continuous bloom. Bachelor's-button likes cool weather. 1–3 feet/Sun or part shade.

Begonia, Wax (*Begonia x semperflorens-cultorum*)
Reliable for nonstop flowers, the neat, compact wax begonia works well as an edging plant or in containers. 6–12 inches/Sun or shade.

Calendula (*Calendula officinalis*)
Calendula likes cool weather. Its bright yellow and orange double daisies serve well as cut flowers. Plant in fall or late winter for early bloom. 10–20 inches/Sun.

Celosia (*Celosia cristata*)
Also called cockscomb, celosia produces two flower types—plumed and crested—that come in a wide range of warm colors. Celosia is ideal for edgings or borders, as a fresh or dried flower, or in containers. It likes heat, and has a long season of bloom. 6 inches–2½ feet/Sun.

Coleus (*Coleus x hybridus*)
Coleus is grown for its variety of foliage colors and shapes. Mass in beds, or use as an edging or container plant. 8 inches–1½ feet/Shade.

Geranium (*Pelargonium* species)
Geranium is one of the most popular and reliable bedding and pot plants. It produces season-long blooms in reds, pinks, and white. 1½–2 feet/Sun.•

Impatiens (*Impatiens wallerana*)
Also called busy lizzy and patience plant, impatiens is a favorite for shady spots. It's neat, has a long season of bloom, and is good in containers. (See also page 129.) 8 inches–2½ feet/Shade.

Marigold (*Tagetes* species)
Many forms of marigold exist; all have the colors of sunshine. They're dependable, have one of the longest seasons of bloom, and make long-lasting cut flowers. Marigolds are good for edgings and borders, and in containers. 6 inches–4 feet/Sun.

Petunia (*Petunia x hybrida*)
Long-blooming petunias come in many colors and are excellent for bedding and edging, and in containers. 10 inches–1½ feet/Sun.

Salvia (*Salvia splendens*)
Salvia now comes in white, pink, rose, and a fine purple. It's easy to grow and likes hot weather. Use it in beds, edgings, mass plantings, or containers. 1–3 feet/Sun.

Snapdragon (*Antirrhinum majus*)
Snapdragon produces spikes of uniquely shaped florets in every color but green and blue and in many sizes. Snapdragon likes cool weather, and occasionally survives the winter. 6 inches–3 feet/Sun.

Zinnia (*Zinnia elegans*)
Zinnia is loved for its durability, speed of growth, and range of heights, colors, and forms, from button size to 7 inches across. Zinnias thrive on heat and like arid climates. 6 inches–3 feet/Sun.

BULBOUS

Daffodil (*Narcissus* species)
Daffodil and jonquil produce delightful spring flowers; some are fragrant. Plant them in front of shrubs or as a border, or naturalize among ivy or vinca. Plants will last for years. 6–20 inches/Zones 3–8/Sun or light shade.

Hyacinth (*Hyacinthus orientalis*)
Perfumed florets of pink, white, or blue bedeck this flower. Use hyacinth in the fronts or corners of borders, or in containers. Replace hyacinth bulbs every three to five years. 9–12 inches/Zones 4–8/Sun.

Iris (*Iris* species)
Easy to grow and quick to multiply, irises range from early-blooming tiny bulbs to late-spring regal beauties. (See also page 203.) 6–50 inches/Zones 3–8/Sun or light shade.

Lily (*Lilium* species)
Aristocratic lilies are easy to grow. Some are fragrant; others are not. Plant in clumps for best effect. 2–9 feet/Zones 4–8/Sun.

Minor Spring Bulbs
These include anemone, crocus, snowdrop, winter aconite, and fritillaria. Plant in gardens or in the grass. Naturalize grape hyacinth and scilla. 3 inches–3 feet/Zones 3–8/Sun.

Tender Bulbs
These include caladium, canna, dahlia, gladiolus, tuberous begonia, agapanthus, and others. These need to be lifted before frost and stored inside. 1–6 feet/Zones 3–10.

Tulip (*Tulipa* species)
Tulips come in a wonderful range of colors and slightly varied forms. Select types for several weeks of spring bloom. 8–28 inches/Zones 3–8/Sun.

PLANTS FOR SHADED AREAS[1]

Understory Trees
Arborvitae
Dogwood
Hemlock
Horse chestnut
Maple, Japanese
Privet
Redbud
Serviceberry
Witch hazel (hybrid)

Flowering Shrubs
Andromeda
Azalea
Buckeye, bottlebrush
Camellia
Clethra
Fuchsia
Hydrangea
Kerria
Mahonia
Mountain laurel

Foliage Shrubs
Boxwood
Cypress, false
Euonymus
Holly
Leucothoe
Privet
Yew

Vines
Akebia
Clematis
Creeper, Virginia
Euonymus
Grape
Honeysuckle
Hydrangea
Ivy: Boston, English
Kiwi
Star jasmine

Ground Covers
Ajuga
Bishop's hat
Euonymus
Fern
Hosta
Ivy
Lily-of-the-valley
Liriope
Mint
Pachysandra
Strawberry
Vinca
Wintergreen

Perennials
Astilbe
Bleeding-heart
Columbine
Daylily
Hosta
Iris
Lobelia
Phlox
Primrose
Trillium
Viola
Virginia bluebells

Biennials and Bulbs
Caladium
Forget-me-not
Foxglove
Pansy
Tuberous begonia

Annuals
Begonia
Browallia
Celosia
Coleus
Coreopsis
Impatiens
Lobelia
Monkey flower
Nicotiana
Snapdragon
Stock
Torenia
Vinca

[1]*For more information on many of the plants listed, see pages 34–37, 67, 82–83, 90, 107–111, 129, 166, 186, 203, 260–261, and 301–323.*

INDEX

INDEX *(continued)*

INDEX *(continued)*

INDEX *(continued)*

Have BETTER HOMES
AND GARDENS.
magazine delivered to
your door. For
information, write to:
MR. ROBERT AUSTIN
P.O. BOX 4536
DES MOINES, IA 50336